MW01073808

Mastering DSM-5™:

Diagnosing Disorders in Children, Adolescents, and Adults

Second Edition

George B. Haarman, Psy.D., LMFT

Foundations: Education and Consultation
Louisville, Kentucky

First Published in the United States in 2015 by:

Foundations: Education & Consultation

FOR INFORMATION ADDRESS:

Foundations: Education & Consultation

1400 Browns Lane

Louisville, Kentucky 40207

Copyright © 2015 by George B. Haarman, Psy.D., LMFT

All Rights Reserved. No part of this publication may be reproduced or transmitted in any form or by any means, electronic or mechanical, including photocopying, recording, or any information or storage retrieval system now known or to be invented, without permission in writing from the publisher, except by a reviewer who wishes to quote brief passages.

ISBN: 13:1500593179

TABLE OF CONTENTS

Haarman

Dedicated to my wife, my daughters, my granddaughters, and my friends of over 50 years, The Flying Pigs.

DSM-5™ is a registered trademark of the American Psychiatric Association. The APA has not participated in the preparation of this book.

Haarman

Mastering DSM-5™

Chapter One: The History of the Diagnostic and Statistical Manual of Mental Disorders: Fifth Edition

Oddly enough, the history of diagnosis in mental health goes back to the 1840 Census. In the 1840 Census, individuals were asked to self-identify as one of two types of individuals. A person could be "normal" or could be classified as "idiot/insane." Imagine yourself a census taker in 1840, walking up to a door, knocking, and asking if there were normal people who lived there or idiots and insane people. The Census was the first attempt, in an organized fashion, to make a distinction between people on the basis of psychological and emotional difficulties.

By 1880, the Census had expanded the dichotomous classification system to seven categories, including: mania, melancholia, monomania, dementia, paresis, epilepsy, and dipsomania. But the first real advances in diagnosis of mental illnesses began to occur after World War II. After WWII, a number of men and women came back from the war who were physically sound, but emotionally and psychologically shattered, distressed, and overwhelmed. The Veterans Administration was overwhelmed by the variety of symptoms and presentations. As a result of the extreme variety of issues that the veterans presented, the Veterans Administration believed they needed some way to classify and organize these individuals based on presenting problems, severity, and behavioral symptoms to ensure proper treatment for these veterans. The goal of the classification system was to appropriately identify the disorders and then house, provide treatment, and manage these individuals on the basis of their disorders. In response, the Veteran's Administration developed their classification system which included 10 psychotic disorders, nine neurotic disorders, and seven disorders of character, behavior and intelligence. The

Haarman

disorders of character, behavior, and intelligence were the precursors of what we now consider to be Axis II Disorders.

Psychiatry, which was the dominant force for the treatment of mental disorders at the time, recognized the work of the Veteran's Administration and its ability to bring organization out of chaos. However, they thought the VA had overstepped its boundaries by diagnosing mental disorders, which was clearly the purview of psychiatry. As a result the American Psychiatric Association began to work on its own classification system which was called the *Diagnostic and Statistical Manual of Mental Disorders.* The *DSM-I,* which was published in 1952, included not only disorders that had a clear medical and organic basis, but also recognized a psychological view and utilized the terminology of psychological reaction. By today's standards, the *DSM-I* was a relatively crude and unsophisticated document, but was embraced by the psychiatric profession. Consequently, by virtue of psychiatry's position in mental health at the time, the *DSM-I* was forced upon all the other professions working in the area of mental health including nursing, psychology, social work, and occupational therapy.

By the mid 60's there was recognition of the need to update the manual with contemporary thinking regarding the major advances in mental health since the publication of *DSM-I.* The changes were largely spurred by the development of the new families of neuroleptic medications that were revolutionizing mental health and allowing many individuals to be treated on an outpatient basis. The *DSM-II* was published in 1968 and was similar to the *DSM-I*, but eliminated the concept of reaction. The revised manual was still a relatively unsophisticated system and only provided a brief two to three sentence description of disorders, leaving much of the actual diagnosis up to the clinical judgment of the individual practitioner. As a result, there was a particularly significant issue with inter-rater reliability. Inter-rater reliability was examined by the Rosencrans Study, in which graduate students were given a protocol and a script to follow and charged with seeking admission at state psychiatric hospitals. Although each student was provided the same script, many different diagnoses were assigned, based on relatively the same presentation. As illustrated by the study, in spite of the revisions to the manual, there still existed a significant problem with inter-rater reliability.

Haarman

In *DSM-II,* the typical descriptions of diagnoses were so vague and amorphous that almost anyone could justify a diagnosis of any particular disorder. For example, in DSM-II (1968), Anxiety Neurosis (300.0) was described as follows, "This neurosis is characterized by anxious over concern, extending to panic, and frequently associated with somatic symptoms." The lack of specificity provided opportunities for incorrect diagnosis, resulted in a high rate of misdiagnosis, and many individuals received inappropriate treatment or failed to make therapeutic progress. Additionally, the *DSM-II* advocated a psychoanalytic approach and focused on disorders as being neuroses or psychoses, a theoretical system that was starting to be questioned by many other professionals in the field, as well as many individuals within the psychiatric community.

Recognizing the problems with reliability and with adopting a system that had at its basis, only one theory, psychoanalysis, work began on the *DSM-III* in 1974. The document was published in 1980 and was a major breakthrough in the field of diagnosis which created a true paradigm shift. Instead of a brief narrative description of disorders, the *DSM-III* developed specific diagnostic criteria for each recognized disorder on the basis of the presence or absence of certain symptoms, occupational, social, and interpersonal impact, and spelled out specific time frames and frequency rates for which symptoms had to be present. The quantification and qualification of each disorder would inevitably help clear up the reliability issues that had been seen in diagnosis under the *DSM-II.*

Another major advance in the *DSM-III* was the recognition that within any given diagnostic classification there was likely to be significant variability in causality, functionality, physical health issues, and environmental factors. Often these individual factors produced significantly different presentations of the same disorder. To address the variability, the Multi-Axial System of Diagnosis was developed, which allowed for a diagnosis on the basis of the proper classification of the disorder, but also allowed for further description, clarification, and qualification of the individual's psychological issue.

Haarman

For example, two individuals may both carry the appropriate diagnosis of Schizophrenia, Paranoid Type; however, individual A has an extremely high Intelligence Quotient, is very well educated, has very good general health with no physical complications, has an active network of friends and supportive family members, and is functioning with the disorder having very little impact on their day to day existence. Individual B may also appropriately carry a diagnosis of Schizophrenia, Paranoid Type, but has very limited intelligence, less than a primary education, has major health issues that contribute to or exacerbate their diagnosis, has a limited or dysfunctional family and poor community support, and is barely functional or responsive. Each of these individuals is appropriately diagnosed, but the presentation of their disorder will require significantly different treatment approaches, and a significantly different level of intervention. The Multi-Axial System of Diagnosis allowed for a description of underlying personality issues and characterological issues, recognition of medical issues, identification of psychosocial stressors, and a general assessment of the individual's level of functioning.

Two other significant shifts in the *DSM-III* were the attempt to develop a document that was "theory-neutral" and an increased recognition of the reality of psychiatric disorders occurring in children. The shift toward a "theory neutral diagnostic system" was an important step in insuring the *DSM-III* would be equally accepted by all professions and all theoretical backgrounds. The terminology of neurosis was dropped and language discussing disorders was refined to be discipline and value neutral. The intent was to develop a system of classification and diagnosis that all professions could readily adopt and feel comfortable operating within that schema and paradigm.

Whenever you drastically alter the schema people rely on to bring meaning and order to their professional life, "all hell will break loose." The *DSM-III* created a firestorm of controversy from the day it was released and created conflict within and between professionals and professions. Some professionals were violently opposed to the "confining" requirements of a diagnostic classification that required the patient to meet certain criteria for a specific diagnosis. Many practitioners were extremely vociferous about objecting to certain classifications and disorders. And still others saw the *DSM-III* as an attempt to

Haarman

further perpetuate the "Myth of Mental Illness" by dressing it up in a pseudoscientific system.

Articles were written roundly criticizing the *DSM-III* and all it stood for; others then wrote articles criticizing the article criticizing the *DSM-III*; and still others wrote articles criticizing the articles that criticized the article criticizing the *DSM-III*; and so on, and so on. As a result a number of committees were almost immediately set in place to address the multitude of objections and criticisms presented about the *DSM-III* in order to develop a revision that would address those concerns. This resulted in the *Diagnostic and Statistical Manual of Mental Disorders: Third Edition- Revised (DSM-III-R)* being published in 1987. One political and philosophical shift that occurred in the DSM-III-R was the elimination of homosexuality as a diagnostic classification through the inclusion of a disorder labeled Ego-Dystonic Homosexuality (this classification was ultimately dropped in *DSM-IV*). The *DSM-III-R* was viewed by many as a "temporary fix" while work was being undertaken to develop a more comprehensive revision to be created in the *DSM-IV*.

Despite the controversies, mental health professionals became comfortable with diagnoses based on criteria and the multi-axial system of diagnosis. Seven years later, the *Diagnostic and Statistical Manual of Mental Disorders: Fourth Edition (DSM-IV)* was published in 1994. The most significant change in the *DSM-IV* was the expansion of the number of diagnostic categories from approximately 220 to 340. Greatly expanding the scope and number of diagnostic categories available, the document was criticized by some as "pathologizing everything." The *DSM-IV* was denounced in some circles for creating "false constructs" for normal behaviors. The categories themselves had a great deal of symptom overlap that blurred the edges between categories and did not satisfactorily address co-morbid conditions. The *DSM-IV* was also criticized for being too "culture bound" and not allowing for behavioral variations that within certain cultures are seen as normal behaviors.

Rapid advances in research, particularly in neurology and neural imaging prompted an update of the *DSM-IV* in 2001. In this update, titled *DSM-IV-TR,* the text sections were updated to reflect advances in research and conceptualization of disorders, but no changes were made to diagnostic criteria and no disorders were added or removed. The specific disorders and criteria remained unchanged from *DSM-IV*. The text changes in *DSM-IV-TR* generated little controversy and were embraced within mental health.

Under a grant from the National Institute of Mental Health, work began in earnest on the *DSM-5* in 2000. A number of issues were identified that became incorporated as goals in the development of the *DSM-5*. A particular goal that was addressed almost immediately was the discrepancies between the *DSM-IV*, a system primarily used in North America, and the *International Classification of Diseases*, the system of diagnosis that is predominately utilized widely in the rest of the world. As part of the preliminary work leading up to the *DSM-5*, a number of meetings were held with the World Health Organization in an attempt to resolve some of the inconsistencies between the two systems of classification. The overall goal was to develop a document that had the highest degree of agreement possible with *ICD,* and minimized the differences in approach. In 2006 and 2007, work on the *DSM-5* began concretely with the appointment of members of the subcommittees and the appointment of Drs. Kupfer and Reigart as the chair and vice chair respectively. The Workgroups began meeting in 2007 and for the next two years, conducted literature searches, reviewed critiques of the *DSM-IV*, and began work on adding disorders, removing or combining disorders, or modifying criteria for disorders.

In order to have a greater openness in the development of the *DSM-5,* the decision was made to publish a first draft and allow for comments, to field test the first draft to see if the changes were workable and productive, and then publish a second draft for public comment. The committees were overwhelmed by the number and volume of comments received through electronic media and in writing. After the second draft was published and the period for comment had expired, the website for the *DSM-5* was closed and the work groups went into a period of quiet isolation to prepare the final draft to be presented to the American Psychiatric Association Board of Directors at their December 2012 meeting. Although the process began with an attempt at transparency, little information was available about what was actually going to be included in the *DSM-5* until it was released for publication at the APA annual meeting on May 18, 2013.

Haarman

Chapter Two: Controversies Generated by the *DSM-5*

Even prior to its release, the *DSM-5* was mired in controversy that was widely covered by the popular press, as well as the professional literature. In a controversial move, Allen Frances resigned his position on the *DSM-5* work group over what Frances has labeled a "lack of scientific integrity." Frances (2013b) openly criticized the *DSM-5* on a number of issues. "All changes to the diagnostic system should be science driven and evidence based, not influenced by my personal whims or anyone else's.....Normal enough people would be captured in *DSM-5*'s excessively wide diagnostic net and exposed to unnecessary medication...the drug companies should be licking their chops." Frances and others are especially critical of new disorders added in *DSM-5* including: Binge-Eating Disorder, Disruptive Mood Dysregulation Disorder, and Mild Neurocognitive Disorder. Paris (2013) commented that these "three new disorders in *DSM-5* share a fuzzy boundary with normality."

Frances (2013b) views the *DSM-5* as taking common, transitional life experiences and creating diagnostic labels that will result in an increase in medication usage and a society that continues to view itself in pathological terms. "*DSM-5* will mislabel normal people, promote diagnostic inflation, and encourage inappropriate medication. The pool of normality is shrinking to a mere puddle. Loose diagnosis is causing a national drug overdose. From 2005 to present, there has been an 800 percent increase in prescriptions among active duty troops. 110,000 soldiers are now taking at least 1 psychotropic drug. 11 percent of all adults took an antidepressant in 2010, 4 percent of children are on stimulants, and 4 percent of teens are on antidepressants. In Canada, SSRIs went up 44 % between 2005 and 2009. Psychiatric meds are the star producers for drug companies."

Frances (2013b) states that "Blurring the lines between normality and pathology are the likely negative effects of a carelessly done *DSM-5*, driven by its grand, but quixotic ambition to be a paradigm shift." A major example of this has been the controversy surrounding dropping the Bereavement Exclusion contained in the diagnostic criteria for Major Depressive Episode. The

Haarman

symptoms of grief (sadness, loss of interest, reduced energy, difficulty with eating and sleeping) are made the equivalent of a Major Depression. Frances (2103a) feels that the *DSM-5* has now taken two weeks of normal grief symptoms and turned these symptoms into Major Depressive Disorder. Frances (2013b) states that "the previous *DSM's* have recognized this distortion by having an explicit 'bereavement exclusion.' *DSM-5* has made a serious error in removing this exclusion." He strongly believes that the Major Depression diagnosis should be reserved for those who are having severe and prolonged depressive symptoms and not the more transitory symptoms of a normal grieving process. Critics fear that many ordinary, but painful reactions to life (grief, anger, angst), will now be labeled as illnesses in the *DSM-5,* and people will be prescribed unnecessary medications.

Paris (2013) also expresses concerns that the *DSM-5* may have gone too far in identifying individual variations in behavior as pathologies. "Some of the problems derive from the concept that psychopathology lies on a continuum with normality. This makes it difficult to separate mental disorders from normal variations and therefore runs the risk of overdiagnosis." The medicalization of ordinary life has sometimes been called "Psychiatric Imperialism" (Moncrieff, 1997). The Kraepelin Model (which has been the basis of *DSM-I* through *DSM-IV)* views psychiatric concerns with mental illnesses, and not the natural pain, discomfort, and unhappiness of life. This has given way to a model which views normality and illness as lying on a vast continuum. The rationale for this change comes from considerable research which suggests the underlying biology of mental disorders is more dimensional than categorical (First, 2014).

DSM-5 states an underlying assumption that all disorders stem from biological brain and neurological disorders. This is commonly referred to in the literature as a "medicalization" of mental disorders and many individuals have rejected this assumption. "Psychiatry has bet on neuroscience as the best way to understand mental disorders.....only time will tell how this wager will pan out" (Paris, 2013). While recognizing the advances in neuroscience and neural imaging, we must also recognize the primitive infancy of current neural imaging. Basing a diagnostic classification system on such primitive data, and attempting a paradigm shift before the reality of the information is fully

Haarman

understood may be a mistake. Pathology is also associated with changes in neurotransmitters, but a theory that chemical imbalances cause mental disorders is overly simplistic. Attempting to fully explain mental disorders as brain disorders may be ill advised. The *DSM-5* "hybrid approach" to diagnosis appears to accept continuing with discrete diagnostic categories as a temporary expedient, rather than making a total shift to viewing illness as a point on a broad continuum that shades into normalcy. Paris (2013) stated, "Mental phenomena reflect the activity of the human brain, which happens to be the most complex structure known in the universe. There are more synapses in the brain than there are stars in the sky." It may be that in attempting to move toward a "medicalization" of mental disorders we are overestimating what we know about brain functioning and are "skating on thin ice" with some of these conclusions.

As mentioned before, others have expressed concern that the *DSM-5* has been overly influenced by the pharmaceutical industry. The pharmaceutical industry has a strong interest in how the *DSM-5* defines and identifies disorders. Maximizing profits means prescribing more drugs to more people, and it is in the pharmaceutical industry's best interest to have an approach that defines more disorders and current disorders in broader inclusionary terms. Paris (2013) has stated that "Some of the most problematic trends in psychiatry have come from attempts to make patients fit into categories that justify the use of prescription drugs. The over-inclusiveness of *DSM-5* should make the pharmaceutical industry very happy." No one can claim the pharmaceutical industry has direct influence over what is included in the *DSM,* but when so many of psychiatry's leaders benefit financially from the pharmaceutical industry, there is room for concern. In 2008, Senator Charles Grassley held public hearings regarding academic and research psychiatrists taking millions of dollars from the pharmaceutical industry in "consulting fees" and for openly, and not so openly, promoting products on lecture tours. The issue of the relationship between psychiatry and the pharmaceutical industry has been further compounded by the fact that over 70 percent of the committee members who served in developing the *DSM-5* have had financial ties to the pharmaceutical industry. The *DSM-5* process required that all *DSM-5* Workgroup members have only minimal involvement with pharmaceutical companies. This "vetting" process slowed down the *DSM-5* development to insure that members of task forces and committees were "clean," but the fact

Haarman

that they have taken money from pharmaceutical companies in the past, or hope for financial support in the future, can raise questions as to whether their objectivity is permanently compromised.

Another major controversy was the Personality Disorders Workgroup. The suggested revised criteria indicated that Personality Disorders were seen as a category that was ripe for "dimensionalization." Many who opposed this approach were left out of the process, or "silenced." However, the proposal for a new classification system for Personality Disorders was roundly attacked through letters of protests and in other public forums. Ultimately, the international members of the committee resigned in protest over the proposed new approach. Their discussions and recommendations were so controversial, that ultimately, the American Psychiatric Association Board of Directors rejected the Personality Disorders Workgroup's proposal on the advice of its scientific advisors (Paris, 2013). The Workgroup's recommendations were placed in Section III, Conditions for Further Study, and *DSM-5* continued the use of the current *DSM-IV-TR* criteria. Thus, controversy was avoided temporarily by "tabling" the new proposal and assigning it to the Conditions for Further Study Chapter.

Two weeks before publication of the *DSM-5*, the National Institute of Mental Health (NIMH) withdrew support from the *DSM-5*, and advocated a biological approach based on their own diagnostic system, the RDoC (Research Domain Criteria). The NIMH system of diagnosis (RDoC) offered a system based on a matrix in which broad spectra of behavior are regulated by a Negative Valence Systems, Positive Valence Systems, Cognitive Systems, Systems for Social Processes, and Arousal/Modulatory Systems. These systems are matched with data based on genes, molecules, neural circuits, physiology, and behaviors. (Paris, 2013). A former director of The National Institute of Mental Health, (Hyman, 2011) notes that when he was in charge, billions of dollars were spent on genetic studies of *DSM* categories, but the money did not produce the clarity of results hoped for when originally funded. The reason for this disappointment was that psychiatric diagnostic labels, as contained in the *DSM,* are not true endophenotypes. The Research Domain Criteria is an idea that may or may not prove valid or viable. The assumption that mental disorders are brain disorders has become a launching point for a new direction in diagnosis. "RDoCs are not a fact, but an ideology used to validate psychiatry and represents the hope that mental illness can be translated into neural science (Paris, 2013)."

Chapter Three: *DSM-5* Philosophy, Cultural Considerations, and Cross-Cutting Dimensional Assessments

Paris (2013) states that traditionally, medicine has attempted to separate pathology from normality. Psychiatry has also traditionally had to make the same distinction, and so "disease-like" disorders such as schizophrenia and bi-polar disorder were separated from reaction patterns like mild depression, anxiety disorders, and difficulties in adjustments to living. All past *DSM*s have been adopted using the Kaeplin assumption that disorders are distinct from non-pathology and distinct from each other. *DSM-5* seeks to overturn the Kraepelinian Model and replace it with one in which illness is not separate from normality, but defined by a cutoff point on a continuum. Kupfer and Reiger (2011) have suggested that diagnostic spectra are supported by neuroscience research rather than categories of unique phenomena.

Many diagnoses that are included in *DSM-5* are conditions that can be found in normal human existence. Poorly behaving children can be diagnosed as Oppositional Defiant; painfully shy adults can be diagnosed with Social Anxiety Disorder; feelings of loss and apathy can justify a diagnosis of Major Depression; episodes of rage can be diagnosed as Intermittent Explosive Disorder; and betting on football games has found a home in *DSM-5's* Gambling Disorder. What is the point at which distress, pain, emotionality, and loss of functioning qualify as mental illness? Thus, everyone has a mental disorder, the only question is one of degree. In *DSM-5, m*any issues of normal living have become diagnosable, and while these conditions are certainly painful and debilitating, they probably lack support in neuroscience as being abnormal or pathological.

Being unable to resolve the basic epistemological question between a categorical approach to diagnosis or a dimensional approach to diagnosis, *DSM-5* has opted to adopt a "hybrid approach." The "hybrid" approach retains many of the familiar categories of the earlier approaches in *DSM-I* through

Haarman

DSM-IV, but attempts to allow for and emphasize a more dimensional approach to diagnosis. *DSM-5 (2013)* has stated that "despite the problems posed by categorical diagnoses, the DSM-5 Task Force recognized that it is premature scientifically to propose alternative definitions for most disorders. The organizational structure is meant to serve as a bridge to new diagnostic approaches without disrupting current clinical practice or research." Many have expressed concerns that mental disorders as classified in *DSM-5* are no more than descriptive syndromes. Children and teenagers may be especially hard to diagnose. They have a short track record, mature at varying rates, are prone to abuse drugs, and are reactive to family stress. The younger, less mature children in classroom settings are at serious risk for a diagnosis of ADHD, and overdiagnosis of ADHD is particularly likely if parents and/or teachers are stressed and overworked. A child's initial diagnosis is likely to be unstable and inappropriate over time as these children catch up to the older "peers" in their class. "Psychiatric diagnosis has an inadequate scientific base, including massive co-morbidity, inadequate coverage, leaving many patients to fit only into an NOS option, while categories obscure a clinically important difference between patients meeting criteria for the same diagnosis. These difficulties have led to the conclusion that categorical diagnosis and psychiatry should either be scrapped entirely, or kept only as a short-term expedient (Kupfer and Reiger, 2011)."

Cultural issues and a lack of cultural sensitivity in *DSM-IV-TR* have lead many minority groups to be particularly wary of any *DSM* classification of disorders. A great deal of time and effort have gone into attempting to make *DSM-5* as culturally sensitive and as culture neutral as possible. In the text section following each diagnostic classification particular attention is paid in discussing cultural aspects, as they might uniquely impact that particular disorder. *DSM-5* has included an *Appendix, The Glossary of Cultural Concepts of Distress* in the document to encourage looking at disorders from a sensitivity as to how different cultures may define the disorder. Cultural Perceptions of Cause, Context, and Support of a mental disorder and Cultural Factors Affecting Self Coping & Past Help Seeking are discussed with the particular implications that those factors might have on diagnostic issues. *DSM-5* also contains a structured 16 question interview format to identify cultural issues. *The Cultural Formulation Interview,* is included in the Section III, Emerging Measures and Models.

Haarman

An additional goal of *DSM-5* was the development of a universal screening and assessment device that could be used by all professionals and in all settings. This cross-cutting and dimensional assessment would look at symptoms more globally and allow for cutting across separate diagnostic classifications to provide a more accurate and thorough assessment and diagnosis. A cross-cutting assessment would also allow for establishing an initial baseline for all individuals requesting assistance from mental health services. The goal of the screening document was to provide additional information for the purpose of assessment, diagnosis, treatment planning, and treatment evaluation. *DSM-5* developers wanted the universal assessment tool to be something that would be useful in clinical practice, brief, simple to read, simple to evaluate, and suitable for most patients in most clinical settings. A practical decision had to be made as to whether the clinician would complete the form or whether it would be a self-report, with the client completing the assessment. Weighing both options, the decision was made that the universal screening and assessment device would be most effective if completed by the client, or in the case of a child by a parent or guardian.

The results of this effort produced *DSM-5 Self-Rated Level I Cross Cutting Symptom Measure-Adult* and the *Parent/Guardian-Rated DSM-5 Level I Cross Cutting Symptom Measure-Child Age 6-17* that are found in Section III of the *DSM-5 (2013)*. These instruments are based on a five point scale with a rating of zero indicating an absence of any symptoms depicted by that item and a rating of four indicating a severe (nearly every day) presence of a symptom or dysfunction. A client who rated themselves as being symptomatic in any area would trigger a further investigation in that symptom area, or a Level II Assessment. A number of devices and screeners were reviewed, and while these were not published in the *DSM-5*, they are listed at the *DSM-5* web site: www.psychiatry.org/DSM-5. The web site also lists a self-report format, *DSM-5 Self-Rated Level I Cross Cutting Symptom Measure (ages 10-17)* for use with children and adolescents who are capable of providing their own self-report.

Many individuals have become increasingly concerned about the nexus between psychiatry and the legal system. An entire section of *DSM-5* has been devoted to clarify that the *Diagnostic and Statistical Manual of Mental Disorders* was designed to assist clinicians in assessment, case formulation and treatment planning. It was never intended to be used in forensic settings, even though it has become increasingly relied upon by the legal system to assess the forensic consequences of mental disorders. Paris (2013) cautions that lawyers have a different agenda, often using the information contained in *the DSM-IV-TR* regarding a diagnosis, to get a client off a charge. "When *DSM-5* categories, texts, and criteria are employed for forensic purposes, there is a risk that diagnostic information will be misused or misunderstood. These dangers arise as a result of the imperfect fit between questions of ultimate concern for the law, and information contained in a clinical diagnosis."

The "McNaghten Rule," establishing that a defendant must be able to distinguish right from wrong has come to rely heavily on the *DSM* criteria for schizophrenia. *DSM-5* cautions that "even when diminished control over one's behavior is a feature of the disorder, having the diagnosis in and of itself does not demonstrate that the particular individual is (or was) unable to control his or her behavior at that particular point in time (Paris, 2013)." The *DSM* has also come to play an important role in civil hearings, particularly child custody cases where nonclinical or nonmedical, or otherwise insufficiently trained persons may have implied or stated the presence of a mental disorder on the basis of an untrained reading of *DSM-5*.

Chapter Four: Major Differences Between DSM-IV-TR and DSM-5

A number of general changes regarding the mechanics of reporting diagnoses are suggested in *DSM-5,* not the least of which is a transition from a pure numerical designation of a diagnosis to an alphanumeric system. This change will undoubtedly require significant environmental and procedural changes for organizations, clinicians, and third party payors who will need to convert existing information systems from a numerical designation to an alphanumeric coding system. For example, Obsessive Compulsive Disorder was coded as 300.3 under *DSM-IV-TR* and will now be coded as F42.0. Organizations will have to plan to transition diagnostic codes to the new alphanumeric system and make decisions about what to do with both paper and electronic records that contain an older *DSM-IV/ICD-9* designation.

Another major logistical change is the elimination of the multi-axial system of diagnosis. While the multi-axial system has been dropped in *DSM-5,* it is a lot like the old parody *"The king is dead; long live the king."* The *DSM-5* has developed a new **"*hybrid diagnostic format*"** that combines what was formerly covered by Axis I and Axis II. The distinction, between Axis I and Axis II, is no longer preserved and should eliminate some problems with billing for services that may have existed in the past where Axis II diagnoses were excluded by some insurance carriers. Medical issues that were formerly addressed by Axis III will now be coded as part of a narrative description of "dimensionalizing" a diagnosis. Axis IV had been reserved for identifying general psychosocial and environmental stressors, yet these factors can now be incorporated in a *DSM-5* diagnosis as "Z" Codes," G" Codes, "T" Codes, and "R" Codes, or as additional narrative descriptors. Axis V, the GAF score has been eliminated from the "hybrid diagnosis," but some authors are advocating including some assessment of level of functioning by also listing the World Health Organization Disability Assessment Score (WHODAS). While this is acceptable, it is not required.

Haarman

A diagnosis that looked like the following under *DSM-IV-TR:*

Axis I: 296.24 Major Depressive Disorder, Single Episode, Severe with Psychotic Features

Axis II: V71.09 No Diagnosis

Axis III: HIV positive

Axis IV: homeless, unemployed

Axis V: GAF 40

Under *DSM-5,* will now be written as:

F32.0 Major Depressive Disorder, Single Episode, Severe with Psychotic Features, HIV positive, Z59.5 Extreme Poverty, WHODAS Score 23.

DSM-5 allows for the identification of the proper diagnostic classification (Major Depressive Disorder) and then allows the clinician to describe or "dimensionalize" the diagnosis by adding specifiers and qualifiers, including what had formerly been contained on Axis III and IV in the Multi-Axial System. This "hybridization" of both a Categorical Model and a Dimensional Model is viewed by some as the first step toward abandoning a Kraeplinian categorical approach and developing a more dimensional and functional diagnostic system. Rather than becoming the paradigm shift that *DSM-5* hoped that it would be, this hybrid approach may ultimately be viewed as a transitional period leading to a true paradigm shift in diagnosis that will be borne out as greater neurological data becomes available.

An additional adjustment proposed in the *DSM-5* is the elimination of the Not Otherwise Specified diagnostic category. Moran (2013) indicates that approximately one-quarter of all diagnoses made under DSM-IV-TR are Not Otherwise Specified diagnoses. This lack of diagnostic clarity and specificity associated with a NOS diagnosis has led to individuals receiving a diagnosis without presenting a clear-cut symptom pattern, often resulting inappropriate treatment regimens. While the designation of Not Otherwise Specified has been eliminated, *DSM-5* allows for some "wiggle room" with the inclusion of two additional categories, Other Specified Disorder and Unspecified Disorder.

Haarman

The *Other Specified Disorder* Category allows clinicians to communicate that the presentation does not meet the criteria for any specific category, followed by the specific criteria that are not met or undetermined. For example, a person who only meets four symptom criteria for Major Depressive Disorder, or who has been symptomatic for less than the required two weeks could be recorded by the clinician as: *Other Specified Depressive Disorder, only presenting with four symptoms and not symptomatic for two weeks.* The *Unspecified* Category can be used when the clinician does not wish to specify the reasons the criteria are not met for a specific disorder. Other options include: 300.9 (F99) *Unspecified Mental Disorder,* in which symptoms of a mental disorder are present, but sufficient information to make a more specific diagnosis is unavailable, and 298.9 (F29) *Unspecified schizophrenia spectrum and other psychotic disorder,* where the patient is having a psychotic episode, but further diagnostic specification is not possible.

A (provisional) diagnosis of a specific disorder indicates that enough information is available to make a "working diagnosis," but the clinician wishes to indicate a significant level of diagnostic uncertainty by recording it as (provisional). A provisional diagnosis can be specified by placing the words (provisional) in parentheses after the diagnosis. This can be used in those situations where there is a strong presumption that this will be the ultimate diagnosis, but further information or time is needed to clarify the diagnosis. As with *DSM-IV-TR,* the words rule/out or rule/in can still be used to indicate a lack of diagnostic certainty that may become apparent at a later point.

DSM-5 encourages using multiple diagnostic categories to reflect the level of co-morbidity that exists for many patients. Many individuals may meet criteria for a number of diagnoses, but there is typically a principal diagnosis that is the focus of treatment at that time. The principal diagnosis can be indicated by placing the words (principal diagnosis) in parentheses right after the listed diagnosis. If the principal diagnosis is not specified, the convention is that whichever diagnosis is listed first in the series is the principal diagnosis and therefore, the focus of treatment. For example, if a child meets criteria for Attention Deficit Hyperactivity Disorder, Major Depressive Disorder, Conduct Disorder, and Alcohol Use Disorder, severe, the diagnosis should be written as: *F10.20 Alcohol Use Disorder, severe, F90.2 Attention Deficit Hyperactivity*

Disorder, combined presentation, mild, F91.1 Conduct Disorder, childhood-onset type, with limited prosocial emotions, moderate, and F32.0 Major Depressive Episode, single episode, mild. The diagnosis could also be augmented by description of relevant health issues and Z Codes, R Codes, or T Codes as are appropriate to describe significant environmental issues and other relevant factors.

The fact that the Alcohol Use Disorder is listed first indicates that the disorder is considered to be the *Principal Diagnosis* and is the focus of treatment. In this particular example the focus of treatment would almost have to be the Alcohol Use Disorder. Without achieving some progress with remediating the symptoms of the Alcohol Use Disorder, treatment for the other disorders would even be ineffective or ill-advised.

DSM-5 has made a number of major conceptual changes and philosophical departures from *DSM-IV-TR.* Diagnostic classes have been added in response to clinical need and scientific advances, including: sections on Trauma and Stress Related Disorders, Obsessive-Compulsive and Related Disorders, and Disruptive, Impulse-control, and Conduct Disorders. Several classes of disorders have been substantially revised, renamed, or reorganized, including: Neurodevelopmental Disorders, Somatic Symptom and Related Disorders, Substance-Related and Addictive Disorders, and Neurocognitive Disorders. Several Classes have been divided or consolidated. Mood Disorders were separated into two chapters: Bipolar and Related Disorders and Depressive Disorders. Sexual and Gender Identity Disorders were split into three chapters: Sexual Dysfunction, Gender Dysphoria, and Paraphillic Disorders. Elimination Disorders now have their own chapter, and Feeding Disorders of *DSM-IV-TR* are combined with Eating Disorders.

New disorders included in *DSM-5*

Autism Spectrum Disorder

The handling of some disorders has been fairly controversial and has generated significant discussion between practitioners and scholars. One of the most controversial changes in *DSM-5* has been the Autism Spectrum Disorder diagnosis. Autism was first described by Leo Kanner (1948) as a syndrome of social communication deficits, combined with repetitive and stereotyped behaviors, and beginning in early childhood. In *DSM-IV,* other related disorders were included in the general category of developmental disorders, including Rett's Disorder, Childhood Disintegrative Disorder, Asperger's Disorder, and Pervasive Developmental Disorder. *DSM-5* has now replaced all of these with a single diagnosis, Autism Spectrum Disorder, which is considered a neurodevelopmental disorder. The belief is that these disorders represent a single continuum from mild to severe impairments in the two domains of social communication and restrictive, repetitive interests and behaviors, rather than separate, distinct disorders.

Opposition to this change has been very vocal with a large grass roots uprising. Many families of patients are very concerned about whether or not their family member would qualify for a diagnosis under broader rules and categories. They are worried that removing these four diagnostic categories could interfere with payments for expensive treatment. Of particular concern to these families is the potential impact the removal of these former diagnostic labels might have on academic accommodations or specialized school services. Thus demonstrating, that the DSM-5 has many constituents, including practitioners, parents, clients, schools, and governmental and private organizations, not all of whom are satisfied by a diagnostic approach driven by pure scientific information (Paris, 2013).

Rationale for the changes included the fact that differentiation between Autism Spectrum DIsorder and other development and "nonspectrum disorders" is done reliably and consistently via neuroimaging; whereas, differentiation among these four disorders is clouded by severity, language, and intelligence

Haarman

issues. The Workgroup concluded that Autism is defined by a common set of behaviors, as a single diagnostic category, adapted to clinical presentation by specifiers and associated features. Gray matter volume can distinguish between Autism and neurotypicals, but there are no apparent neurological distinctions between Autism and Pervasive Developmental Disorder, Childhood Disintegrative Disorder, and Asperger's Disorder. It would appear that the distinction between Asperger's, Pervasive Developmental Disorder, Childhood Disintegrative Disorder, and Autism is an artificial one. The essential features of Autism Spectrum Disorder are persistent deficits in reciprocal social communication, in nonverbal communicative behaviors used for social interaction, and in developing and maintaining social relationships, and restricted and repetitive patterns of behavior, interests, or activities. Because Autism is defined by a common set of behaviors, it was felt that Autism is best represented by a single diagnostic category, *Austism Spectrum Disorder,* adapted to the individual's clinical presentation, as reflected through specifiers. These specifiers include the level of support required by the individual, intellectual impairment, language impairment, and associated features (Paris, 2013).

One essential feature of Autism Spectrum Disorder is a persistent impairment in reciprocal social communication. Typically this symptom is pervasive and sustained across the developmental continuum. Language ability can be impacted, but communication skills will be impaired even if vocabulary and grammar are intact. Young children may show little or no initiation of social interaction, no sharing of emotion, and poor or absent eye contact. These individuals may not develop a pattern of smiling or respond to cuddling. The second essential feature of Autism Spectrum Disorder is a restrictive and repetitive pattern of behavior and interests. These individuals often prefer rigid routines and sameness in their daily activities. An intense interest in particular topics, high or low reactivity to sensory input, and stereotyped or repetitive motor movements are also frequently observed. In adulthood, rigidity and difficulty with novelty may limit independence even in highly intelligent people with Autism Spectrum Disorder (Black and Grant, 2014).

First (2014) indicates that Autism Spectrum Disorder is characterized by persistent deficits in social communication and social interaction across

Haarman

multiple contexts, accompanied by restricted, repetitive patterns of behavior, interests, and activities. This is in contrast to childhood-onset Schizophrenia in which early development is near-normal. Schizophrenia in children, as a part of the prodromal state, may include social impairment and atypical interests and beliefs; however, hallucinations and delusions, which are the more defining features of Schizophrenia, are not typically observed in Autism Spectrum Disorder. Intellectual Developmental Disorder involves a general impairment in intellectual functioning, but there is not a discrepancy between the level of social communication skills and other intellectual abilities. A dual diagnosis of Autism Spectrum Disorder and Intellectual Developmental Disorder is now appropriate under *DSM-5,* when social communication and interaction are significantly impaired relative to the developmental level of the individual's nonverbal skills.

Frazier et al., (2012) have suggested that adopting the Autism Spectrum Disorder requirements would mean that 12% of the current patients carrying one of the five eliminated diagnoses would no longer meet criteria for a diagnosis of Autism Spectrum Disorder. *DSM-5* offers a new category called Social Communication Disorder, which will address many of these individuals. Social Communication Disorder describes a milder constellation of symptoms in which impaired verbal and non-verbal communication are the dominant symptom pattern, but the restrictive and repetitive behaviors are absent. A note at the end of diagnostic criteria for Autism Spectrum Disorder would seem to allow "grandfathering in" those individuals who formerly held one of the four diagnoses. Individuals with "a well-established *DSM-IV* diagnosis of Autistic Disorder, Asperger's Disorder, or Pervasive Developmental Disorder should be given the diagnosis of Autism Spectrum Disorder, unless Social (Pragmatic) Communication Disorder is more appropriate (*DSM-5*, 2013)."

Social (Pragmatic) Communication Disorder

Social (Pragmatic) Communication Disorder is a disorder evidenced in children who have difficulty with the pragmatic or practical aspects of social communication. It is a category that is supported by a body of research

Haarman

identifying a group of children who have a dominant symptom pattern of difficulty with language comprehension, formulation, and idiomatic or non-literal language (Bishop, 2000). The impetus to include this category is, at least in some part, an attempt to provide an accurate diagnosis for the majority of those 12% of current patients who would not appear to meet criteria for a diagnosis of Autism Spectrum Disorder. Research indicates that these children exhibit socially inappropriate behavior and significant communication issues, but do not meet criteria Autism Spectrum Disorder (Bishop and Norbury, 2002).

Children with this disorder display the difficulties in social communication, but not the restrictive and repetitive behaviors or restrictive interests consistent with Autism Spectrum Disorder. Moran (2013) stated that many of these individuals had been diagnosed with Pervasive Developmental Disorder Not Otherwise Specified in the past and had significant difficulty using language to narrate, explain, or carry on a conversation. While these children had many similar characteristics of children with Autism, they lacked the restrictive and repetitive behaviors. Autism Spectrum Disorder, Intellectual Disability and Global Developmental Delay must first be ruled out before utilizing this diagnostic category. First (2014) states that Autism Spectrum Disorder is characterized by restricted, repetitive patterns of behavior, interests, or activities, in addition to social communication deficits; whereas, with Social (Pragmatic) Communication Disorder, the restrictive, repetitive behaviors, interests, and activities are virtually absent. Social (Pragmatic) Communication Disorder is distinguishable from Social Anxiety Disorder, in that with the onset of Social Anxiety Disorder, the lack of communication and social interaction is due to anxiety and fear, or distress about social interactions. The affective component, present in Social Anxiety Disorder is typically absent in individuals who meet criteria for Social (Pragmatic) Communication Disorder.

Binge Eating Disorder

Binge Eating Disorder has now been included in *DSM-5,* but has generated little controversy or discussion. Perhaps this is due to Binge Eating Disorder having taken the most appropriate and planful route for inclusion in *DSM-5.* Binge

Haarman

Eating Disorder was first discussed as a part of the development of *DSM-IV-TR*. At that time there was some disagreement as to the legitimacy of this category as a separate disorder, and many individuals questioned its existence as a separate and distinct diagnosis from Bulimia Nervosa. At the time the disagreements could not be resolved, so Binge Eating was included in the chapter for further study in *DSM-IV* and *DSM-IV-TR*. The studies have been done, and there is a substantial archive of data suggesting that Binge Eating Disorder is a diagnosis of its own, separate and distinct from Bulimia Nervosa. The new disorder has essentially the same criteria that were included in *DSM-IV* for further study, with the exception of lowering the minimum average frequency of binge eating required to once weekly over the past three months, similar to the revised criteria for Bulimia Nervosa.

Binge Eating Disorder is characterized by recurrent episodes of binge eating accompanied by marked emotional and psychological distress. While both Bulimia Nervosa and Binge Eating Disorder may be characterized by binge eating, in Bulimia Nervosa, there are recurrent inappropriate compensatory behaviors (e.g., purging, exercise, laxatives, diuretics, enemas, fasting, etc.). Both Major Depressive Disorder and Bipolar I Disorder may involve overeating, but the overeating does not necessarily occur in the form of, or meet the specific diagnostic criteria for binge eating. The impulsivity criteria of Borderline Personality Disorder does include binge eating, and these two disorders can certainly exist in a co-morbid fashion. If the full criteria for Binge Eating Disorder and Borderline Personality Disorder are met, both diagnoses should be given (First, 2014).

Binge Eating Disorder is characterized by recurrent episodes of binge eating without the use of compensatory behaviors. Binge eating is the most common eating disorder in the United States with estimates of 1.6% of all women and 0.8% of all men. Compared with individuals with Bulimia Nervosa, people with Binge Eating Disorder are generally older, more likely to be male, and have a later age of onset. Although weight and body shape concerns are not required for the diagnosis, they are a common part of the presentation. The clinician can rate the current severity of the disorder based on the number of binge eating episodes per week, and can also specify whether the disorder is in partial or full remission. Binge eating is controversial for the same reason that

Haarman

most of the innovations in *DSM-5* are controversial, as it may "widen the nets" and "pathologize" individuals who may fall within normal limits. Frances (2010) has recommended that clinicians not utilize the diagnosis, and that eating disorders be restricted to the classical forms that are known to produce severe dysfunction. He feels that Binge-Eating Disorder describes symptoms that are fairly common, fall within the "normal range," and probably do not deserve to be classified as a mental disorder.

Conduct Disorder and the Limited Prosocial Emotions Specifier

Conduct Disorder is relatively unchanged, but a new specifier has been added in *DSM-5* to reflect a discussion in the literature of a subset of Conduct Disordered Individuals who present as calloused and unemotional. The Workgroup added this new specifier using the terminology of Limited Prosocial Emotions. This terminology was seen as a less pejorative and judgmental way of describing these individuals who are the childhood equivalent of adults with psychopathy, a syndrome falling within the antisocial spectrum, which is characterized by a lack of empathy and concern for the feelings and well-being of others. These traits are found in a very small percentage of youth with Conduct Disorder. Individuals with Conduct Disorder who demonstrate this lack of prosocial emotions have a poorer prognosis and response to treatment than those who still demonstrate prosocial emotions. Individuals with a lack of prosocial emotions typically display deficits in processing signs of fear and distress in others, less sensitivity to punishment, and more fearlessness or thrill-seeking behaviors. The limited prosocial emotions are relatively stable from childhood to early adolescence and early adulthood, and may be genetically influenced (Black and Grant, 2014).

DSM-5 requires that clinicians utilize a specifier to indicate the age of onset for these behaviors: *Childhood-Onset Type (one symptom prior to age ten), Adolescent-Onset Type (no symptoms prior to age ten), or Unspecified Onset (criteria are met, but there is no information about the age of onset available).*

Haarman

The older the child is before the Conduct Disorder starts, the better the prognosis. Cases with an onset during adolescence usually recover by young adulthood (Moffitt, 1993). But when conduct disorder begins in the preschool and elementary school years, the syndrome is most likely to continue into adulthood and is likely to result in an antisocial personality disorder (Zoccolillo et al., 1992.

Disruptive Mood Dysregulation Disorder

Disruptive Mood Dysregulation Disorder is new to *DSM-5* and was an attempt to address a diagnostic controversy regarding pediatric Bipolar Disorder, but has also become controversial in its own right. A petition by 51 mental health agencies requested that the *DSM-5* change, adding Disruptive Mood Dysregulation Disorder, be reviewed by independent experts. This was rejected without explanation (Division 32 Committee on *DSM-5* (2012): The open letter to the *DSM-5* Task Force. http://DSM-5reform.com/the-open-letter-to-DSM-5-task force). Frances (2013) has stated that "Disruptive Mood Dysregulation Disorder is included in *DSM-5*, despite having been studied by one group for only six years. It is included based on minimal research and was justified on the basis of needing to reduce the over diagnosis of childhood bipolar disorders. I strongly recommend that it be used extremely sparingly, if at all. It should certainly not be regarded as an indication for medication. In my view Disruptive Mood Dysregulation Disorder was "not ready for Prime Time."

The addition of Disruptive Mood Dysregulation Disorder in *DSM-5* has generated considerable controversy. It was created in part to address concerns about the possible overdiagnosis of bipolar disorder in children under the age of 12 who display irritability and extreme behavioral dyscontrol (Alexson et al., 2006). In the past 20 years, there has been a 40-fold increase in the number of youth diagnosed with Bipolar Disorder. It was hoped that the diagnosis of Disruptive Mood Dysregulation Disorder would help fill an important gap for children with mood dysregulation characterized by chronic, severe, and persistent irritability. Brottman et al., (2006) introduced a different term,

Haarman

Severe Mood Dysregulation, to describe children whose behavior presents in a very similar fashion to Bipolar Disorder, but who don't accurately meet criteria for a diagnosis of Bipolar Disorder.

This terminology was eventually replaced by Disruptive Mood Dysregulation Disorder. The terminology views the syndrome as a variant of a new disorder, not as a classical behavior disorder such as Oppositional Defiant Disorder, Conduct Disorder, or Bipolar Disorder. Research shows that children with Disruptive Mood Dysregulation Disorder have a different outcome, gender ratio, and family history than those with Bipolar Disorder, and do not necessarily go on to develop a full-blown manic or hypomanic episode. Originally, the Workgroup considered naming the disorder Temper Dysregulation Disorder, a term used in earlier research, but felt like the word "temper" indicated a willfulness or voluntary aspect of a disorder that is typified by an inability to regulate affective states (Black and Grant, 2014).

One of the purposes of this new terminology would be to discourage automatic prescription of mood stabilizers and antipsychotics typically used to treat Bipolar I. However, the practice of prescribing drugs to seriously disturbed and acting out children does not depend solely on diagnosis. In contrast, when we give drugs to young children seen as bipolar, we do not have the same evidence base and do not know the long-term consequences. No one would be shocked to learn that children diagnosed with Disruptive Mood Dysregulation Disorder (DMDD) might ultimately receive antipsychotics or mood stabilizers. However, the new diagnosis may also prevent some children from being diagnosed Bipolar inaccurately, and automatically placed on mood stabilizers and antipsychotics.

Olfson et al. (2006) states that the members of the *DSM-5* task force were cautious about the concept of bipolar disorder in pre-pubertal children, in part because it leads to frequent prescriptions of mood stabilizers and antipsychotics, many of which have significant side effects. "Many of these medications have broad sedative effects that are often helpful to reduce anger, even if the diagnosis is inappropriate. No one would claim that pain relief from analgesics proves that all patients have the same illness, and psychiatry would not claim that medications typically used for Bipolar individuals prove that a Bipolar diagnosis is appropriate. The medications may have a broad and nonspecific effect in reducing anger, even if the diagnosis is inaccurate (Frances, 2013)."

There is concern that this new diagnosis of Disruptive Mood Dysregulation Disorder may "widen the nets" to include children displaying "normal" temper tantrums, leading to an increased use of inappropriate psychotropic medications with children. Some individuals are concerned that Disruptive Mood Dysregulation Disorder could become the new "fad" diagnosis. Frances (2010) has expressed grave concerns about pediatric Bipolar Disorder as an example of a diagnostic fad. "To become a fad, psychiatric diagnosis requires three preconditions: a pressing need, an engaging story, and influential Prophets." In Frances' opinion, Disruptive Mood Dysregulation Disorder has all the components necessary to become the new "fad" diagnosis.

In *DSM-5,* Disruptive Mood Dysregulation Disorder is viewed as "severe recurrent temper outbursts that are out of proportion in intensity and duration to the situation or the child's developmental level." These outbursts occur, on average, at least three times per week, have been present for 12 months or more, and the child has never had a period of three months where outbursts were not evident. Onset of symptoms is prior to age 10, distinguishing it from Bipolar Disorder, which typically has a much later onset. The outbursts must occur in multiple settings and mood between outbursts is persistently irritable or angry. The diagnosis is not made before age five and does not persist beyond age 18. This diagnosis is not for any individuals who have met the full criteria for a manic or hypomanic episode for at least one day. It is a diagnosis that cannot coexist with Oppositional Defiant Disorder, Intermittent Explosive Disorder, or Bipolar Disorder. If a child's symptoms meet criteria for both Disruptive Mood Dysregulation Disorder and Oppositional Defiant Disorder, *DSM-5* directs that only the Disruptive Mood Dysregulation Disorder diagnosis should be given. Estimates indicate that about 15% of children currently diagnosed with Oppositional Defiant Disorder will have symptoms that meet criteria for Disruptive Mood Dysregulation Disorder (Black and Grant, 2014). First (2014) has recognized the difficulty of distinguishing Disruptive Mood Dysregulation Disorder from a variety of other disorders or issues that children

Haarman

and adolescents might present. Disruptive Mood Dysregulation Disorder is characterized by severe, recurrent temper outbursts that are grossly out of proportion in intensity and duration to the provocation. These outbursts are accompanied by a persistent irritable or angry mood, most of the day, nearly every day. Disruptive Mood Dysregulation Disorder is distinguishable from Bipolar I and Bipolar II Disorders which are episodic illnesses with cycling and discrete episodes of mood perturbation that are clearly distinguishable from the child's baseline behavior. In addition, the change in mood during a Manic or Hypomanic Episode, required for a Bipolar I or II diagnosis, is accompanied by increased energy and activity as well as cognitive and behavioral symptoms. In contrast, the irritability of Disruptive Mood Dysregulation Disorder is present chronically and persistently over many months. *DSM-5* specifically prohibits a co-morbid diagnosis of both Bipolar Disorder and Disruptive Mood Dysregulation Disorder.

Additionally, Oppositional Defiant Disorder, Intermittent Explosive Disorder, and Autism Spectrum Disorder are clearly distinguishable from Disruptive Mood Dysregulation Disorder and cannot be diagnosed as co-morbid conditions in a child. Oppositional Defiant Disorder is characterized by a pattern of angry, irritable mood, argumentative, defiant behaviors, and/or vindictiveness. As indicated previously, If criteria are met for both Oppositional Defiant Disorder and Disruptive Mood Dysregulation Disorder, only Disruptive Mood Dysregulation Disorder is diagnosed. Intermittent Explosive Disorder is characterized by aggressive outbursts that can resemble the severe temper tantrums in Disruptive Mood Dysregulation Disorder; however, there is no persistent irritable or angry mood between outbursts as in Disruptive Mood Dysregulation Disorder. Intermittent Explosive Disorder requires only three months of active symptoms, in contrast to the twelve month requirement for Disruptive Mood Dysregulation Disorder. Furthermore, Intermittent Explosive Disorder is not diagnosed if criteria are met for Disruptive Mood Dysregulation Disorder. Individuals diagnosed with Autism Spectrum Disorder may typically display temper outbursts, particularly when routines are disrupted. If then

Haarman

Temper outbursts are better explained by Autism Spectrum Disorder, then *DSM-5* Disruptive Mood Dysregulation Disorder is not diagnosed (First, 2014). While *DSM-5* specifically prohibits a co-morbid diagnosis of both Oppositional Defiant Disorder, Intermittent Explosive Disorder, and Autism Spectrum Disorder and Disruptive Mood Dysregulation. Disruptive Mood Dysregulation Disorder can coexist with Attention Deficit Hyperactivity Disorder, Substance Use Disorder, Depressive Disorders, and Anxiety Disorders if the angry, irritable episodes extend outside the anxiety-provoking situations or the depressed episodes (First, 2014).

Excoriation (Skin Picking) Disorder

Excoriation (Skin Picking) Disorder was first proposed in *DSM-IV,* but research data to justify including it as a disorder at that time was insufficient. In *DSM-IV,* specific criteria for a diagnosis were developed, but Excoriation Disorder was assigned to the chapter for further study. Since that time, sufficient data has been gathered to justify its inclusion in *DSM-5.* Excoriation Disorder is characterized by recurrent, compulsive picking of the skin, resulting in skin lesions. Black and Grant (2014) report that Excoriation Disorder has long been recognized in medical literature, and is now in *DSM-5* due to a growing body of data emphasizing its prevalence and disabling nature. There are a number of similarities between Excoriation Disorder and Trichotillomania and the criteria for the two disorders parallel each other.

DSM-5 Excoriation Disorder criteria call for recurrent skin picking of sufficient intensity and frequency that it results in skin lesions. The individual has tried and failed to stop the picking, and the disorder causes significant distress in important areas of functioning. The disorder is not better explained by the physiological effects of substance abuse, a medical condition, or another mental disorder. Prevalence studies have found that Excoriation Disorder occurs in 1.4% to 5.4% of the general population. Often considered chronic, the disorder may fluctuate over time and in intensity.

First (2014) describes Excoriation Disorder as recurrent skin picking resulting in skin lesions despite repeated attempts to stop. Other diagnoses that involve some picking at the skin include Obsessive-Compulsive Disorder, Body Dysmorphic Disorder, Psychotic Disorders, and Stereotypic Movement Disorder. In Obsessive-Compulsive Disorder and Body Dysmorphic Disorder, if either of these diagnoses better explain the skin picking or skin lesions, those diagnoses should be used rather than Excoriation Disorder. Psychotic disorders may include skin picking in response to delusions, hallucinations, and other repetitive behaviors. In those cases, Excoriation Disorder should not be diagnosed.

Hoarding Disorder

Hoarding disorder may be the first diagnostic category that received its impetus for inclusion in *DSM-5* as a result of a popular cable television show. *Hoarders* has appeared on the A&E cable channel since 2006. As a result, the show's popularity has also spurred considerable scientific research into Hoarding Disorder. Substantial data exists indicating that Hoarding Disorder is a unique and separate diagnostic category not reflected in a diagnosis of Obsessive Compulsive Disorder. In *DSM-IV,* Hoarding was listed as part of the symptom pattern in the criteria for a Compulsive Personality Disorder. In the past, individuals with Hoarding Disorder were typically diagnosed Obsessive Compulsive Disorder. Individuals who meet diagnostic criteria for Hoarding Disorder do not exhibit a classical symptom pattern of Obsessive Compulsive Disorder (OCD) or respond to medications known to be effective with OCD. Hoarding may be a symptom of OCD, but data indicate that hoarding is a separate phenomenon and must be addressed through its own unique set of treatment strategies.

Black and Grant (2014) describe Hoarding Disorder as a persistent difficulty discarding or parting with possessions. In most situations, the quantity of the items retained and the disorganization of those items distinguishes Hoarding Disorder from normal messy and disorganized behavior. There also appears to be a set of uniquely neurological correlates that set Hoarding Disorder apart

Haarman

from normal "collecting" behaviors or Obsessive Compulsive Disorder. The high prevalence and serious consequences of Hoarding Disorder, together with the research on its distinctiveness from Obsessive Compulsive Disorder and Obsessive-Compulsive Personality Disorder, have led the authors of *DSM-5* to classify Hoarding Disorder as a new diagnostic category. Hoarding is fairly common, significantly disabling, and has been shown to be present in 2% to 6% of the general population.

DSM-5 diagnostic criteria for Hoarding Disorder includes persistent difficulty discarding or parting with their possessions and a perceived "need" to save the items regardless of their actual value. The clutter is due to purposeful saving, rather than just an inability to throw away items, due to attaching emotional significance to the items. The criteria for this disorder can also be met if the living areas are uncluttered, "but only because of the interventions of third parties such as family member or hired cleaners (*DSM-5, 2013*)." Criteria also call for the accumulation of these possessions to congest and clutter living areas to the point they can no longer be used for their intended purpose (Frost et al., 2012). The criteria emphasize the living areas of the home or workplace, rather than unused space like basements or storage facilities. The hoarding symptoms cause significant impairment in functioning and are not better attributable to a medical condition or another mental disorder. *DSM-5* diagnostic criteria also include a number of specifiers such as "with excessive acquisition," "with good or fair insight," "with poor insight," and "with absent insight/delusional beliefs."

First (2014) provides insight and guidance for making a differential diagnosis between Hoarding Disorder and Obsessive-Compulsive Disorder. In Obsessive-Compulsive Disorder, the individual feels driven to perform repetitive behaviors in response to an obsession or set of rules that are generally experienced by the individual as ego-dystonic; whereas, Hoarding Disorder is typically ego-syntonic. When the accumulation of objects is a direct consequence of the Obsessive-Compulsive Disorder, a diagnosis of Hoarding Disorder is not made. However, when hoarding appears concurrently with typical symptoms of Obsessive-Compulsive Disorder and are independent of those symptoms, both Hoarding Disorder and Obsessive-Compulsive Disorder may be diagnosed. When the accumulation of objects relates to a fixated

Haarman

interest that is a part of Autism Spectrum Disorder or the delusions/hallucinations associated with psychotic disorders, the diagnosis of Hoarding Disorder is not made. *DSM-5* also encourages clinicians to make a distinction between "normal collecting behavior" which is organized and systematic, even if the amount of possessions is similar in quantity to individuals with Hoarding Disorder.

Disinhibited Social Engagement Disorder

Disinhibited Social Engagement Disorder is new in *DSM-5,* having been split off from the *DSM-IV-TR* Reactive Attachment Disorder of Infancy or Early Childhood. What distinguishes these two, both of which have an assumed etiology of pathogenic childcare, is the behavioral response the child makes to being exposed to inadequate or abusive child caring practices. The dominant feature of Disinhibited Social Engagement Disorder is a pattern of behavior that involves inappropriate and overly familiar behavior with unfamiliar adults or strangers. Young children are typically reticent when interacting with unfamiliar adults, but children with this disorder not only lack such reticence, but willingly engage strangers and have no fear of going off with them. The child must have reached a cognitive capacity of a nine-month-old child and the disinhibited social behaviors are frequently observed in children between the ages of two years and adolescence (Black and Grant, 2014).

In Disinhibited Social Engagement Disorder, pre-school children's verbal and social intrusiveness and attention seeking behaviors are common. In the middle years, verbal and physical over familiarity are common and by adolescence, the indiscriminate and overly familiar behaviors may extend to peers. Like Reactive Attachment Disorder, Disinhibited Social Engagement Disorder is associated with cognitive, language, and developmental delays as well as signs of neglect like poor nutrition and poor hygiene. Signs of the disorder may persist even when the neglect is no longer present. The diagnosis requires that two or more examples of disinhibited behavior are present. These include a reduced or absent reticence in interacting with adults, overly familiar verbal or physical behaviors with adults, diminished "checking back" behaviors,

Haarman

and a willingness to go off with an unfamiliar adult with no hesitation. These disinhibited behaviors are not just simple impulsivity, as frequently observed in children with Attention Deficit Hyperactivity Disorder, but are more of a social impulsivity, where the child does not recognize boundaries or limitations with adults (Black and Grant, 2014).

Post Traumatic Stress Disorder

While not a new disorder in *DSM-5*, there have been extensive changes in Posttraumatic Stress Disorder, including a separate set of diagnostic criteria for Posttraumatic Stress Disorder in Children Under Six, Dissociative Features, Delayed Onset, and the removal of the criteria calling for an excessive reaction to the traumatic situation.

Black and Grant (2014) describe the lengthy history of the development of Posttraumatic Stress Disorder (Post Traumatic Stress Disorder) which was initially recognized in *DSM-I* as "gross stress reaction." Post Traumatic Stress Disorder is common in the general population and can occur at any age, even in young children. In women, the most frequent precipitating event is a physical or sexual assault; whereas, in men, the traumatic event often involves a combat experience. Post Traumatic Stress Disorder generally begins soon after the event is experienced, but the onset can be delayed.

The *DSM-5* criteria depart from those in *DSM-IV* in several important aspects (Friedman et al., 2011). The stressors that trigger the Post Traumatic Stress Disorder are more explicitly described, requiring the individual to have had exposure to actual or threatened death, serious injury, or sexual violence. As Nally (2009) points, this change is significant because over diagnosis weakens the main concept of the disorder and fails to focus on the disorder's key idea - the impact of severe trauma. The *DSM-5* criteria specifically state that the trauma cannot be a result of exposure to trauma through electronic media, television, movies, or pictures. Paris (2000) believes there is substantial evidence that most people exposed to trauma, even severe trauma, never

Haarman

develop Post Traumatic Stress Disorder.   Post Traumatic Stress Disorder is likely as much a consequence of personality traits, as it is of life events. For example, Post Traumatic Stress Disorder in firefighters was best predicted by traits of neuroticism prior to exposure, rather than by the severity of the fire.

The excessive reaction to the stressor, that was an integral part of the *DSM-IV* criteria for Post Traumatic Stress Disorder, has been eliminated.   Many individuals who are first responders do not necessarily show an excessive reaction to trauma, but do display symptoms consistent with a diagnosis of Post Traumatic Stress Disorder. *DSM-5* also dropped *DSM-IV* criteria A2, which required individuals to have subjectively experienced fear, helplessness, or horror at the time of the traumatic event.   Research indicates that an individual's initial response to the stressor is not always useful in predicting who will later exhibit symptoms of Post Traumatic Stress Disorder. Furthermore, criteria A2 did not take into account that some individuals who experience trauma as a result of an occupational hazard, for which they have been extensively trained, often viewed the event as "just doing my job."

While *DSM-IV* had three major symptom clusters re-experiencing, avoiding, and changes in arousal levels, *DSM-5* has added a new, fourth symptom cluster identified as negative alterations in cognitions and mood. The new symptom cluster includes persistent, exaggerated, negative expectations about one's self, others, and the world itself.   The new symptom cluster also includes avoidance and numbing symptoms. Criteria call for an individual to have displayed two or more of seven specified symptoms, including: an inability to remember, persistent and exaggerated negative beliefs, persistent and distorted cognitions, persistent negative emotional states, a diminished interest or participation in activities, feelings of detachment or strangeness, and an inability to experience positive emotions (Black and Grant, 2014).

DSM-5 criteria also call for alterations in arousal associated with the traumatic event. These include irritable behavior and angry outbursts, hypervigilance, an exaggerated startle response, problems with concentration, and disturbances in sleep. The new criteria also allow for specifiers of Dissociative Symptoms that may involve depersonalization or derealization, as well as the possibility of

Haarman

delayed expression. In some cases, the individual may not meet full criteria for a diagnosis of Post Traumatic Stress Disorder until at least six months after the traumatizing event. This is not to be confused with the "recovered memory syndrome."

A major addition to *DSM-5* Post Traumatic Stress Disorder provides for specific diagnostic criteria for Post Traumatic Stress Disorder for Children Six Years or Younger. Specifically, symptom thresholds were lowered or eliminated for some symptoms that are difficult to assess in preschool children. A child's exposure to the threat of death, serious injury, or sexual violence may have been a result of directly experiencing a traumatic event, witnessing the event as it occurred to others, learning that the traumatic event occurred to a close family member, or experiencing repeated or extreme exposure to the details of the trauma. The spontaneous and intrusive memories, so typical with adults, may not necessarily appear as distressing for children under six. In some situations it may not be possible to ascertain that the frightening content of memories or dreams is related to the traumatic event. For many children, their posttraumatic stress may be reflected as enactments in play, as well as, substantially increased frequency of negative emotions, socially withdrawn behavior, or a general reduction in the expression of positive emotions.

First (2014) describes Post Traumatic Stress Disorder as exposure to actual or threatened death, serious injury, or sexual violence, followed by the development of intrusive symptoms, persistent avoidance of stimuli associated with the trauma, negative alterations of cognitions and mood, and marked alterations in arousal and reactivity. Post Traumatic Stress Disorder is distinguished from Adjustment Disorder, which is characterized by a stressor of any level of severity and does not have a specific response pattern. The diagnosis of Adjustment Disorder is used when the response to an extreme stressor does not meet criteria for Post Traumatic Stress Disorder or when the symptom pattern of Post Traumatic Stress Disorder occurs in response to a non-traumatizing stressor.

While there is an overlapping symptom pattern, Post Traumatic Stress Disorder is distinct from Obsessive Compulsive Disorder, Panic Disorder, and

Haarman

Generalized Anxiety Disorder. In Obsessive Compulsive Disorder, there may be recurrent and intrusive thoughts, but these are experienced as inappropriate and not related to an experienced, traumatic event. Panic Disorder may be characterized by arousal and dissociative symptoms, but these occur during Panic Attacks and are not associated with a traumatic stressor. Unlike Post Traumatic Stress Disorder, the persistent symptoms of Generalized Anxiety Disorder, irritability and anxiety, are not associated with any identifiable traumatic stressor. A relatively recent phenomena is the co-occurrence of Traumatic Brain Injury and Post Traumatic Stress Disorder. With Traumatic Brain Injury, neurocognitive symptoms (disorientation, confusion, and memory deficits) develop after a traumatic brain injury which can also lead to Post Traumatic Stress Disorder. In that case, both disorders should be diagnosed (First, 2014).

Premenstrual Dysphoric Disorder

The Mood Disorders Workgroup recommended that Premenstrual Dysphoric Disorder should receive full disorder status in *DSM-5*. In *DSM-IV* it was included in the appendix for further study and if present, was coded as Depressive Disorder Not Otherwise Specified. Research evidence has accumulated that would indicate the disorder is a significant cause of distress. It was also felt that information on the diagnosis, treatment, and validation of the disorder has matured to the point that the disorder qualified for inclusion in *DSM-5*. Additionally, the studies identified a subset of women (about 2%) who suffer intermittently from severe affective symptoms associated with the luteal phase of their menstrual cycle (Black and Grant, 2014).

Premenstrual Dysphoric Disorder is characterized by marked affective lability, irritability, anger, increased interpersonal conflicts, depressed mood, feelings of hopelessness, self-deprecation, anxiety and tension, and feelings of being "keyed up" or "on edge" regularly developing in the final week before the onset of menses. These symptoms start to improve within a few days after the onset of menses, and become minimal or absent in the week post menses (First, 2014). This disorder has a distinctive pattern of onset and resolution that is dissimilar from Bipolar Disorder and Major Depressive Disorder, as in both these, the affective symptoms are unrelated to the menstrual cycle. Prospective daily symptom ratings are important for documenting the time of onset and offset of mood symptoms. Premenstrual Dysphoric Disorder should only be used when there are prominent psychological symptoms not just difficult physical symptoms (Francis, 2103). Premenstrual Dysphoric Disorder is divergent from dysmenorrhea in which painful symptoms begin with the onset of menses.

Bereavement Exclusion

In *DSM-5,* the core criterion items for the diagnosis of Major Depressive Disorder, as well as the two weeks duration criterion, are unchanged from *DSM-IV,* with minor wording changes. The Mood Disorders Workgroup concluded that the Major Depressive Disorder criteria have accumulated considerable research support and have held up well over the past 30 years. One important change in *DSM-5* is the deletion of the "bereavement exclusion." The deletion of this diagnostic criteria has led to controversy in which critics have claimed eliminating the "bereavement exclusion," has medicalized the normal process of grief. In *DSM-IV*, Major Depressive Episode criteria required that the symptoms are "not better accounted for by bereavement" (Black and Grant, 2014). This exclusion applied to symptoms lasting less than two months following the death of a loved one. Rationale for the change has been provided by many individuals, and included: any stressor, not just grief, is capable of triggering a Major Depressive Episode, the time span specified is arbitrary, and the treatment of both Major Depressive Episode and grief have been shown to respond to a combination of antidepressants and psychotherapy, specifically, cognitive behavioral therapy.

One argument for dropping the "bereavement exclusion" was the lack of evidence to support the unique loss of a loved one as different from other stressors in terms of its likelihood of precipitating a major depressive episode. Any significant stressor is capable of triggering a Major Depressive Episode. There is no justification for excluding bereavement. The same rationale could

Haarman

result in a "divorce exclusion," "loss of employment exclusion," "a major health issue exclusion, etc." Additionally, the time period of two months implies that "normal grief" should only last for two months, which is not substantiated by the available research. Although bereavement may be painful, most persons do not develop a Major Depressive Episode. Those who do, however, typically experience more suffering, feel worthless, and may have suicidal ideation. For others, bereavement is a severe psychosocial stressor capable of precipitating Major Depressive Episodes in vulnerable persons.

 Bereavement-related depression has some of the characteristics of a major depressive episode and is most likely to occur in individuals with a personal or family history of Major Depressive Episodes. Finally, the symptoms associated with the bereavement-related Major depressive disorder respond to antidepressant medication and psychotherapy. Many clinicians prefer to observe an individual, within the first two months following the death of a loved one, to determine an appropriate treatment for either Major Depressive Disorder, or to continue to treat the client's reaction as a part of the normal grieving process (Black and Grant, 2014).

Other authors including, Paris (2013) and Frances (2013) have provided cogent arguments for continuing the "bereavement exclusion." While Bereavement and Major Depression have a number of symptoms that are common, there are enough distinctions to insist they be regarded as two separate phenomena. A comparison of the symptom criteria for Major Depression and the proposed Complex Bereavement Disorder would reveal that of the nine symptoms of Major Depression, only four have a comparable counterpart in Complex Bereavement Disorder. There are three symptoms of Complex Bereavement Disorder that have no counterpart in Major Depression criteria. So while both disorders have some common symptoms, they are viewed as separate phenomena. In Bereavement, the symptoms seem to come in waves and then reside from awareness, having minimal impact on the individual's behavior; whereas, in Major Depression, the symptoms are chronic, ongoing, and tend to have a cumulative impact on individuals. The thought content associated with Bereavement generally features a preoccupation with thoughts and memories of the deceased, rather than the self-critical or pessimistic ruminations of a Major Depressive Episode. In Bereavement, the individual's self-esteem is not

Haarman

significantly impacted: whereas, in Major Depression, chronic depression tends to grind away at self-esteem, and many individuals may reach the point of feeling, helpless, hopeless, and worthless.   Finally, in Bereavement, the individual may experience some suicidal ideation as a part of a desire to be reunited with a loved one; whereas, in Major Depressive Disorder, the symptom of suicidal ideation is more reflective of a desire for the emotional pain to stop.

Responding to the maelstrom of criticism, *DSM-5 has also provided a note in the diagnostic criteria to address this issue.* "Responses to a significant loss (e.g. Bereavement, financial ruin, losses from a natural disaster, a serious medical issue or disability) may include the feelings of intense sadness, ruminations about the loss, insomnia, poor appetite and weight loss noted in Criterion A, which may resemble a depressive episode.   Although such symptoms may be understandable or considered appropriate to the loss, the presence of a major depressive episode in addition to the normal response to a significant loss should also be carefully considered.   The decision inevitably requires the exercise of clinical judgment based on the individual's history and cultural norms for the expression of distress in the context of loss (*DSM-5, 2013*)."

Clinicians are urged not to diagnose major depression if grief, even if prolonged, best accounts for the symptoms. *DSM-5* also provides a category for further study called Complex Bereavement Disorder (Paris, 2013). The resolution of this controversy has been to provide a note to the diagnostic criteria for a Major Depressive Episode and to establish a category for further study labeled Complex Bereavement Disorder.   It remains an issue of great debate and one that will only be resolved by the passage of time and the development of clinical practices (Paris, 2013).

Haarman

Substance Use Disorder

Black and Grant (2014) describe the evolving history of diagnosing individuals who use substances inappropriately. In *DSM-I,* addictions were placed within the umbrella category of "sociopathic personality disturbance," reflecting a belief that these individuals were violating the norms of society. *DSM-II* placed alcoholism and the renamed drug dependence in the group of "personality disorders and certain other non-psychotic mental disorders." Alcoholism was subdivided into *Episodic Excessive Drinking, Habitual Excessive Drinking, and Alcohol Addiction* (those considered to be dependent on alcohol). Furthermore, ten categories of Drug Dependencies were created to reflect the fact that many drugs were commonly misused. *DSM-III* gave substance use disorders, separate diagnostic criteria as well as divisions of abuse and dependence. The construct of Abuse and Dependence has continued until *DSM-5.* Dependence was thought to have a different cause and course of development from abuse which only resulted in social and personal problems. Substance Intoxication was considered a reversible substance-specific syndrome and likewise, Substance Withdrawal was an identifiable syndrome related to a particular drug and associated with medically important consequences.

DSM-5 defines a Substance Use Disorder as a maladaptive pattern leading to clinically significant impairment or distress for at least 12 months (Paris, 2013). It must be distinguished from non-pathological use of a substance which is characterized by the repeated use at relatively low doses, possibly involving periods of intoxication, but not associated with significant negative behavioral consequences. Substance Use Disorders are characterized by heavy use, leading to significant distress or impaired functioning. Many individuals with Conduct Disorder or Antisocial Personality Disorder also abuse substances and these disorders are often co-morbid with Substance Use Disorder (First, 2014). Importantly, the distinction between Substance Abuse and Substance Dependence defined in *DSM-IV-TR* no longer exists. The two former diagnoses are merged into a single Substance Use Disorder, because the distinction between abuse and dependence was often arbitrary, had limited utility, and was often confusing. A new symptom - Craving - or a strong desire or urges to use a substance has been added, while the symptom of recurrent legal problems has been dropped. Simultaneously, Criterion A3 (legal problems) was eliminated as it had a low prevalence rate relative to other criteria. The severity of the new Substance Use Disorder is specified based on the number of symptoms observed.

Black and Grant (2014) reported there were several reasons to combine abuse and dependence into a single category of Substance Use Disorder. First, many clinicians had trouble distinguishing the two, and while there was good reliability with Substance Dependence diagnoses, Substance Abuse diagnoses were much less reliable and more variable. Substance Abuse was often seen as the prodromal phase of Substance Dependence. Second, most studies indicated that a Substance Abuse diagnosis was most commonly based on hazardous use (driving and drinking or using) with that being the sole basis for the diagnosis. Third, the division between abuse and dependence led to many "diagnostic orphans," i.e. an individual who met only two criteria for dependence and none of the criteria for abuse, resulting in a "no diagnosis." Considering the evidence, the Workgroup recommended Abuse and Dependence be combined into a single disorder of graded clinical severity, and established the symptom threshold as a minimum of two symptoms (Helzer et al., 2006). Mild Substance Use Disorder requires 2 -3 symptoms; Moderate Substance Use Disorder requires 4 - 5 symptoms; and Severe Substance Use Disorder requires more than 6 symptoms.

A number of individuals have expressed concern that the elimination of the abuse/dependence distinction may lead to an "artificial epidemic" in the diagnosis of individuals who have a substance disorder. An Australian study (Mewton et al., 2011) predicts a 60% increase in prevalence, as a whole; whereas, an American study (Agrawal et al., 2011) projected only a 10% increase. The chair of the Workgroup (O'Brien, 2011) has defended eliminating the terminology of "dependence" because it was a confusing concept that conflates physical and psychological need for the substance. This logic was based on research by (Hasin & Beseler, 2009) which suggests alcoholism is a dimensional disorder that can be rated on a continuum of severity, and then be coded for physiological dependence.

Haarman

Critics continue to express concern that *DSM-5* relabels individuals with a *DSM-IV-TR* Substance Abuse diagnosis in a way that includes them with end-stage addicts. Statistical analysis suggests that there are no sharp boundaries between these groupings. Some argue that it is unfair and inaccurate to label someone whose substance abuse problems are intermittent, temporary, or contextual (college), the same as a chronic substance abuser. In addition, being labelled as dependent, or self-labeling oneself as Substance Dependent can become a self-fulfilling prophecy and a great excuse for not meeting personal responsibilities (O'Brien, 2011). Caffeine Withdrawal and Cannabis Use Disorder and Cannabis Withdrawal have also been added in *DSM-5* as new diagnostic categories.

Gambling Disorder

Black and Grant (2014) state that gambling is encountered in almost all cultures and has been present throughout history. For most individuals gambling is not considered pathological. Disordered gambling was first introduced in *DSM-III*, as *Pathological Gambling*. It was included in the chapter on impulse control disorders, along with pyromania and kleptomania. In *DSM-5*, the disorder has been included in the chapter on Substance-Related and Addictive Disorders because of high rates of co-morbidity, similar presentations, and genetic and physiological overlap. The criteria are relatively unchanged from Pathological Gambling contained in *DSM-IV-TR*. Significantly the name itself was changed from Pathological Gambling to Gambling Disorder to avoid the stigma of "pathological," and the number of symptoms required has been reduced from five to four.

DSM-5 puts one and only one "behavioral disorder" on a par with addiction to substances, Gambling Disorder. Pathological Gambling was listed as a disorder in *DSM-IV-TR* under the chapter of Impulse Control Disorders and has a lengthy history with extensive studies to back it up. Other "disordered" behaviors such as internet use, sex, eating, shopping, video gaming, etc. aren't included, but are likely to have their "day in court" in due time. (Potenza, 2006) concluded "There is substantive research to support the position that pathological

Haarman

gambling and substance use disorders are very similar in the ways that they affect the neurological reward system in the brain. PET scans and MRIs have demonstrated these physical changes in the brains of people with behavior disorders and substance disorders alike."

Some fear that *DSM-5* has introduced the concept of Behavioral Addictions. The concept suggests that behavior originally intended for pleasurable recreation is now compulsively driven, performed in a repetitive fashion, despite negative consequences, and there is an escalating sense of loss of control. A behavior has now become an addiction. "The new concept of behavioral addictions has created potentially millions of new "patients" and created excuses for irresponsibility (O'Brien, 2011)." First (2014) separates Gambling Disorder, which is a persistent and recurrent, problematic gambling behavior leading to clinically significant impairment or distress. He makes a distinction between Professional Gambling, which is highly disciplined and has limited risk taking Social Gambling, which usually occurs with friends and is characterized by limited time spent on gambling activities, and Gambling Disorder.

Chapter Five: Conditions for Further Study

Finally, a number of possible Disorders have been introduced by *DSM-5* in a section entitled Conditions for Further Study. These diagnostic categories are not available for use, but have become useful in providing criteria for further study and research with a temporary criteria set and are "intended to provide a common language for researchers and clinicians who are interested in studying these disorders. It is hoped that this will promote understanding and inform decisions about their placement in future *DSM* editions (*DSM-5, 2013*)."

Attenuated Psychosis

The Psychotic Disorders Workgroup proposed a new diagnosis in order to identify persons at risk for the development of Schizophrenia and to facilitate early identification and treatment. The disorder consists of mild psychotic like symptoms, with the assumption that conversion to Schizophrenia or a full-blown psychosis is likely, at a future point. The proposed diagnosis became a focus of controversy. Critics within and outside the field expressed concerns that Attenuated Psychosis might lead to psychiatric labeling of individuals who are not ill, and who, in most cases, would never develop a psychotic disorder. Concerns were also expressed this disorder might lead to an overuse of antipsychotic medications, in individuals who do not require them, with the possibility of significant side effects (*DSM-5*, 2013).

Depressive Episodes with Short Duration Hypomania

The Mood Disorders Workgroup proposed a diagnosis of individuals with short duration hypomania (2-3 days) who met the criteria for a Major Depressive Episode. Research indicates that these individuals show increased co-morbidity with Substance Use Disorder and Bipolar Disorder. Estimates place the rate of incidence at 2.8% of the general population and a greater prevalence in women than men. Critics were concerned this diagnosis could lead to confusion with Bipolar II Disorder, Major Depressive Disorder With Mixed Features, Cyclothymic Disorder, or Borderline Personality Disorder (*DSM-5,* 2013).

Persistent Complex Bereavement Disorder

The Anxiety, Obsessive-Compulsive Spectrum, Posttraumatic, and Dissociative Disorders Workgroups proposed a new category entitled, Persistent Complex Bereavement Disorder. This new diagnosis was seen to address some of the controversy surrounding the elimination of the bereavement exclusion and simultaneously acknowledging the significant distress and functional impairment that some individuals experience after the loss of a close family member or friend. The Workgroups felt that these circumstances are not adequately covered by *DSM-5,* and may need to be addressed in future editions (*DSM-5,* 2013).

Caffeine Use Disorder

The Substance-Related Disorders Workgroup proposed inclusion of Caffeine Use Disorder in recognition that chronic caffeine users develop features of substance dependence: continued use despite recognizable harm, unsuccessful efforts to quit or cut down, and continued use to avoid withdrawal. Recognition of a diagnosis of inappropriate use of caffeine as a disorder could lead to the development of specific cessation strategies and interventions. Critics objected out of concern that recognizing excessive caffeine use as a disorder might trivialize Substance Use Disorders and label a large portion of the adult population, who use caffeine regularly and extensively, as disordered (*DSM-5,* 2013).

Haarman

Internet Use/Gaming Disorder

Criteria were proposed by the Substance-Related Disorders Workgroup to recognize a new condition that is the result of rapidly expanding technology. Internet/Gaming Disorder is excessive or inappropriate use of the internet to engage in games. Although the condition is relatively common, particularly in Asian countries, Workgroup members felt that it is not reflected in the *DSM*. Concerns were expressed that Internet/Gaming Disorder can only exist in countries where individuals have ready access to technology and the internet and is not a concern in some cultures. The disorder captures the same common clinical features that link it to substance addictions: repetitive and driven behaviors despite the consequences, diminished control, cravings, and experiencing pleasure while engaged in the behavior. Symptoms of tolerance, dependence, and withdrawal similar to substance use disorders have also been observed. This proposed diagnosis has been met with extreme criticism. Some believe its inclusion in a future edition of *DSM* would medicalize "bad behavior" and expand behavioral addictions. Others believe that it is too narrowly defined and a broader category of "Internet Addiction" or "Compulsive Computer Use Disorder" should have been proposed instead (*DSM-5,* 2013).

Neurobehavioral Disorder Associated with Prenatal Alcohol Exposure

There was a proposal for a neurobehavioral disorder associated with in utero exposure to alcohol. The proposed disorder is reflected by impaired neurocognitive functioning, impaired self-regulation, and impaired adaptive functioning. The rationale for including this diagnosis was to increase recognition and to facilitate treatment and referral for children exposed to alcohol during the prenatal period. Others argued that the symptoms of this disorder are already adequately captured in the *DSM-5* and clinicians need simply be more alert to the symptoms. Others are concerned that this disorder assumes a causal relationship to alcohol, which is difficult to prove, and overlaps other disorders, including Conduct Disorder and Antisocial Personality Disorder (*DSM-5,* 2013).

Suicidal Behavior Disorder

This ++disorder was proposed to remedy a diagnostic coding problem. Suicidal behavior is limited to E Codes drawn from the ICD-9-CM (E50-E59). Although suicidal behavior and ideation are listed as symptoms of Major Depressive Disorder and Borderline Personality Disorder, it may be recorded as a separate diagnostic category and as a primary focus of treatment. The absence of an approved code may lead to incomplete and misleading information in clinical records. Also, the availability of a codeable disorder might help with prevention and safety monitoring (*DSM-5,* 2013).

Nonsuicidal Self-Injury

The Child and Adolescent Disorders Workgroup proposed Nonsuicidal Self-Injury with the rationale that these behaviors are not represented in *DSM*. While this behavior is reflected in item 5 of Borderline Personality Disorder, it is common in children and adolescents who would not meet criteria for that diagnosis. Research has shown that repeated self-injury co-occurs with a variety of diagnoses, and many of these individuals do not meet criteria for a diagnosis of Borderline Personality Disorder.

Separate diagnostic criteria would clear up two misconceptions regarding self-injury: 1) that self-injury is exclusively part of a Borderline Personality Disorder, and 2) that it is a form of attempted suicide. For most individuals, self-injury is not intended to result in death, but rather to bring relief from tension or other negative affective states. The definition proposes that the injuries (e.g., cutting, burning) are superficial, frequently repeated, and are viewed as non-life threatening. Nevertheless, recurrent self-injurious behaviors are associated with increased risk for inadvertent suicide (*DSM-5,* 2013).

Haarman

At some point in the future, these disorders, or Conditions for Further Study, may or may not be included in future *DSM's* based on the results of the ongoing studies and scientific investigation. At a minimum, they are useful for further study and research.

Chapter Six: Chapter by Chapter Highlights of Changes Between the DSM-IV-TR and DSM-5

One significant change between the *DSM-IV-TR* and the *DSM-5* was a restructuring of the chapters and presentation of the disorders. In *DSM-IV-TR* there was a specific chapter (Chapter two) which covered the disorders typically associated with children and adolescents. Chapter Two, Disorders Usually First Diagnosed in Infancy, Childhood or Adolescence, has been eliminated and the disorders typically diagnosed in children and adolescents have been spread throughout the structure of the new *DSM-5*. A listing of the chapters within the *DSM-5* is presented in the illustration.

Figure 1: DSM-5 Table of Contents

1.	Neurodevelopmental Disorders
2.	Schizophrenia Spectrum and Other Psychotic Disorders
3.	Bipolar and Related Disorders
4.	Depressive Disorders
5.	Anxiety Disorders
6.	Obsessive-Compulsive and Related Disorders
7.	Trauma and Stressor-Related Disorders
8.	Dissociative Disorders
9.	Somatic Symptoms and Related Disorders
10.	Feeding and Eating Disorders
11.	Elimination Disorders
12.	Sleep-Wake Disorders
13.	Sexual Dysfunctions
14.	Gender Dysphoria
15.	Disruptive, Impulse Control, and Conduct Disorders
16.	Substance-Related and Addictive Disorders
17.	Neurocognitive Disorders
18.	Personality Disorders
19.	Paraphilic Disorders

In the *DSM-5,* chapters were assigned based on a continuum. Disorders that were viewed as occurring earlier in the normal developmental cycle were listed in the early chapters of the document; whereas, disorders that more typically occurred in later development were listed later in the document. In addition to the developmental perspective that occurred in the structuring of the chapters, the disorders that were viewed as more internalized (i.e., likely present through genetic transmission) were included earlier in the document; whereas disorders which were viewed as externalized or more an indication of inappropriate learning or behavioral conditioning were listed in later chapters. An attempt was made to place disorders and groups of disorders on these two continua within the *DSM-5*.

In the following sections, **Disorders** and appropriate **Specifiers** are listed in bold to focus the discussion of each chapter and for easy reference.

Section I: Neurodevelopmental Disorders: Chapter 1

In this particular chapter of the *DSM-5*, disorders such as **Intellectual Disability, Communication Disorders, Autism Spectrum Disorder, Attention Deficit Hyperactivity Disorder, Specific Learning Disorders, and Motor Disorders** are covered. The fact that these are listed in Chapter One indicates that these disorders were viewed as highly internalized, and are usually evident in the early developmental period.

Intellectual Disability is a renaming of what was considered in DSM-IV-TR as Mental Retardation. The terminology of Mental Retardation was eliminated to be consistent with what advocacy and client groups suggested was a more appropriate designation, as well as, an attempt to be consistent with how the disorder was referred to in the various laws and legislation regarding these individuals. ICD-11 has already determined that this disorder will be renamed Intellectual Developmental Disorder. Certainly either Intellectual Disability or Intellectual Development Disorder is preferable to terminology reflecting a category of Mental Retardation.

In *DSM-IV-TR*, Mental Retardation was primarily diagnosed based on IQ scores. A substantial change in the conceptualization of Intellectual Developmental Disorder resulted in a twofold approach to this disorder which looks at both deficits in intellectual functioning and deficits in adaptive functioning for a diagnosis of Intellectual Disability. This disorder requires deficits in both cognitive, social, and adaptive behaviors (identified through a comprehensive assessment) as well as deficits indicated by traditional IQ scores. While *DSM-5* does not include a specific IQ score as a part of its criteria, language in the text specifically indicates that there is an assumption that IQ functioning will be approximately two standard deviations below the mean, or approximately 70. The *DSM-5* diagnostic criteria include the same severity measures, that were present in *DSM-IV-TR*, **Mild, Moderate, Severe, and Profound Intellectual Disability**; yet the severity is not based solely on IQ scores, but

Haarman

rather adaptive functioning. A comprehensive chart for determining the severity level based on adaptive domains, is presented in *DSM-5*, page 5.

This diagnosis must be distinguished from a Specific Learning Disability in which the impairment is confined to academic areas such as reading, mathematics, and written expression. While Intellectual Disability is frequently co-morbid with Autism Spectrum Disorder, and both disorders should be diagnosed if full criteria are met, in some situations the deficits in social-communication skills may simply be a reflection of a deficit in intellectual ability. Major and Mild Neurocognitive Disorders are characterized by a loss of intellectual functioning from previous ability and are distinct from Intellectual Disability which is viewed as a neurodevelopmental disorder observable in early development.

Intellectual Disability must also be differentiated from **Borderline Intellectual Functioning.** Borderline Intellectual Functioning is coded as R41.83 and is more appropriate for those situations where a lesser degree of intellectual functioning impairment is observed or where there are no problems with adaptive functioning, but significant intellectual impairment is evident. In children under age five, when data is confounded or when an objective assessment of intellectual ability is difficult or impossible due to sensory complications, a diagnosis of Global Developmental Delay may be more appropriate.

Global Developmental Delay is a new diagnosis that is reserved for children under the age of five. It was designed for individuals who fail to meet developmental milestones in several areas of intellectual functioning, but who are unable to undergo a systematic assessment of intellectual functioning due to age or other physical or sensory limitations. This category requires a reassessment after age five, but can serve as a "bridge" diagnosis until a more accurate and comprehensive evaluation can be conducted.

Communication Disorders have undergone significant modifications in comparison to *DSM-IV-TR*. Communication Disorders have been restructured

Haarman

by eliminating, combining, renaming, and adding additional disorders. Language Disorders, Speech Sound Disorders, Childhood-Onset Fluency Disorder (Stuttering), and Social (Pragmatic) Communication Disorder are included in this section. **Language Disorder** is a category which covers disorders formerly listed in the *DSM-IV-TR*, as Mixed Receptive-Expressive Language Disorder and Expressive Language Disorder. This new disorder would include individuals who have difficulty with both expressive and receptive language development, including limited vocabulary, making errors in tense, or having difficulty recalling words or producing sentences. Typically, these individuals would not meet criteria for an Intellectual Developmental Disorder, Global Developmental Delay, or other sensory, motor, or neurological conditions. Language Disorder differs from Selective Mutism which is characterized by a lack of speech in specific settings, whereas, the individual speaks normally in "safe" settings (e.g., home). With Language Disorder, the communication problems are consistent across settings and situations. Some children may develop a co-morbid Selective Mutism due to embarrassment about their Language Disorder.

Speech Sound Disorder is a diagnosis that was identified as Phonological Disorder in *DSM-IV-TR*, and had formerly been identified as Developmental Articulation Disorder in *DSM-III-R*. Individuals with this disorder show errors in sound production that are inconsistent with their developmental phase in life. These errors in sound production produce difficulties in speech intelligibility or prevent verbal communication. These difficulties are not attributable to congenital or acquired conditions.

Childhood-Onset Fluency Disorder (Stuttering) is a speech difficulty of fluency and time patterning of speech that causes significant anxiety. Anxiety can also create a more serious disruption in speech fluency. The onset typically occurs in the early developmental period, but later onset cases require a coding variation. It is not typically associated with sensory difficulties or neurological insult.

Social (Pragmatic) Communication Disorder is a new category in *DSM-5*. This new diagnostic category was created to differentiate between those individuals who are on the autism spectrum and should be diagnosed as Autism Spectrum Disorder, and those individuals who in the past may have carried a diagnosis of Asperger's Disorder, Childhood Disintegrative Disorder, or Pervasive Developmental Disorder (NOS). These individuals show difficulty using language to narrate, explain, or conduct a simple conversation. They may struggle with using communication for social purposes, are unable to change communication to match circumstance or context, have difficulties following the rules of conversation, and have display problems understanding what is not explicitly stated. Social (Pragmatic) Communication Disorder is not typically explained by low cognitive ability, global developmental delays, or other mental disorders. Diagnostic criteria for Social (Pragmatic) Communication Disorder require that individuals must first be considered for Autism Spectrum Disorder prior to being considered for Social Communication Disorder. These individuals present many of the social communication and interaction deficits found in individuals with an Autism Spectrum Disorder diagnosis, but do not show the repetitive behaviors/interests, and activities that characterize individuals on the autism spectrum.

Autism Spectrum Disorder is an extremely controversial diagnosis created by *DSM-5*. This diagnostic classification reflects a consensus of the scientific community, but has generated enormous controversy in the general public and therapeutic communities. Autism Spectrum Disorder combines four disorders contained in *DSM-IV-TR* into a single category, Autism Spectrum Disorder. In *DSM-5*, Autistic Disorder, Asperger's Disorder, Childhood Disintegrative Disorder, and Pervasive Developmental Disorder have all been eliminated. This decision was based primarily on neurological studies indicating no clear-cut differentiation between the four categories. These four disorders are now viewed as a single-category disorder that is characterized by deficits in social communication and interaction, as well as, the presence of restricted, repetitive behaviors, interests, and activities. Both the social deficits and the repetitive and restricted behaviors are required for a diagnosis of Autism Spectrum Disorder. If the restricted and repetitive behaviors are absent, a diagnosis of Social Communication Disorder is more appropriate.

Haarman

Individuals in this population show an extreme range of behaviors and dysfunction. In order to acknowledge the extreme variability, an extensive set of specifiers has been created. The *DSM-5* diagnosis of Autism Spectrum Disorder allows for a number of specifiers in terms of presentation, including intellectual, language, genetic/medical, and severity indicators. In a very unique approach, the *DSM-5* diagnostic criteria for Autism Spectrum Disorder requires an assessment of the person's needs, based on the overall level of support services required. Specifiers of **Requiring Support, Requiring Substantial Support,** and **Requiring Very Substantial Support** for both the social/communication and repetitive behavior domains are to be utilized. Severity of social communication difficulties and restrictive, repetitive behaviors should be assessed and rated separately, rather than making a global assessment of severity. *DSM-5* also provides a matrix of the specific behavioral indicators required to assist in determining the appropriate specifier for the level of support required.

Applying the specifier of **With or Without Accompanying Intellectual Impairment** requires an understanding of the often uneven intellectual profile of a client with Autism Spectrum Disorder. The **With or Without Accompanying Language Impairment** specifier necessitates some attempt to spell out the specific language impairment (e.g. No intelligible speech, phrase speech, single words only, receptive speech deficit, etc.) that the individual demonstrates. If the child has a known medical or genetic condition (e.g. Rett syndrome, Down syndrome, Fragile X syndrome, epilepsy, environmental exposures), the specifier of **Associated with a Known Medical or Genetic Condition or Environmental Factor** should be used and may require an additional ICD-10-CM or ICD-11 code as a part of the diagnosis. A specifier of **Associated with Another Neurodevelopmental, Mental, or Behavioral Disorder** (e.g. ADHD, Impulse Control, Conduct Disorder, Anxiety Disorders, Tourette's Disorder, etc.) may be recorded through additional codes or as co-morbid disorders. The **With Catatonia** specifier can be used when the individual displays catatonic symptoms, but not at a level that would justify a separate diagnosis of Catatonia Associated with Another Mental Disorder. To emphasize the early developmental aspects of this disorder, DSM-5 indicates that symptoms must be present in the "early developmental period," which, as defined in the *DSM-5* text, is roughly prior to 24 months of age.

Childhood-Onset-Schizophrenia, typically occurring after a period of normal, or near normal, development may include social impairment and atypical beliefs and interests. This should not be confused with the social deficits seen in Autism Spectrum Disorder.   Hallucinations and delusions, which are the defining features of Schizophrenia, are not typically seen in Autism Spectrum Disorder. Selective Mutism is distinguishable from Autism Spectrum Disorder in its normal early development and appropriate social communication in "safe" contexts and settings. The key differential between Social (Pragmatic) Communication Disorder and Autism Spectrum Disorder is the lack of the restricted and repetitive behaviors that characterize Autism Spectrum Disorder. A dual diagnosis of Autism Spectrum Disorder and Intellectual Disability is appropriate when social communication and interaction are significantly impaired relative to the developmental level of the individual's nonverbal skills.

Interestingly enough, *DSM-5* allows for individuals who formerly carried a diagnosis of Autistic Disorder, Asperger's Disorder, Childhood Disintegrative Disorder, or Pervasive Developmental Delay to be included in the category of Autism Spectrum Disorder, or "grandfathered in," despite not meeting full criteria for a diagnosis of Autism Spectrum Disorder. This exception is allowed unless those individuals reach full diagnostic criteria for a diagnosis of Social (Pragmatic) Communication Disorder, in which case they are not "grandfathered in," but should carry a diagnosis of Social Communication Disorder. The key differential between Autism Spectrum Disorder and Social Communication Disorder is the absence of the restrictive and repetitive behaviors.

Attention Deficit Hyperactivity Disorder in many ways is relatively unchanged in *DSM-5*, but in other ways is substantially different. While the same 18 symptoms (nine symptoms of inattention and nine symptoms of hyperactivity/impulsivity) promulgated in *DSM-IV-TR* are included in *DSM-5*, almost verbatim.   *DSM-5* also adds behavioral examples for each of the diagnostic symptoms. These behavioral examples provide behavioral descriptions of the observed symptoms for children and adolescents, as well as, adults. Other changes include requiring that symptoms must be present prior to age 12, rather than age 7 and allowing for co-morbidity with Autism Spectrum Disorder. The biggest shift in criteria is lowering the diagnostic threshold of symptoms for older adolescents and adults from six of nine symptoms to five of nine symptoms. More substantially, Attention Deficit Hyperactivity Disorder is now included under a grouping of neurodevelopmental disorders rather than as a behavioral disorder, as it was in *DSM-IV-TR*.

Subtypes of ADHD have been eliminated based on neurological findings, which view these three disorders as a single disorder. In *DSM-5*, Attention Deficit Hyperactivity Disorder is to be diagnosed as **Attention Deficit Hyperactivity Disorder, Combined** *Presentation*, **Attention Deficit Hyperactivity Disorder, Predominately Hyperactive/Impulsive** *Presentation*, **or Attention Deficit Hyperactivity Disorder, Predominately Inattentive** *Presentation.* In addition to the specifiers of **Mild, Moderate, and Severe,** a new specifier for ADHD of **In Partial Remission** has been added. This is to be utilized when full criteria were previously met, but less than the full criteria have been observed for the past six months, but the symptoms still interfere with functioning. The implication is that Attention Deficit Hyperactivity Disorder is a lifelong condition that may be in remission, to an extent, given appropriate medication and treatment.

In contrast to Attention Deficit Hyperactivity Disorder, Oppositional Defiant Disorder individuals may resist school work or tasks as a way of nonconforming through negativity and defiance. This is in contrast to individuals with ADHD, who resist mentally demanding activities or school work due to the difficulty in sustaining mental effort, forgetting instructions, and/or impulsivity. Complicating the differential diagnosis is the fact that some individuals with ADHD may develop secondary oppositional behaviors and negative attitudes toward school out of frustration. ADHD and Intermittent Explosive Disorder share high levels of impulsive behavior; however, Individuals with Intermittent Explosive Disorder show serious aggression toward others, which is not characteristic of ADHD, and they do not show the inattention and disorganization that is characteristic of ADHD.

Haarman

Symptoms of ADHD are common among children placed in academic settings inappropriate to their Intellectual Disability. The symptoms of ADHD are not usually observed during non-academic tasks. A dual diagnosis of ADHD and Intellectual Disability requires that the symptoms of inattention and hyperactivity are excessive given the individual's mental age. Individuals with ADHD and those with Autism Spectrum Disorder exhibit inattention, social dysfunction, and disruptive behaviors. The social dysfunction and peer rejection in individuals with ADHD should be distinguished from the social disengagement, isolation, and indifference to the tonal and facial cues of others that is seen in individuals with Autism Spectrum Disorder. Children with ADHD may display a temper tantrum or other misbehaviors during transitions due to impulsivity or poor self-control; whereas, children with Autism Spectrum Disorder may display tantrums due to an inability to tolerate a change from an expected routine or course of events.

ADHD shares symptoms with Anxiety Disorders. In ADHD, inattention is the result of attraction to external stimuli. This is distinguished from the inattention due to the internalized worry and rumination seen in Anxiety Disorders. Individuals with depressive disorders may also present with an inability to concentrate; however, the poor concentration becomes prominent only during a depressive episode. In older adolescents and adults, it may be difficult to distinguish ADHD from Borderline, Narcissistic, and other Personality Disorders. All these disorders tend to share features of disorganization, social intrusiveness, emotional dysregulation, and cognitive dysregulation. However, ADHD is not characterized by fear of abandonment, self-injury, extreme ambivalence, antisocial behavior, and a lack of empathy. If criteria are met for both ADHD and a Personality Disorder, both should be diagnosed.

Specific Learning Disorder in *DSM-5* combines four categories formerly contained in the *DSM-IV-TR* into a single category called Specific Learning Disorder. Reading Disorder, Mathematics Disorder, Disorder of Written Expression, and Learning Disorder (NOS) have been subsumed under a single category. Neurological studies indicate very small differences between the various learning disabilities specified under the public laws, ICD 10, or *DSM-IV-TR*. The assumption was that a single category, which can then be specified as to the specific nature of the difficulty, was a more appropriate line of thinking in this regard. The ability/achievement discrepancy model formulated in *DSM-IV-TR* has been abandoned in favor of a diagnosis that looks at individuals who are substantially below average in academic achievement in specific areas. Disorders will be diagnosed as Specific learning Disorder, **With an Impairment in Reading, With an Impairment in Written Expression, With an Impairment in Mathematics**, or combinations thereof. Alternative terminology utilized in ICD-10-CM, Dyslexia and Dyscalculia, is also not recognized in *DSM-5*. *DSM-5* also requires a specifier of **Mild, Moderate, or Severe.**

Motor Disorders contains a number of disorders that are included *in DSM-IV-TR*, including **Developmental Coordination Disorder, Stereotypic Movement Disorder, Tourette's Disorder, Persistent Vocal or Motor Tic Disorder, and Provisional Tic Disorder.** Slight wording changes have been developed in *DSM-5* to clarify specific issues. Perhaps the most significant development in this area is the consistent definition of a "tic" across all disorders. For the most part, these disorders remain unchanged.

Section II: Schizophrenia Spectrum and Other Psychotic Disorders: Chapter 2

Schizophrenia, Schizoaffective Disorder, Delusional Disorder, Brief Psychotic Disorder, Schizophreniform Disorder, and a specifier of **Catatonia** have undergone some substantive changes as well as some more cosmetic changes. In addition, for many of the disorders in this chapter, an optional severity specifier rating, on a scale of 0 to 4, has been added. (See Clinician-Rated Dimensions of Psychosis Symptoms Severity in the chapter "Assessment Measures"). A specifier of **With Catatonia** has also been included in many of these disorders.

Schizophrenia under *DSM-IV-TR* was prone to a number of false positive diagnoses. As a result the "diagnostic bar" for schizophrenia has been raised from a single Criterion A symptom of bizarre delusions or auditory hallucinations to a minimum of two Criterion A symptoms, and at least one of those symptoms must be an active symptom of Schizophrenia (i.e. delusions, hallucinations, or disorganized speech). Subtypes of Schizophrenia that were included in *DSM-IV-TR*, such as paranoid, disorganized, catatonic, undifferentiated, and residual have all been eliminated due to limited diagnostic stability, low reliability, and poor validity. Instead, an optional dimensional approach to rating severity for core symptoms of schizophrenia is included in the chapter on Measurement and Emerging Trends to express the severity across all individuals with psychotic disorders. Additionally, specifiers for the majority of psychotic disorders are based on the number of prior psychotic episodes, and only after a one year duration of the disorder. Schizophrenia Spectrum Disorders are specified as: **First Episode Currently Acute, First Episode in Partial Remission, First Episode in Full Remission, Multiple Episodes Currently Acute, Multiple Episodes in Partial Remission, Multiple Episodes in Full Remission, Continuous, and With Catatonia.**

Neither Schizophrenia nor Schizophreniform Disorder are diagnosed if the psychotic symptoms are due to the direct effects of a medical condition or the

Haarman

direct physiological effects of a substance, including medications. Schizophrenia is distinguishable from Schizoaffective Disorder in that it requires a Major Depressive or a Manic Episode occuring concurrently for the majority of the total duration of the disorder and that the mood symptoms be present for a majority of the total duration of the active period. In Schizophrenia, the mood episodes may have been present for a minority of the total duration of the active and residual periods. Schizophrenia differs from Schizophreniform and Brief Psychotic Disorder primarily on the basis of the duration of the symptoms. Schizophrenia requires six months of symptoms; whereas, Schizophreniform Disorder requires that the disturbance is less than six months, and in Brief Psychotic Disorder, symptoms are present at least one day, but less than one month. In Bipolar Disorders with Psychotic Features, the psychotic or catatonic symptoms occur exclusively during Manic or Major Depressive Episodes.

Individuals with Obsessive-Compulsive Disorder or Body Dysmorphic Disorder may present with Poor or Absent Insight, which approaches delusional proportions, but are distinguished from Schizophrenia by their prominent obsessions, compulsions, and preoccupations with the body or body-focused repetitive behaviors. Posttraumatic Stress Disorder may include flashbacks that have a hallucinatory quality, and hypervigilance that may reach paranoid proportions, but it is distinguished from Schizophrenia by the requirement of exposure to a traumatic event and a characteristic PTSD symptom cluster. Autism Spectrum Disorder is characterized by an early onset, typically before age three, and an absence of delusions or hallucinations. A co-morbid diagnosis of Schizophrenia and Autism Spectrum Disorder is only warranted if prominent hallucinations or delusions have been present for at least one month. Schizotypal, Schizoid, and Paranoid Personality Disorders are characterized by subthreshold symptoms of Schizophrenia that are associated with persistent personality features.

Schizophreniform Disorder remained relatively unchanged with the exception of a requirement to rule out Schizoaffective Disorder, Major Depressive Disorder with Psychotic Features, and Bipolar Disorder with Psychotic Features prior to diagnosing an individual with Schizophreniform Disorder. The optional dimensional approach to rating severity for core symptoms of psychosis can be utilized. Specifiers of **With Good Prognostic Features, Without Good Prognostic Features, and With Catatonia** can also be used with this diagnosis. The primary differential with Schizophrenia is the duration of symptoms in Schizophreniform Disorders have only persisted for one day, but less than one month.

Schizoaffective Disorder has remained relatively unchanged, except for language to emphasize that in Schizoaffective Disorder, the mood episode is present for a majority of the disorder's total duration, including active and residual periods of the illness. The specifiers of **Bipolar Type and Depressive Type** were retained from *DSM-IV-TR* as well as course specifiers: **First Episode Currently Acute, First Episode in Partial Remission, First Episode in Full Remission, Multiple Episodes Currently Acute, Multiple Episodes in Partial Remission, Multiple Episodes in Full Remission, Continuous, and With Catatonia.** The optional dimensional approach to rating severity for core symptoms of psychosis can also be utilized.

Distinguishing Schizoaffective Disorder from Schizophrenia and Depressive or Bipolar Disorders with Psychotic Features is often difficult. Criterion C, symptoms of a Major Mood Episode requiring the presence of symptoms for the majority of the total duration of the illness, is designed to separate Schizoaffective Disorder from Schizophrenia. Criterion B, delusions or hallucinations for two or more weeks in the absence of a Major Mood Episode, is designed to separate Schizoaffective Disorder from a Depressive or Bipolar Disorders with Psychotic Features.

Delusional Disorder no longer requires that delusions are non-bizarre in nature. If the individual meets diagnostic criteria for a Delusional Disorder, bizarre delusions can be covered by a specifier: **With Bizarre Content.** Traditional specifiers of Delusional Disorder (**Erotamanic, Grandiose, Jealous, Persecutory, Somatic, Mixed, and Unspecified**) have been retained. Additional specifiers have been added in *DSM-5*, including: **First**

Episode Currently Acute, First Episode in Partial Remission, First Episode in Full Remission, Multiple Episodes, Currently Acute, Multiple Episodes in Partial Remission, Multiple Episodes in Full Remission, and Continuous. An optional severity specifier based on the new assessment measure was also included in *DSM-5*.

Brief Psychotic Disorder has remained relatively unchanged with the exception of requiring at least one active psychotic symptom. Specifiers of With Marked Stressors (symptoms occur in response to events that would be markedly stressful to almost anyone in similar circumstances and culture), Without Marked Stressors (symptoms do not occur in response to events that would be markedly stressful to almost anyone in similar circumstances and culture), With Catatonia, and With Postpartum Onset (during pregnancy or within four weeks of delivery. The optional dimensional approach to rating severity for core symptoms of psychosis can also be utilized. Schizotypal Personality Disorder is detailed in the chapter on Personality Disorders, but it was also listed in this chapter because it is considered part of the schizophrenia spectrum. Shared Psychotic Disorder (Folie a Deux) has been eliminated in *DSM-5*.

Section III: Bipolar and Related Disorders: Chapter 3

A major conceptual change Between *DSM-IV-TR* and *DSM-5* Is the separation of Bipolar and Related Disorders from Depressive Disorders, highlighting both an issue of severity, as well as, perhaps a different organic basis for the disorders. The chapter on Bipolar and Related Disorders is placed between Schizophrenia and Other Psychotic Disorders chapter and Depressive Disorders chapter as a "bridge" between the two groups of disorders. This chapter includes: **Bipolar I Disorder, Bipolar II Disorder, Cyclothymic Disorder, Substance/Medication-Induced Bipolar Disorder, and Bipolar Disorder Due to a Medical Condition.**

Bipolar I Disorder criteria have been modified slightly to reflect a modern understanding of the disorder, in that neither psychosis nor the presence of a major depressive episode are required, although they may be present. Individuals must meet the full criteria for a manic episode. Additional language has been included in *DSM-5* to reflect "abnormally and persistently increased goal-directed activity or energy" to emphasize the changes in behavior, as well as the changes in mood. The manic symptoms must also "represent a noticeable change from usual behavior." An additional note has been added to the *DSM-5* definition to include a manic episode that results from treatment of depression (medication or electroconvulsive therapy), but persists beyond the physiological effects. The manic episode must not be a response to a significant loss (e.g. Bereavement, a natural disaster, and/or medical issues), and the individual must have at least one lifetime manic episode.

Major Depressive Disorder is distinguishable from Major Depressive Disorder by the absence of a Manic or Hypomanic Episode. A Major Depressive Episode may be accompanied by hypomanic or manic symptoms, but the symptoms may fail to meet criteria for a Hypomanic Episode or a Manic Episode due to an insufficient number of symptoms or shorter duration of symptoms. In those cases a diagnosis of Major Depressive Disorder with Mixed Features may be more appropriate. A diagnosis of Bipolar I Disorder is differentiated from Bipolar II Disorder by determining if there have been any past episodes of Mania. If the individual has ever met criteria for a Manic Episode, then a

Haarman

diagnosis of Bipolar I Disorder is appropriate. If the individual has ever met criteria for a Hypomanic Episode (symptoms are typically less severe and are of shorter duration), then a diagnosis of Bipolar II is utilized.

Cyclothymia is discernibly different from Bipolar I and Bipolar II by numerous periods of hypomanic symptoms that do not meet the criteria for a Manic or Hypomanic Episode and periods of depressive symptoms that do not meet the criteria for a Major Depressive Episode. If criteria have ever been met for a Manic, Hypomanic, or Depressive Episode, Cyclothymic Disorder should not be diagnosed. A careful history is needed to differentiate Anxiety Disorders from Bipolar Disorders, as anxious ruminations may be mistaken for racing thoughts, and efforts to minimize anxious feelings may be mistaken as impulsive behaviors.

Attention Deficit Hyperactivity Disorder may be mistaken for Bipolar Disorder, especially in children and adolescents. ADHD is characterized by persistent, ongoing symptoms of inattention, hyperactivity, and impulsivity, which may resemble the symptoms of a Manic Episode, and have their onset prior to age 12; whereas, the symptoms of Mania in Bipolar Disorder occur in distinct periods and typically begin in late adolescence or early adulthood. Many Personality Disorders, especially the Borderline Personality Disorder, are characterized by symptoms of mood lability and impulsivity which are persistent and have their onset in early adulthood. The mood symptoms in Bipolar I Disorder occur in distinct episodes that represent a noticeable change from baseline functioning.

Bipolar II Disorder has also been modified slightly to emphasize the need for a distinct period of "abnormally and persistently increased activity or energy," lasting four consecutive days, most of the day, nearly every day. Additional notes have been added to the *DSM-5* definition, including a hypomanic episode that results from treatment of depression (medication or electroconvulsive therapy) that persists beyond the physiological effects. The hypomanic episode is not a response to a significant loss (e.g. Bereavement, a natural disaster, and/or medical issues).Bipolar II Disorder cannot be diagnosed if the person has ever met criteria for Bipolar I Disorder

Haarman

A number of new specifiers have been developed that are shared by both Bipolar I and Bipolar II. **With Mixed Features** is a new specifier for Bipolar I and Bipolar II, which has been added to those cases in which the individual does not meet full diagnostic criteria. If the individual meets criteria for a manic or hypomanic episode, and does not meet the full criteria for a depressive episode, but has at least three of the symptoms of a depressive episode, a specifier of **Manic or Hypomanic Episode, With Mixed Features** is utilized. If the individual meets criteria for a major depressive episode, and does not meet the full criteria for a manic or hypomanic episode, but has at least three of the symptoms of a manic or hypomanic episode, a specifier of **Depressive Episode, With Mixed Features** is utilized.

A specifier of **With Anxious Distress** has also been added as an option for Bipolar I and Bipolar II to reflect individuals with significant anxiety symptoms, and secondary specifiers of either **Mild, Moderate, Moderate-Severe, or Severe** should accompany the modifier of with anxious distress. **With Melancholic Features, With Atypical Features, With Psychotic Features (with mood-congruent psychotic features or with mood-incongruent features),** and **With Catatonia** remain relatively unchanged. **With Rapid Cycling** (the presence of at least four mood episodes in the previous 12 months) **and With Seasonal Pattern** (applies to a lifetime pattern of a temporal relationship between mood episodes and a particular time of the year, full remission occurs at a characteristic time, there is at least a two year history, and seasonal mood episodes outnumber non-seasonal mood episodes) are retained in *DSM-5*, with modifications and numerous clarifying notes. The With Postpartum Onset specifier of *DSM-IV-TR* has been changed to **With Peripartum Onset** to include the course of the pregnancy and four weeks following delivery. Severity specifiers of **Mild, Moderate, and Severe** are required as part of the diagnosis and are based on the number and severity of symptoms and the degree of functional disability. **In Partial Remission** (a period of less than two months without significant symptoms of a mood episode) **and In Full Remission** (during the past two months no symptoms of a significant mood episode were present) are retained, relatively unchanged. The Chronic, With Full Interepisode Recovery,

Haarman

and Without Full Interepisode Recovery specifiers for Bipolar I and II have been dropped in *DSM-5*.

Cyclothymic Disorder, with some minor wording clarifications remains unchanged. For at least two years (one year in children and adolescents) there are periods of hypomanic symptoms that do not meet criteria for a Hypomanic Episode and numerous periods with depressive symptoms that do not meet the criteria for a Major Depressive Episode. These sub threshold symptoms are typically present for at least half the time, and the individual has never been symptom free for a two month period. Under *DSM-5*, an added specifier of **With Anxious Distress** can be utilized.

Substance/Medication Induced Bipolar and Related Disorder criteria remain relatively unchanged, but coding has become significantly more complicated based on whether or not there is a co-morbid substance use disorder present. If there is a mild substance use disorder present, the fourth digit is "1" and the substance use disorder is listed prior to the co-morbid Substance/Medication Induced Bipolar and Related Disorder. If there is a moderate or severe substance use disorder present, the fourth digit is "2" and the substance use disorder is listed prior to the co-morbid Substance/Medication Induced Bipolar and Related Disorder. The fourth digit is an indicator of the level of substance use disorder present. If there is no co-morbid substance use disorder present, the fourth position character is a "9" and only the Substance/Medication Induced Bipolar and Related Disorder is narrated.

The classification of **Other Specified Bipolar and Related Disorder** includes individuals with a past history of Major Depressive Disorder, whose symptoms meet all criteria for hypomania except the duration criteria. Other atypical presentations may be coded with this diagnosis. This would include a situation where too few symptoms of hypomania are present although the duration, at least four consecutive days, is sufficient.

Haarman

Section IV: Depressive Disorders: Chapter 4

Major changes have occurred in this chapter of *DSM-5*, including creation of new disorders, elimination of some diagnostic classifications, modifications of diagnostic criteria, elimination of certain symptom criteria or exclusions, and combining disorders into a new diagnostic category.   Unlike *DSM-IV-TR*, Depressive Disorders have been separated from Bipolar and Related Disorders. The common feature of all the Depressive Disorders is the presence of sad, empty, or irritable mood, accompanied by somatic and cognitive changes that significantly impact functioning. What distinguishes these disorders from each other is duration, timing, and presumed etiology. The Depressive Disorders chapter includes **Disruptive Mood Dysregulation Disorder, Major Depressive Disorder, Persistent Depressive Disorder, Premenstrual Disorder, Substance/Medication-Induced Depressive Disorder, and Depressive Disorder due to Another Medical Condition.**

In order to address concerns over the apparent overdiagnosis of Bipolar Disorder in children and adolescents, a new diagnosis, **Disruptive Mood Dysregulation Disorder,** was created. This diagnosis was designed to cover those children and adolescents who present with persistent irritability and frequent episodes of extreme behavioral dyscontrol. The placement of this disorder in the Depressive Disorders chapter reflects the finding that children with this symptom pattern typically develop unipolar depressive disorders or anxiety disorders, rather than bipolar disorders, as they mature into adolescence and adulthood. This disorder originally appeared in the professional literature as Temper Dysphoria Disorder as an explanation for the persistent irritability and behavioral dyscontrol.   This extreme irritability presents in these individuals without the mood changes that so typically accompany the clinical picture of bipolar disorders.   While these behavioral episodes are typically dramatic and reflect a seeming inability to control, they do not usually meet the criteria necessary for a diagnosis of a manic or hypomanic episode.   There have been a promising number of brain imaging studies that have distinguished between individuals with Bipolar Disorder I and II Disorder and Disruptive Mood Dysregulation Disorder (Leibenluft, 2012).

Haarman

Diagnostic criteria call for severe, recurrent temper outbursts, inconsistent with developmental level, occurring three or more times per week, and where the mood between outbursts is persistently angry. Outbursts have been present for 12 or more months in at least two settings, and the age of onset is prior to age 10. This diagnosis should not be made before six years of age or after age 18. A **coding note** specifies that Disruptive Mood Dysregulation Disorder **cannot coexist** with Oppositional Defiant Disorder, Intermittent Explosive Disorder, or Bipolar Disorder. It **can be co-morbid** with Major Depressive Disorder, Attention Deficit/Hyperactivity Disorder, Conduct Disorder, and Substance Use Disorder. Individuals who meet criteria for both Disruptive Mood Dysregulation Disorder and Conduct Disorder should only be given the Diagnosis of Disruptive Mood Dysregulation Disorder. Also, if an individual has ever experienced a manic or hypomanic episode, the diagnosis of Disruptive Mood Dysregulation Disorder should not be assigned.

The central feature differentiating Disruptive Mood Dysregulation Disorder from Bipolar Disorders in children and adolescents is the longitudinal course of the core symptoms. Bipolar I and II manifest as an episodic illness with discrete episodes of mood alteration that can be differentiated from the child's typical presentation. With Bipolar Disorders, the mood alteration that occurs in a Manic or Hypomanic Episode is distinctly different from the child's usual mood. In contrast, the irritability of Disruptive Mood Dysregulation Disorder is persistent and present for many months and is characteristic of the child prior to age ten. While Bipolar Disorders are episodic conditions, Disruptive Mood Dysregulation Disorder is relatively continuous. Another differential is that while elevated or expansive mood and grandiosity are essential components of the Manic or Hypomanic Episodes of Bipolar Disorder, these are not typically observed in Disruptive Mood Dysregulation Disorder.

While symptoms of Oppositional Defiant Disorder typically occur in children with Disruptive Mood Dysregulation Disorder, the mood symptoms of DMDD are relatively rare in children classified as ODD. The presence of severe and frequently recurring outbursts and persistent disruption in mood between outbursts is essential to the criteria for a diagnosis of Disruptive Mood Dysregulation Disorder These symptoms are not core elements of the criteria for a diagnosis of Oppositional Defiant Disorder. If criteria are met for both disorders, only Disruptive Mood Dysregulation Disorder is diagnosed. Placing Disruptive Mood Dysregulation Disorder in the "Depressive Disorders" chapter and placing Oppositional Defiant Disorder in the chapter "Disruptive, Impulse-Control, and Conduct Disorders" reflects the more prominent mood component of Disruptive Mood Dysregulation Disorder.

Temper outbursts are common in individuals diagnosed with Autism Spectrum Disorder, especially when routines are disrupted. If the temper outbursts are better explained by Autism Spectrum Disorder, the child should not receive a diagnosis of Disruptive Mood Dysregulation Disorder. Intermittent Explosive Disorder is dominated by aggressive outbursts that can resemble the severe temper tantrums of Disruptive Mood Dysregulation Disorder; however, in Intermittent Explosive Disorder there is no persistent irritability or angry mood between outbursts. In addition, Intermittent Explosive Disorder only requires three months of active symptoms, in contrast to the 12 month active symptom requirement of DMDD. Intermittent Explosive Disorder is not diagnosed if criteria are met for Disruptive Mood Dysregulation Disorder.

The nine symptom criteria for **Major Depressive Disorder** appear to have weathered the test of time and have been incorporated into *DSM-5* virtually unchanged. The criteria still call for five of nine symptoms of a major depressive episode for a period of two weeks. Notes reflecting some of the more subtle presentations of depression in children have also been retained. The biggest and most controversial change in Major Depressive Episode criteria is the elimination of criteria E, or the so called "Bereavement Exclusion." The bereavement exclusion has been a part of the diagnostic criteria for Major Depressive Disorder since *DSM-III*. Its purpose was to prevent over diagnosis of Major Depressive Disorder in those situations where the symptoms could be easily understandable in the context of an individual who became symptomatic after the loss of a loved one. The controversy surrounding dropping the bereavement exclusion and the arguments, pro and con, are discussed in an earlier chapter. Nevertheless, it is covered in *DSM-5* criteria by a note, as well as, an extensive footnote detailing some of the more subtle differences between Major Depressive Disorder and normal grief or bereavement. Ultimately, this becomes an individual clinician's decision and clinical judgment. "This decision inevitably requires the exercise of clinical judgment based on the individual's history and cultural norms for the expression of distress in the context of loss (*DSM-5*, 2013)."

Severity specifiers of **Mild, Moderate, and Severe** are required as part of the diagnosis and are based on the number and severity of symptoms and the degree of functional disability. Specifiers of **With Melancholic Features, With Atypical Features, With Psychotic Features (with mood-congruent psychotic features or with mood-incongruent features),** and **With Catatonia** remain relatively unchanged. **With Seasonal Pattern** (applies to a lifetime pattern of a temporal relationship between mood episodes and a particular time of the year, full remission occurs at a characteristic time, there is at least a two year history, and seasonal mood episodes outnumber non-seasonal mood episodes) is retained in *DSM-5*, with modifications and numerous clarifying notes. The With Postpartum Onset specifier of *DSM-IV-TR* has been changed to **With Peripartum Onset** to include the course of the pregnancy and four weeks following delivery.

Major Depressive Episodes with irritable mood may be difficult to distinguish from a Manic or Hypomanic Episode. Major Depressive Disorder cannot be diagnosed if a Manic or Hypomanic Episode has ever been present; however, a diagnosis of Major Depressive Disorder can be compatible with some manic or hypomanic symptoms that do not reach the level of Bipolar criteria and a diagnosis of Major Depressive Disorder with Mixed Features may be appropriate. In Persistent Depressive Disorder, the criteria call for the person to have a depressed mood, more days than not, for at least two years. If criteria are met for both Major Depressive Disorder and Persistent Depressive Disorder, both can be diagnosed with appropriate specifiers.

Distractibility and low frustration tolerance can occur in both Attention Deficit Hyperactivity Disorder and Major Depressive Disorder, and if the criteria are met for both, each should be listed as a part of the diagnosis. *DSM-5* specifically cautions clinicians not to over diagnose Major Depressive Disorder in children with Attention Deficit Hyperactivity Disorder, particularly if the mood disturbance is characterized by irritability rather than by sadness or loss of interest. Schizoaffective Disorder requires that a Major Depressive Episode is concurrent with the active phase symptoms of Schizophrenia, hallucinations and delusions occur for at least 2 weeks in the absence of a Major Depressive Episode, and the Major Depressive Episode is present for a majority of the total duration of the illness. The diagnosis of Major Depressive Disorder with Psychotic Features is appropriate if the psychotic symptoms have occurred exclusively during Major Depressive Episodes. A diagnosis of Adjustment Disorder with Depressed Mood is utilized when the depressive symptoms occur in response to a stressor and do not meet criteria for a Major Depressive Episode.

Persistent Depressive Disorder, a new diagnostic category in *DSM-5*, is a combination of what was covered by two different *DSM-IV-TR* diagnoses, Dysthymia and Major Depressive Disorder, Chronic. The focus of this new disorder is on the chronicity involved in this affective dysfunction, which often requires treatment approaches that are very different than for a Major Depressive Disorder. Many individuals see this combination of diagnostic categories as the first step toward conceiving all affective disorders on a continuum that may be differentiated by severity, chronicity, and level of dysfunction. The diagnostic criteria are an interesting amalgamation of *DSM-IV-TR* criteria for Dysthymia and Major Depression with a greatly expanded list of specifiers. The dominant symptom is a depressed mood for most of the day and most days for a period of at least two years. Criteria for a Major Depressive Disorder may, or may not, have been met continuously for the two year period, but there has never been a manic or hypomanic episode and the criteria for Cyclothymic Disorder have never been met. A note in the criteria clarifies a unique situation that may occur in some individuals. The criteria for a major depressive episode includes four symptoms that are not reflected in the symptom list for Persistent Depressive Disorder. Some individuals may have depressive symptoms that have persisted longer than two years, but will not satisfy the criteria for Persistent Depressive Disorder. In this case, if the full criteria for a major depressive episode have been met at some point in the current episode, they should be given a diagnosis of Major Depressive Disorder. Otherwise, a diagnosis of Other Specified Depressive Disorder or Unspecified Depressive Disorder is warranted.

Haarman

Persistent Depressive Disorder has an extensive list of specifiers that must be considered with this diagnosis. As with many other affective disorders, a specifier of **With Anxious Distress** has also been added as an option to reflect individuals with significant anxiety symptoms, and secondary specifiers of either **Mild, Moderate, Moderate-Severe, or Severe** should accompany the modifier of with anxious distress. Specifiers of **With Melancholic Features, With Atypical Features, With Psychotic Features (with mood-congruent psychotic features or with mood-incongruent features),** and **With Catatonia** remain relatively unchanged. The With Postpartum Onset specifier of *DSM-IV-TR* has been changed to **With Peripartum Onset** to include the course of the pregnancy and four weeks following delivery. Additionally, specifiers for onset and remission are also available, including **In Partial Remission** (symptoms of a major depressive episode are present, but full criteria are not met, or there is a period of less than 2 months without any significant symptoms), **In Full Remission** (during the past 2 months, no significant symptoms have been present**, Early Onset** (prior to age 21) and **Late Onset** (onset is at age 21 years or older**.**

A set of specifiers unique to Persistent Depressive Disorder describes the most recent two year period: **With Pure Dysthymic Syndrome** (full criteria for a major depressive episode have not been met in the preceding 2 years), **With Persistent Major Depressive Episode** (full criteria for a major depressive episode have been met throughout the preceding 2 year period), **With Intermittent Major Depressive Episodes with Current Episode** (full criteria for a major depressive episode are currently met, but there have been periods of at least 8 weeks in at least the preceding 2 years with symptoms below the threshold of a full major depressive episode), and **With Intermittent Major Depressive Episodes without Current Episodes** (full criteria for a major depressive episode are not currently met, but there has been at least one or more major depressive episodes in at least the preceding 2 years). As with almost all *DSM-5* disorders, a specifier is required to indicate the level of severity as **Mild, Moderate, and Severe.**

Haarman

Major Depressive Disorder requires a period of depressed mood, diminished interest, or a lack of pleasurable experience, most nearly every day, for two weeks and five of the nine symptoms of a Major Depressive Episode. Persistent Depressive Disorder has a lower symptom threshold (two symptoms plus depressed mood), and a lower severity threshold (more days than not for a two year period), but requires a two year duration. A Major Depressive Episode lasting at least two years will meet criteria for a Persistent Depressive Disorder. If criteria are met for both Major Depressive Disorder and Persistent Depressive Disorder, both should be diagnosed. Personality Disorders commonly co-occur with Persistent Depressive Disorder. If criteria are met for Persistent Depressive Disorder and a Personality Disorder, both should be diagnosed and listed as part of the diagnosis.

A Disorder with a very lengthy history has finally been accepted for inclusion in *DSM-5*. **Premenstrual Dysphoric Disorder** was first included *in DSM-III-R in* the Needing Further Study Chapter as Late Luteal Phase Dysphoric Disorder and was met with extreme controversy. It was considered again and continued in the Needing Further Study Category in *DSM-IV-TR* under the designation of Premenstrual Dysphoric Disorder and has been formally accepted as a diagnostic category in *DSM-5*. Criteria call for an individual to have experienced (for a majority of their menstrual cycles) five symptoms in the final week before menses which improve at the onset of menses, and become minimal or absent in the week post menses. Symptoms include marked affective lability, irritability, depressed mood, anxiety, decreased interest, concentration difficulties, lethargy, changes in appetite or sleep patterns, feeling out of control, and physical discomfort. The criteria call for prospective daily ratings by the individual for two cycles, but allow for a provisional diagnosis until ratings can be completed. The diagnosis of Premenstrual Dysphoric Disorder continues to generate some controversy, primarily around fears of the societal implication of the disorder, "pathologization" of women, and the potential for using this diagnosis to limit women's role in society and the marketplace.

Major Depressive Disorder and Persistent Depressive Disorder involve depressive symptoms that are unrelated to a woman's menstrual cycle. *DSM-5* requires that the timing of the depressive symptoms in Premenstrual Dysphoric

Disorder be confirmed by prospective daily ratings during at least two symptomatic menstrual cycles. Without this documentation, the diagnosis can be made provisionally until documentation is available.

Substance/Medication-Induced Depressive Disorder and **Depressive Disorder Due to Another Medical Condition** remain relatively unchanged in *DSM-5* with some minor language clarifications, but coding has become significantly more complicated based on whether or not there is a co-morbid substance use disorder present. If a mild substance use disorder is present, the fourth digit is "1" and the substance use disorder is listed prior to the co-morbid Substance/Medication Induced Depressive Disorder. The fourth digit is an indicator of the level of substance use disorder present. If there is a moderate or severe substance use disorder present, the fourth digit is "2" and the substance use disorder is listed prior to the co-morbid Substance/Medication Induced Depressive Disorder. If there is no co-morbid substance use disorder present, the fourth position character is a "9" and only the Substance/Medication Induced Bipolar and Related Disorder is narrated. Specifiers for these disorders are slightly changed, and coding numbers have been modified to reflect ICD-10-CM numbering.

Section V: Anxiety Disorders: Chapter 5

A major conceptual and organizational change that occurred with *DSM-5* is the removal of a number of disorders from the Anxiety Disorders section. The *DSM-5* chapter on Anxiety Disorders no longer includes Obsessive- Compulsive Disorder (now contained in *DSM-5*, Chapter 6: Obsessive-Compulsive and Related Disorders) or Posttraumatic Stress Disorder and Acute Stress Disorder (now covered in *DSM-5*, Chapter 7: Trauma and Stressor-Related Disorders). Anxiety Disorders typically contain an element of fear, an emotional response to the real or perceived threat, anxiety, and anticipation of future threat. In Anxiety Disorders, the fear and anxiety persist beyond normal development, beyond the degree of persistence, with an overestimation of the danger, and are not attributable to substances or medication. The chapter attempts to arrange the anxiety disorders developmentally, with disorders sequenced according to typical age of onset. Disorders included in this chapter are **Separation Anxiety Disorder, Selective Mutism, Specific Phobia, Social Anxiety Disorder, Panic Disorder, Agoraphobia, and Generalized Anxiety Disorder.**

Separation Anxiety Disorder was contained in the *DSM-IV-TR* chapter on Disorders of Childhood and Adolescence, and has been moved to the Anxiety Disorders Chapter. While little has changed in the symptom criteria of Separation Anxiety Disorder, the disorder has been expanded beyond simply children and adolescents to also include adults, and the onset specifier has been eliminated. Adults with this disorder are overly concerned about their children, spouses, or significant caregivers, and may spend excessive effort and time checking on the whereabouts of their significant individuals.

In contrast to Separation Anxiety Disorder, Generalized Anxiety Disorder is characterized by anxiety and worry in a multitude of different areas and not limited to issues involving separation from family. Posttraumatic Stress Disorder may also involve fear of separation from loved ones, but occurs in the context of a traumatic event. However, in Posttraumatic Stress Disorder, the symptoms involve re-experiencing memories or avoiding situations associated with the traumatic event; whereas, in Separation Anxiety Disorder, the worries and avoidance concern the well-being of attachment figures and fears of being

Haarman

separated from them. The dominant dynamic of Social Anxiety Disorder is the fear of being judged, ridiculed, or rejected by other people, but in Separation Anxiety Disorder, the worry is about being separated from major attachment figures.

Children with Separation Anxiety Disorder can become very oppositional and defiant, but only in the context of being required to leave an attachment figure. Oppositional Defiant Disorder should be considered only when there is a persistent oppositional behavior unrelated to the anticipation or occurrence of separation from an attachment figure. A Dependant Personality Disorder involves an indiscriminate tendency to rely on others, whereas Separation Anxiety Disorder involves concern about the proximity and safety of primary attachment figures. Borderline Personality Disorder is characterized by fear of abandonment, but there are also problems with identity, self-direction, interpersonal functioning, and impulsivity. If criteria are met for both Separation Anxiety Disorder and a Personality Disorder, both may be diagnosed.

Selective Mutism criteria are essentially unchanged from *DSM-IV-TR*, but were felt to be an appropriate fit for the Anxiety Disorders Chapter. The anxiety and avoidance present in Social Anxiety Disorder may become associated with Selective Mutism. If criteria are met for both disorders, both disorders should be diagnosed.

The criteria for a **Specific Phobia** were modified slightly between *DSM-IV-TR* and *DSM-5*. The recognition that the fear is excessive and/or unreasonable on the part of the client has been removed. Instead, the anxiety must be out of proportion to the actual danger or threat, taking into consideration cultural contexts. In addition, the duration criteria of six months only applied to children and adolescents in *DSM-IV-TR*; whereas, the six month duration criteria applies to all ages in *DSM-5*. Specifiers to be coded include: **Animal, Natural Environment, Blood-Injection Injury, Situational, and Other.** A **coding note** indicates that when more than one phobic stimuli is present, all appropriate ICD-10-CM codes should be listed.

Haarman

A situational specific phobia may resemble Agoraphobia in presentation. If the individual fears only one agoraphobic situation, then a Specific Phobia should be diagnosed. If two or more agoraphobic situations are feared, a diagnosis of Agoraphobia is warranted. Agoraphobia may also have some symptoms of fear and avoidance of social situations, but with Agoraphobia, the individual's fear is that escape might be difficult or that help might not be available to deal with the incapacitation of the panic attack feelings. In Social Anxiety, the fear is the scrutiny of others, resulting in humiliation, and rejection. Additionally, individuals with Social Anxiety Disorder are typically calm when left alone, which is often not the case in Agoraphobia.

Social Anxiety Disorder (Social Phobia) criteria have undergone some minor conceptual changes as well as some language clarifications. In a manner consistent with the changes applied to criteria for Specific Phobia, the recognition that the fear is excessive and/or unreasonable on the part of the client has been removed. Instead, the anxiety must be out of proportion to the actual danger or threat, taking into consideration sociocultural contexts. In addition, the duration criteria of six months only applied to children and adolescents in *DSM-IV-TR*; whereas, the six months duration applies to all ages in *DSM-5*. An interesting addition to the criteria in *DSM-5* is a new specifier of **Performance Only.** This is to be used in those situations where the symptoms of social anxiety are restricted to speaking or performing in public situations.

Individuals with Social Anxiety Disorder may experience panic attacks, but the fear is about the negative evaluation of others; whereas, in Panic Disorder, the concern is about the panic attacks themselves or a re-occurrence of panic attacks. Social worries are also common in Generalized Anxiety Disorder, but the focus is more on the nature and quality of ongoing relationships rather than on a fear of negative evaluation. Individuals with Generalized Anxiety Disorder may be excessively worried about their social performance, but they also are excessively worried about their performance in non-social situations where evaluation by others is not an issue. In Social Anxiety Disorder, the worries are exclusively focused on social performance and the evaluation by others. Separation Anxiety Disorder may also result in avoidance, but the concern is about being separated from attachment figures. Individuals with

Haarman

Social Anxiety Disorder tend to be uncomfortable even in social situations where attachment figures are present.

Autism Spectrum Disorder is characterized by social anxiety and social communication deficits that typically result in a lack of age appropriate social relationships. Individuals with Social Anxiety Disorder typically have age appropriate relationships and social communication capacity, but may appear to have impairment in these areas when first meeting people. An apparent overlap with Social Anxiety Disorder is Avoidant Personality Disorder. Individuals with Avoidant Personality Disorder may have a broader avoidance pattern than those with Social Anxiety Disorder. Nevertheless, there is a high comorbidity rate between Social Anxiety Disorder and the Avoidant Personality Disorder. If criteria are met for Social Anxiety Disorder and Avoidant Personality Disorder, both diagnoses should be given.

Panic Disorder and Agoraphobia are unlinked in *DSM-5*. *DSM-IV-TR* diagnoses of Panic Disorder with Agoraphobia, Panic Disorder without Agoraphobia, and Agoraphobia without a History of Panic Disorder are now replaced by two diagnoses, **Panic Disorder** and **Agoraphobia,** each with separate criteria. *DSM-IV-TR* diagnoses of Panic Disorder Without Agoraphobia and Panic Disorder With Agoraphobia have been combined in *DSM-5* to a single category of **Panic Disorder.** There have been minor wording changes in the description and symptoms, and a note details that culturally expected symptoms should not be included in meeting diagnostic criteria. A differential as to whether or not the client shows agoraphobic behaviors is not required.

Under *DSM-IV-TR*, Agoraphobia was not a codeable disorder, but the specific disorder in which the Agoraphobia occurred was coded. In *DSM-5*, **Agoraphobia** is a codeable disorder, which requires marked fear or anxiety about at least two specific situations which the individual avoids, for fear that escape might not be possible, or the individual requires the presence of a companion. Additionally, Agoraphobia requires that the fear is out of proportion and has persisted for at least six months. Agoraphobia is diagnosed irrespective of the presence of Panic Disorder. If the full criteria for Panic

Disorder and Agoraphobia are met, both diagnoses should be assigned and coded.

The **Panic Attack Specifier** has been added in *DSM-5*. Panic Attacks can now be listed as a specifier that is applicable to all *DSM-5* disorders. A panic attack, in and of itself, is not a mental disorder. Many "normal" individuals can experience an abrupt surge of intense fear that reaches a peak in a matter of minutes, in response to disasters, threats of violence, accidents, etc. Panic attacks can be ***Expected,*** in that there is an obvious cue or trigger, or ***Unexpected***, when there is no obvious cue or trigger at the time of occurrence such as relaxing or asleep. When the presence of a panic attack is identified, it should be coded as a specifier (e.g. Major Depressive Disorder with Panic Attacks, Bipolar I Disorder with Panic Attacks, etc.). For Panic Disorder, the presence of panic attacks is contained within the criteria for the disorder and Panic Attack is not used as a specifier.

Generalized Anxiety Disorder is virtually unchanged between *DSM-IV-TR* and *DSM-5* and the requirement of only one symptom for children is also continued. **Anxiety Disorder Due to a Another Medical Condition** also remains essentially unchanged with the exception that, With Generalized Anxiety, With Panic Attacks, and With Obsessive-Compulsive Symptoms have been eliminated as specifiers.

Panic Disorder is also characterized by anxiety and worry, but the worry is about having additional Panic Attacks, as opposed to Generalized Anxiety Disorder which is less specific and applicable across situations. An additional diagnosis of Generalized Anxiety Disorder should be used only if there are additional anxieties and worries unrelated to the Panic Attacks. Social Anxiety Disorder focuses exclusively on being evaluated by others in social situations An additional diagnosis of Generalized Anxiety Disorder should be used only if there are additional anxieties and worries regarding non-social situations. Obsessive-Compulsive Disorder focuses on repetitive anxiety provoking thoughts and typically compulsive behaviors that serve to reduce the anxiety;

whereas, the worries in Generalized Anxiety Disorder typically arise from everyday routine life experiences.

Substance/Medication-Induced Anxiety Disorder criteria have remained relatively unchanged and a note has remained that indicates this diagnosis should be made only when the symptoms of anxiety or panic dominate the clinical picture and are sufficiently severe to warrant clinical attention. Specifiers of With Generalized Anxiety, With Panic Attacks, With Phobic Symptoms, and With Obsessive-Compulsive Symptoms have been eliminated. Specifiers of **With Onset During Intoxication,** and **With Onset During Withdrawal** have been continued in *DSM-5* and a new specifier **With Onset After Medication Use** has been added. Coding has become significantly more complicated based on whether or not there is a co-morbid substance use disorder present. If there is a mild substance use disorder present, the fourth digit is "1" and the substance use disorder is listed prior to the co-morbid Substance/Medication Induced Anxiety Disorder. If there is a moderate or severe substance use disorder present, the fourth digit is "2" and the substance use disorder is listed prior to the co-morbid Substance/Medication Induced Anxiety Disorder. The fourth digit is an indicator of the level of substance use disorder present. If there is no co-morbid substance use disorder present, the fourth position character is a "9" and only the Substance/Medication Induced Anxiety Disorder is narrated.

Section VI: Obsessive-Compulsive and Related Disorders: Chapter 6

The Chapter, "Obsessive-Compulsive and Related Disorders," is new to *DSM-5* and includes **Hoarding Disorder, Excoriation (Skin-Picking) Disorder, Substance/Medication Induced Obsessive-Compulsive, Obsessive-Compulsive and Related Disorder Due to a Medical Condition, Trichotillomania (Hair-Pulling Disorder), Obsessive-Compulsive Disorder, and Body Dysmorphic Disorder.** The addition of "insight specifiers," including: **With Good or Fair Insight, With Poor Insight, and With Absent Insight/Delusional Beliefs,** for most of the disorders in this chapter reflects a change between *DSM-IV-TR* and *DSM-5*.

In **Obsessive-Compulsive Disorder,** the criteria for what constitutes an obsession have been somewhat altered to emphasize that the obsessions are not pleasurable or experienced as voluntary, and that attempts to neutralize them have not been successful. Criteria for what constitutes a compulsion are essentially unchanged. The note indicating that young children may not be able to articulate the aims of the behaviors or thoughts has been retained in *DSM-5*. In diagnosing Obsessive-Compulsive Disorder, new specifiers have been added under *DSM-5*, including **With Good or Fair Insight, With Poor Insight, With Absent Insight/Delusional Beliefs, and Tic-Related.**

In contrast to Obsessive-Compulsive Disorder, Hoarding Disorder involves a persistent difficulty discarding or parting with possession, and an excessive accumulation of objects, materials, or animals. However, for an individual with obsessions about completion or incompleteness, with associated hoarding behaviors, a diagnosis of OCD should be given. Tic Disorder and Stereotypic Movement Disorder require a subtle differentiation with Obsessive-Compulsive Disorder. A tic is a sudden, rapid, recurrent, nonrhythmic motor movement or vocalization. Stereotyped movement is repetitive, seemingly driven, nonfunctional motor behavior. Tics and stereotyped movements are typically less complex than compulsions and are not aimed at neutralizing the anxiety and negative affect associated with the obsessions. Some individuals have

Haarman

symptoms of both Obsessive-Compulsive Disorder and a Tic Disorder, in which case both diagnoses are warranted.

Obsessive-Compulsive Disorder can be distinguished from the ruminations of a Major Depressive Disorder, in which thoughts are usually mood-congruent, and not necessarily experienced as intrusive. OCD can be distinguished from Eating Disorders as typically in Obsessive-Compulsive Disorder, the obsessions are not limited to concerns about weight and food. Although Obsessive-Compulsive Disorder and Obsessive-Compulsive Personality Disorder have similar names, the clinical manifestations of these disorders are quite different. In contrast to Obsessive-Compulsive Disorder, the Obsessive-Compulsive Personality Disorder involves an enduring and pervasive, maladaptive pattern of excessive perfectionism and rigid control and is not characterized by the presence of obsessions or compulsions.

Body Dysmorphic Disorder was considered to be a Somatoform Disorder in *DSM-IV-TR*, but has been moved to the "Obsessive-Compulsive and Related Disorders" Chapter of *DSM-5*. This change reflects the dynamic of a "tension-building, tension-release" force, which appears to be an underlying motivation for this group of disorders. Criteria have been modified to reflect the underlying "preoccupation" about defects in appearance, which result in repetitive behaviors or mental acts that cause an impairment in functioning. A specific exclusion states that the preoccupation is not better accounted for by symptoms that would meet the criteria for an eating disorder. Insight specifiers including **With Good or Fair Insight, With Poor Insight, and With Absent Insight/Delusional Beliefs** are to be utilized, as well as a new specifier, **With Muscle Dysmorphia.** This occurs almost exclusively in males, where the preoccupation is that one's body is too small or insufficiently muscular.

In an individual with an eating disorder, concerns about being fat are considered an integral symptom of the eating disorder, rather than Body Dysmorphic Disorder which focuses on "physical defects." However, weight concerns can occur in Body Dysmorphic Disorder and can be co-morbid with a specific eating disorder, in which case both disorders are diagnosed. Gender Dysphoric Disorder involves bodily concerns that are limited to wanting to get rid of primary or secondary sexual characteristics. Body Dysmorphic Disorder should only be diagnosed if appearance issues go beyond the physical manifestation of gender. Many individuals with Body Dysmorphic Disorder hold ideas and opinions about their appearance with almost delusional conviction. These individuals are diagnosed with Body Dysmorphic Disorder with Absent Insight, as opposed to Delusional Disorder

Hoarding Disorder is a new disorder included in *DSM-5*. It does not purely focus on the acquisition of things, but on the difficulty and distress in discarding or parting with possession, despite their actual value. This inevitably results in excessive clutter, and makes living space unusable unless others expend significant effort in reducing the clutter. *DSM-5* emphasizes the living space or work area rather than attics, basements, and closets, which may be cluttered in normal individuals. This inability to discard or part with items causes significant impairment in functioning and is not a result of another disorder or a medical condition like traumatic brain injury or Prader-Willi syndrome. Typical specifiers regarding insight: **With Good or Fair Insight, With Poor Insight, and With Absent Insight/Delusional Beliefs** may also be accompanied by a specifier that focuses on acquisition, as well as inability to discard items: **With Excessive Acquisition.**

In contrast to Hoarding Disorder, Obsessive-Compulsive Disorder typically involves repetitive behaviors that the individual feels driven to perform and are generally experienced by the individual as ego-dystonic. Hoarding Disorder is not diagnosed if the symptoms are judged to be a direct consequence of typical obsessions or compulsions. In OCD, the behavior is generally unwanted and highly distressing and the individual experiences no pleasure or reward and excessive acquisition is not usually present. When an accumulation of objects occurs as a consequence of OCD (e.g., paper clips, rubber bands, urine, hair, nails, etc.) a diagnosis of hoarding disorder is not made.

However, when severe hoarding appears concurrently with other typical symptoms of OCD, both Hoarding Disorder and Obsessive-Compulsive Disorder can be diagnosed. Many individuals with Autism Spectrum Disorder may also excessively accumulate objects, but this usually relates to a fixated interest (matchbox cars, model dinosaurs, etc.), in which case a diagnosis of Hoarding Disorder is not made.

Criteria for **Trichotillomania (Hair-Pulling Disorder)** has been modified somewhat to focus on the behavior of pulling out one's hair, despite repeated attempts to stop. The requirement for experiencing a sense of tension and pleasure or relief after pulling has been eliminated, since not all individuals with this disorder report this experience. Trichotillomania has been moved from the Chapter on Impulse-Control Disorders in *DSM-IV-TR* to the "Obsessive-Compulsive and Related Disorders" Chapter of *DSM-5*. Some children excessively play with their hair or even "chew on" their hair; these behaviors do not constitute a diagnosis of Trichotillomania. Individuals with a psychotic disorder may remove hair in response to a delusion or hallucination. Trichotillomania is not diagnosed in such cases.

The criteria for **Excoriation (Skin-Picking) Disorder** roughly parallels the criteria for Trichotillomania. Excoriation Disorder is a new disorder in *DSM-5*. It had been in the Chapter for Further Study in the DSM-IV-TR. The recurrent skin picking results in skin lesions, despite repeated attempts to stop, and significantly disrupt functioning. These individuals normally use their fingernails to pick at healthy skin, pimples, calluses, or scabs from previous lesions, but may also use instruments such as pins, tweezers, or other objects. Excoriation Disorder is not diagnosed if the skin picking is attributable to the direct physiological effects of a dermatological condition.

Substance/Medication-Induced Obsessive-Compulsive and Related Disorder and **Obsessive-Compulsive and Related Disorder Due to Another Medical Condition** have also been added in *DSM-5*, primarily to be consistent with other chapters in *DSM-5*.

Haarman

Section VII: Trauma-Stressor-Related Disorders: Chapter 7

Trauma and Stressor-Related Disorders is a new Chapter in *DSM-5* and includes disorders in which exposure to a traumatic or stressful event is listed specifically as a part of the diagnostic criteria. These include **Reactive Attachment Disorder, Disinhibited Social Engagement Disorder, Posttraumatic Stress Disorder, Acute Stress Disorder, and Adjustment Disorders.** The placement of this chapter reflects the close relationship between these diagnoses and the disorders in the surrounding chapters. Psychological distress and behavioral symptoms following exposure to traumatic or stressful events are quite variable. Important changes have been made to the *DSM-5* criteria to reflect our current understanding of trauma related psychological disorders.

Reactive Attachment Disorder as defined in *DSM-IV-TR* has been split into two disorders in *DSM-5*: **Reactive Attachment Disorder** and **Disinhibited Social Engagement Disorder.**

Reactive Attachment Disorder requires that the individual displays a pattern of inhibited, emotionally withdrawn behavior toward adult caregivers. Specifically, the child rarely or minimally seeks comfort when distressed and rarely or minimally responds to comfort when distressed. The child also displays a persistent social and emotional disturbance in terms of emotional responsiveness to others, through limited positive affect, and unexplained episodes of irritability, sadness, or fearfulness. This lack of emotional responsiveness is assumed to be the result of patterns of extreme insufficient child care as evidenced by a persistent lack of having basic emotional needs met, repeated changes of primary caregivers, or being reared in extreme or unusual settings. Criteria also require that the individual does not meet the criteria for Autism Spectrum Disorder and the disturbance is evident before five years of age. This diagnosis is not appropriate for children developmentally unable to form selective attachments, and for this reason the child must have a developmental age of at least nine months. Additional specifiers of **Persistent**

Haarman

and **Severe** are provided to reflect descriptions of the chronicity and severity. A new diagnostic category has been included in *DSM-5*, that is a split off from the *DSM-IV-TR* Reactive Attachment Disorder of Infancy or Early Childhood.

Young children with Reactive Attachment Disorder or Autism Spectrum Disorder can manifest dampened expression of positive emotions, language delays, and impairments in social reciprocity. As a result, Reactive Attachment Disorder must be differentiated from Autism Spectrum Disorder. These two disorders can be distinguished typically based on differential histories of neglect, on the presence of restricted interests and ritualized behaviors, deficits in social communication, and selective attachment behaviors. Children with Reactive Attachment Disorder often have experienced a history of severe social neglect; whereas, children with Autism Spectrum Disorder will rarely have a history of neglect. The restricted interests and repetitive behaviors so characteristic of Autism Spectrum Disorder are not typically a feature of Reactive Attachment Disorder. However, it is important to note that children with either disorder can exhibit stereotypic behaviors such as rocking, hand-wringing, or flapping of arms. Finally, children with Autism Spectrum Disorder typically show attachment behavior consistent with developmental level. In contrast, children with Reactive Attachment Disorder do so only rarely, or inconsistently, if at all.

Disinhibited Social Engagement Disorder has at its etiology an assumption of "pathogenic" childcare. This results in social neglect or deprivation in the form of a persistent lack of having basic emotional needs met, repeated changes in primary caregivers, and being reared in unusual settings that limit opportunities to form selective attachments. These children typically display a pattern of behavior in which the child actively approaches and interacts with unfamiliar adults. These disinhibited social behaviors are evidenced by a reduced, or absent, reticence in approaching or interacting with unfamiliar adults, overly familiar verbal or physical behaviors with adults, a diminished or absent checking back behavior, and a willingness to go off with an unfamiliar adult with minimal hesitation. These behaviors are not limited to impulsivity (as in Attention Deficit Hyperactivity Disorder) but are dominated by socially disinhibited behavior. The child must have a developmental age of at least nine months. Additional specifiers of **Persistent** and **Severe** are provided to reflect descriptions of the chronicity and severity.

Major conceptual and diagnostic criteria changes have occurred *between DSM-IV-TR* and *DSM-5* in the diagnosis of **Posttraumatic Stress Disorder**, not the least of which is a separate set of diagnostic criteria for children under the age of six. Post traumatic Stress Disorder was included in the chapter on anxiety disorders in *DSM-IV-TR*, and has been moved to the Trauma-and Stressor-Related Disorders chapter of *DSM-5*. This is consistent with the belief that these disorders are directly the result of exposure to a traumatic or stressful event.

Posttraumatic Stress Disorder has become "watered-down" by clinicians applying it to a vast array of situations. Criteria A has been reworked to emphasize the fact that the traumatic event to which the individual has been exposed was actual or threatened death, serious injury, or sexual violence. This does not include exposure through electronic media, television, movies, or pictures. Criteria B calls for intrusive symptoms associated with the traumatic events, including involuntary and distressing memories, recurrent distressing dreams, dissociative reactions in which the individual feels and acts as if the traumatic events were re-occurring, intense physiological distress at exposure to cues that symbolize the event, and marked physiological reactions to cues that symbolize the event. Criterion C, which calls for a persistent avoidance of stimuli associated with the event, has been significantly rewritten. Three of six symptoms were required under *DSM-IV-TR*; whereas, *DSM-5* requires one or both of the following: avoidance efforts to minimize distressing memories, thoughts and feelings, and avoidance efforts to circumvent external reminders that arouse distressing memories.

A new symptom cluster, Criteria D, has been added to post traumatic stress disorder in *DSM-5*. This cluster of symptoms involves negative alterations in cognitions and mood associated with the traumatic event. It is evidenced by two of the following: an inability to remember important aspects of the traumatic events, persistent and exaggerated negative beliefs about one's self, persistent and distorted cognitions about the cause or consequences of the

Haarman

traumatic events, persistent negative emotional states, diminished interest or participation in significant activities, feelings of detachment or estrangement, and a persistent inability to experience positive emotions. As with *DSM-IV-TR*, Criterion E in *DSM-5* calls for marked alterations in arousal and reactivity associated with the traumatic event. Symptoms must have persisted for at least one month, causing significant distress or impairment in functioning, and are not attributable to the effects of a substance. The Acute and Chronic specifiers of *DSM-IV-TR* have been eliminated and replaced in *DSM-5* with specifiers of **With Dissociative Symptoms of Depersonalization** (experiences of feeling detached from oneself, as if an outside observer) and **With Dissociative Symptoms of Derealization** (experiences of the unreality of surroundings). The *DSM-IV TR* specifier of With Delayed Onset has been replaced with a specifier of **With Delayed Expression** (when diagnostic criteria are not met until at least six months after the stressor).

A separate set of diagnostic criteria has been developed for **Posttraumatic Stress Disorder for Children Six Years and Younger** to reflect the intellectual, conceptual, and emotional development of these individuals. The subtype for children six years and younger was created to lower the symptom threshold and eliminate some symptoms that are difficult to assess in preschool children. The requirement for experiencing repeated or extreme exposure to aversive details about the event is eliminated in criterion A, but a new criteria recognizes that children this age have not fully individuated. For children this age, simply learning that traumatic events have occurred to a primary caregiver can be traumatizing. Criterion B has been modified to acknowledge the fact that the spontaneous and intrusive memories may not necessarily appear distressing and may be expressed as play reenactment. Negative alterations in cognition and mood are typically reflected in children under the age 6 in very different ways than with adults, and may be evidenced as: an increased frequency of negative emotional states, marked or diminished interest or participation in activities, socially withdrawn behavior, and an overall persistent reduction in the expression of positive emotions. The specifiers in *DSM-5* for children under six are identical to those used for adults.

In contrast to Posttraumatic Stress Disorder, Adjustment Disorder is characterized by a stressor of any severity level, or one that fails to meet Criterion A of PTSD, and does not have a specific response pattern such as intrusion symptoms. In addition, the diagnosis of an Adjustment Disorder is used when the response to a stressor that meets Criterion A does not meet all the other criteria for a diagnosis of PTSD, or when the symptom pattern of PTSD occurs in response to a stressor that does not meet PTSD Criterion A.

Not all psychopathology that occurs in response to an extreme stressor should be diagnosed as PTSD. The diagnosis requires that the trauma exposure precede the onset or exacerbation of pertinent symptoms. If the symptom response pattern meets criteria for another disorder, these diagnoses should be given instead of, or in addition to, PTSD. Other diagnoses are excluded if they are better explained by PTSD. Acute Stress Disorder is distinguished from PTSD because the symptom pattern is greater than three days, but less than one month in duration. Major Depressive Disorder may or may not be preceded by a traumatic event and should be diagnosed if other PTSD symptoms are absent.

Traumatic Brain Injury is typified by neurocognitive symptoms that develop after a traumatic brain injury. Symptoms can overlap between Traumatic Brain Injury and Posttraumatic Stress Disorder. However, re-experiencing and avoidance which are characteristic of PTSD and not the effects of TBI; whereas, persistent disorientation and confusion are more specific to TBI than to PTSD. In those situations where this physically traumatic occurrence can also lead to the development of PTSD, both diagnoses should be considered and diagnosed. Malingering is characterized by feigning of symptoms and must always be ruled out when legal, financial, and other benefits play a role.

Acute Stress Disorder criteria have been reworked to be consistent with Posttraumatic Stress Disorder. The presence of nine or more symptoms, from any of the five categories: intrusion, negative mood, dissociation, avoidance, and arousal after a traumatic event are required for a diagnosis of Acute Stress Disorder. The duration of the symptoms is three days to one month after the trauma exposure. It is noted in the diagnostic criteria that symptoms typically begin immediately after the trauma, but the persistence of symptoms, for at least three days, is required to differentiate from a transitory disturbance. Persistence for greater than one month is required to differentiate Acute Stress Disorder from Posttraumatic Stress Disorder, in which symptoms last for more than a month.

Adjustment Disorders were included in a separate chapter in *DSM-IV TR*, but are included in the Trauma-and Stress or-Related Disorders Chapter of *DSM-5*. Diagnostic criteria have remained essentially unchanged, in that, symptoms must occur within three months of the stressor, create clinically significant distress or impairment, do not represent normal bereavement, and do not persist for more than an additional six months. The Acute and Chronic specifiers included in *DSM-IV-TR* have been dropped, but the traditional specifiers of: **With Depressed Mood, With Anxiety, With Anxiety and Depressed Mood, With Disturbance of Conduct, With Disturbance of Emotions and Conduct, and Unspecified** have been retained in DSM-5.

Adjustment disorders may be diagnosed following the death of a loved one when the intensity, quality, or persistence of grief reactions exceeds what might be normally expected. A more specific set of bereavement-related symptoms has been designated as Persistent Complex Bereavement Disorder and has been included in *DSM-5,* Section III as a Condition For Further Study. It is not available for use as a diagnosis at this time. In those situations where bereavement presents outside the diagnostic criteria due to onset or duration, F43.8, Other Specified Trauma-and Stressor-Related Disorder, Persistent Complex Bereavement Disorder can be utilized.

Section VIII: Dissociative Disorders: Chapter 8

Dissociative Disorders are frequently found in the aftermath of trauma, and many of the symptoms are influenced by the proximity to trauma. In *DSM-5*, the Dissociative Disorders were placed next to, but are not a part of, the Trauma and Stress or-Related Disorders Chapter. These disorders include: **Dissociative Identity Disorder, Dissociative Amnesia, Depersonalization/Derealization Disorder.**

Dissociative Identity Disorder criteria have been reworked in *DSM-5* to reflect the disruption of identity characterized by two or more distinct personality states. The disruption involves marked discontinuity in the sense of self, accompanied by related alterations in affect, behavior, consciousness, and memory. The disorder also includes recurrent gaps in the recall of everyday events, which are not consistent with ordinary forgetting. Diagnostic criteria also note, that in children, the symptoms are not better explained by imaginary playmates or other fantasy play.

Individuals with Dissociative Identity Disorder are often depressed, but rigorous assessment typically indicates that the depression does not meet full criteria for Major Depressive Disorder. Many times the depressed mood fluctuates because depressive symptoms are experienced in some identity states but not others. Individuals with Dissociative Identity Disorder may frequently be misdiagnosed as Bipolar. The relatively rapid shifts in mood and energy with Dissociative Identity Disorder typically contrast with the slower mood changes seen in individuals with Bipolar Disorder.

Some traumatized individuals have both Posttraumatic Stress Disorder and Dissociative Identity Disorder. It becomes critical to distinguish individuals with only PTSD and those who have both PTSD and Dissociative Identity Disorder. Some individuals with PTSD manifest dissociative symptoms that occur in the context of the trauma and the intrusive thinking or avoidance behaviors, alterations in cognition or mood, and hyperarousal are focused around the traumatic event. Individuals with Dissociative Identity Disorder more often

Haarman

manifest dissociative symptoms that are not part of the trauma and more related to day-to-day existence.

Individuals with dissociative identity disorder often present activities that have a number of Personality Disorder features, especially of Borderline Personality type. Importantly, however, the variability of personality style differs from the pervasive and persistent dysfunctions in affect management and interpersonal relationships, which are typical of those who have Personality Disorders. Individuals who feign Dissociative Identity Disorder often do not present the subtle symptoms of intrusion, which are characteristic of the disorder. Instead, they tend to over report the well-publicized symptoms of the disorder such as Dissociative Amnesia, while under reporting the less publicized co-morbid symptoms such as depression. Individuals who fake Dissociative Identity Disorder tend to be undisturbed by or even enjoy having the disorder. In contrast, individuals with genuine Dissociative Identity Disorder tend to be ashamed of and under report symptoms. Malingering individuals who present with Dissociative Identity Disorder usually create limited, stereotyped, dichotomous identities, such as the "all good" or "all bad" personalities.

DSM-IV-TR contained diagnostic categories of Dissociative Amnesia and Dissociative Fugue. These two diagnostic categories have been combined with the use of a specific specifier. **Dissociative Amnesia** primarily affects the ability to recall personal information about one's self, and it may be selected for specific events or more global information. Criteria call for an inability to recall important autobiographical information, usually of a traumatic or stressful nature, that is inconsistent with ordinary forgetting. A new specifier, **With Dissociative Fugue** can be used to designate apparently purposeful travel or bewildered wandering that is associated with amnesia for identity or for other important autobiographical information. Dissociative Amnesia with Dissociative Fugue requires a separate coding number under *DSM-5*. **Dissociative Fugue** as a separate diagnostic category has been dropped in *DMS-5*.

Individuals with Dissociative Amnesia display an inability to recall autobiographical information. Amnesia that is present in Dissociative Identity

Haarman

Disorder may include amnesia for everyday events and brief amnestic gaps in interpersonal interactions. Some individuals with PTSD cannot recall part or all of a specific traumatic event (e.g., a rape victim who cannot recall the events for the entire day on which the rape occurred). When the amnesia extends beyond the time of the immediate time of the trauma, a comorbid diagnosis of Dissociative Amnesia may be warranted.

Repeated intoxication with alcohol or other substances may produce "blackouts" or periods for which the individual has no memory. Distinguishing these episodes from Dissociative Amnesia may require a longitudinal history demonstrating that the episodes occur only in the context of intoxication and not in other situations. Amnesia may also occur in the context of a traumatic brain injury (TBI). Other diagnostic characteristics of TBI, including loss of consciousness, disorientation, and confusion are not typically observed in Dissociative Amnesia.

In *DSM-5*, Depersonalization Disorder of *DSM-IV-TR* has been rewritten as **Depersonalization/Derealization Disorder.** While transient depersonalization and derealization symptoms are fairly common, Depersonalization/Derealization Disorder criteria call for the presence of persistent or recurrent episodes of either depersonalization, derealization, or both. During the depersonalization or derealization, reality testing typically remains intact, but the disorder does cause significant impairment in important areas of functioning.

In contrast to Depersonalization/Derealization Disorder, Dissociative Identity Disorder is characterized by symptoms of depersonalization and accompanying pervasive discontinuities in the sense of self. Depersonalization/Derealization Disorder is not diagnosed if the symptoms are better explained by Dissociative Identity Disorder. Depersonalization/Derealization symptoms that develop in response to exposure to a traumatic stressor would be indicated by using the specifier With Dissociative Symptoms for the diagnosis of PTSD. Depersonalization/Derealization Disorder is not diagnosed if the symptoms are better explain by Posttraumatic Stress Disorder or Acute Stress disorder.

Haarman

Feelings of numbness, deadness, apathy, and being in a dream state are not uncommon in Major Depressive Disorder. If the depersonalization/derealization symptoms precede the onset of of Major Depressive Episode, or continue after its resolution, the diagnosis of Depersonalization/Derealization Disorder applies. Depersonalization/Derealization symptoms are common symptoms of a Panic Attack and typically increase as the severity of the panic attack increases. Therefore, Depersonalization/Derealization Disorder should not be diagnosed when the symptoms occur exclusively during a panic attack.

Section IX: Somatic Symptom and Related Disorders: Chapter 9

Somatic Symptom Disorder and other disorders with prominent somatic symptoms now constitute a new category in *DSM-5* called Somatic Symptom and Related Disorders. This chapter includes: **Somatic Symptom Disorder, Illness Anxiety Disorder, Conversion Disorder (Functional Neurological Symptom Disorder),** and **Factitious Disorder (imposed on Self and Imposed on Another).**

Somatization Disorder and Undifferentiated Somatoform Disorder of *DSM-IV-TR* have been combined into a single category under *DSM-5* called **Somatic Symptom Disorder.** The diagnosis deemphasizes medically unexplained symptoms, which had a central organizing role in many of the somatoform disorders. Instead, the category is defined on the basis of distressing somatic symptoms and the excessive thoughts, feelings, and behaviors that arise in response to the symptoms. Diagnostic criteria call for one or more somatic symptoms that create a significant disruption in daily living through excessive thoughts, feelings, or behaviors. Although any one somatic symptom may not be continuously present, the state of being symptomatic is persistent (typically lasting more than six months). Specifiers of severity, **Mild, Moderate, or Severe** are utilized, as well as specifiers of **With Predominant Pain** (previously Pain Disorder, where pain is the dominant symptom) and **Persistent** (severe symptoms have lasted for longer than six months).

A distinguishing aspect of Somatic Symptom Disorder, as contrasted with Illness Anxiety Disorder, is that Illness Anxiety Disorder Is characterized by Extensive Worries about Health with Minimal Somatic Symptoms. In Somatic Symptom Disorder, the dominant focus is on the distressing somatic complaints. Generalized Anxiety Disorder is typified by worry about multiple events, situations, or activities which may include concerns about health. The main focus of worry in Somatic Symptom Disorder is on somatic symptoms and health concerns.

Haarman

Obsessive-Compulsive Disorder involves recurrent thoughts that are experienced as intrusive and unwanted, and the person attempts to ignore or suppress through repetitive behaviors which the individual feels driven to perform. In Somatic Symptom Disorder, the recurrent concerns are about the somatic symptoms themselves, and the thoughts are less intrusive and typically not associated with repetitive behaviors that the person feels driven to perform.

The diagnostic category of Hypochondriasis contained in DSM-IV-TR has been dropped in favor of a less judgmental terminology, **Illness Anxiety Disorder.** *DSM-5* diagnostic criteria call for a preoccupation with having or acquiring a serious illness. This occurs in situations where the presence of somatic symptoms is relatively mild. This is important because the essence of this disorder is not the presence of symptoms, but rather the presence of health-related anxieties and preoccupations. There is a high level of anxiety about health, involving excessive health-related behaviors, or maladaptive avoidance of medical services. Illness preoccupation has been present for at least six months, but the specific illness that is feared may change over time. Specifiers of **Care-Seeking Type** (a variety of medical services and activities are frequently used) and **Care-Avoidant Type** (medical care is rarely used) are utilized to reflect the specific symptom presentation.

Concern and distress about a medical condition that is proportionate to the severity should not be considered Illness Anxiety Disorder. A co-morbid diagnosis of Illness Anxiety Disorder is appropriate only if the health-related anxiety is clearly disproportionate to the actual medical condition. Individuals with Illness Anxiety disorder may have intrusive thoughts about having a disease, and also may have associated compulsive behaviors. However, in Illness Anxiety Disorder, the preoccupations are usually focused on having a disease or illness, whereas, in OCD, the thoughts are intrusive and are usually focused on fears of getting a disease in the future. Most individuals with OCD have obsessions or compulsions involving other concerns in addition to fears about contracting disease or becoming ill.

Haarman

The Conversion Disorder criteria of *DSM-IV-TR* have been somewhat reworked in the *DSM-5* as **Conversion Disorder (Functional Neurological Symptom Disorder).** Diagnostic criteria continue to call for one or more symptoms of altered voluntary motor or sensory function. The requirement that psychological factors are judged to be associated with the symptoms, because the initiation or exacerbation of the symptoms was preceded by conflicts or other stressors, has been dropped. Also the *DSM-IV-TR* criteria required that the symptom was not intentionally produced (as in Factitious Disorder or Malingering) has also been dropped. Specifiers have been changed dramatically between *DSM-IV-TR* and *DSM-5* and now include**: Acute Episode** (less than six months)**, Persistent** (more than six months)**, With Psychological Stressor,** or **Without psychological Stressor.** Coding under DSM-5 requires the specification of the symptom type: **With Weakness or Paralysis, With Abnormal Movement, With Swallowing Symptoms, With Speech Symptoms, With Attacks or Seizures, With Anesthesia or Sensory Loss, With Special Sensory Symptom,** or **With Mixed Symptoms.**

The diagnostic criteria for Factitious Disorder contained in *DSM-IV-TR* have been significantly reworked in *DSM-5*. **Factitious Disorder** involves the intentional falsification of physical or psychological signs or symptoms, or induction of injury or disease, associated with the identified deception. These individuals present themselves to others as well, impaired, or injured and the disruptive behavior is evident, even in the absence of obvious external rewards. Specifiers include **Single Episode** or **Recurrent Episodes.** The *DSM-IV-TR* designation of Factitious Disorder by Proxy has been renamed as **Factitious Disorder Imposed on Another (Previously Factitious Disorder by Proxy).**

Section X: Feeding/Eating Disorders: Chapter 10

The chapter on Feeding and Eating Disorders has combined the feeding disorders from the *DSM-IV-TR* chapter "Disorders Usually First Diagnosed in Infancy, Childhood, or Adolescents" with eating disorders (Anorexia Nervosa, Bulimia Nervosa) to better reflect their shared pathophysiology. Chapter 10 in *DSM-5* contains the following disorders: **Pica, Ruminations Disorder, Avoidance/Restrictive Through Intake Disorder, Anorexia Nervosa, Bulimia Nervosa,** and **Binge-Eating Disorder.**

In *DSM-IV–TR*, Pica was included in the chapter on children's disorders, but under *DSM-5* has been expanded to include all ages. The essential feature of **Pica** is eating non-nutritive, non-food substances on a persistent basis for a period of at least one month. This eating behavior is not a part of a culturally supported or socially normative practice. A **coding note** calls for two different ICD–10–CM codes, (F 98.3) for children and (F 50.8) in adults. A specifier of **In Remission** is available for individuals after the full criteria were previously met, but the criteria have not been met for a sustained period of time.

Pica can usually be distinguished from the other feeding and eating disorders by the consumption of non-nutritive, nonfood substances. It is important to note that some presentations of Anorexia Nervosa include ingestion of nonfood substances, such as paper or tissues, as a means of attempting to control appetite. In such cases, when the eating of nonfood substances is primarily used for weight control, Anorexia Nervosa should the primary diagnosis.

The diagnostic criteria for **Rumination Disorder** are relatively unchanged from *DSM-IV-TR*. Individuals with this disorder repeatedly regurgitate swallowed or partially digested food, which then may be re-chewed or re-swallowed. Adolescents and adults may be less likely to re-chew regurgitated

Haarman

material. Criteria have been modified to ensure they are appropriate for individuals of any age, and a specifier of **In Remission** is also available.

The *DSM-IV–TR* disorder, Eating Disorder of Infancy or Early Childhood has been subsumed under a broader category in *DSM-5*, called **Avoidant/Restrictive Food Intake Disorder.** The change in the name of the disorder reflects the fact that there are a number of types of presentations that occur across the age continuum, rather than being restricted to infancy or early childhood. The disorder is characterized as an eating or feeding disturbance, as manifested by persistent failure to meet appropriate nutritional and/or energy needs. This is evidenced by weight loss or nutritional deficiency, dependence on nutritional supplements, and interference with psychosocial functioning. The disturbance is not better explained by a lack of available food or by a culturally sanctioned practice. The feeding disturbance does not occur exclusively during the course of Anorexia Nervosa or Bulimia Nervosa, and there is no evidence of a disturbance in the way in which one's body weight or shape is experienced. An additional specifier of **In Remission** is available for individuals after the full criteria were previously met, but currently, the criteria have not been met for a sustained period of time.

The disturbance in the caregiver-child relationship observed in Reactive Attachment Disorder may also affect feeding and the child's food intake. A diagnosis of Avoidant/Restrictive Food Intake Disorder (ARFID) may be appropriate if the feeding disturbance is a primary focus of intervention. Many individuals with Autism Spectrum Disorder display rigid eating behaviors and heightened sensitivity to foods; however, this typically does not result in a level of impairment that would be required for a diagnosis of ARFID. ARFID should be diagnosed only if the feeding disturbance requires specific treatment.

Individuals with a Specific Phobia may avoid situations that could lead to choking or vomiting, resulting in food avoidance or restriction. In addition, individuals with the Major Depressive disorder frequently experience appetite loss to such an extent that the individual may present with significantly restricted food intake, which usually dissipates with the resolution of the

Haarman

depression. A diagnosis of ARFID in addition to a Specific Phobia, or Major Depressive Disorder should be utilized only when the problem becomes a primary focus of clinical attention or requires specific treatment.

Avoidant/Restrictive Food Intake Disorder and Anorexia Nervosa are both characterized by food restrictions and low weight; however, individuals with Anorexia Nervosa also have a fear of gaining weight or becoming fat, or engage in persistent behaviors that interfere with weight gain, as well as, specific disturbances in their perception and experience of body weight and shape.

Anorexia Nervosa has undergone some significant criteria changes in *DSM-5*. The criteria related to a body weight of less than 85% of that which is expected has been changed in *DSM-5* to a *significantly low weight* as defined by a weight that is less than minimally normal or, for children and adolescents, less than that minimally expected. Intense fear of gaining weight or becoming fat persists even though the person is significantly low in weight. There is also a disturbance in body image. Also the requirement of amenorrhea in postmenarcheal females has been dropped, as many individuals with anorexia nervosa may exhibit all of the symptoms, but report at least some menstrual activity. The **Restricting Type (F50.01)** (the individual has not engaged in binge-eating or purging for the last three months. Weight loss is accomplished by dieting, fasting, and/or excessive exercise) and **Binge-Eating/Purging type (F50.02)** (during the last three months, the individual has engaged in recurrent episodes of binge-eating or purging) specifiers will be reflected in an ICD-10-CM coding exception. A specifier of **In Partial Remission** is available for individuals who have met full criteria for Anorexia Nervosa, but where appropriate body weight has been sustained for a period of time. The individual may still experience intense fear of gaining weight or disturbances in self perception. The **In Full Remission** specifier is available in those situations where a full criteria for Anorexia Nervosa were previously met, but none of the criteria have been met for a sustained period of time. Severity specifiers of **Mild, Moderate, Severe, and Extreme** are to be utilized based on body mass index.

Haarman

Individuals with Substance Use Disorders might experience low weight, due to poor nutritional intake, but generally do not fear gaining weight or have a significant body image disturbance. Some individuals abuse substances that reduce appetite and also have a fear of weight gain. These individuals should be carefully evaluated for the possibility of co-morbid Anorexia Nervosa, in which case, both diagnoses would be appropriate. In both Obsessive-Compulsive Disorder and Anorexia Nervosa, there may be repetitive and intrusive thoughts and compulsive behaviors. With Anorexia Nervosa, however, these thoughts and behaviors are limited to weight, eating, or food. An additional diagnosis of Obsessive-Compulsive Disorder should be considered only if there are additional obsessions and/or compulsions unrelated to weight, eating, or food.

In both Bulimia Nervosa and Anorexia Nervosa, the person may engage in recurrent episodes of binge eating, engage in inappropriate behavior to avoid weight gain (e.g., self-induced vomiting), and be overly concerned with body shape and weight. The two conditions are primarily differentiated based on body weight. Individuals with Bulimia Nervosa typically maintain body weight at or above the minimal normal level, whereas those with Anorexia Nervosa maintain a significantly low body weight. In Body Dysmorphic Disorder and Anorexia Nervosa, individuals may be preoccupied with imagined defects in bodily appearance. With Anorexia Nervosa, the preoccupation is limited to body shape and weight. In addition, a diagnosis of Body Dysmorphic Disorder is warranted only if there are distortions about the body that are unrelated to weight or being fat.

Bulimia Nervosa is characterized by episodes of binging on food, followed by efforts to purge the body of the food, via vomiting, laxatives, diuretics, fasting, or excessive exercise. In *DSM-5*, the criteria have been modified to slightly lower the diagnostic bar for the frequency of the purging behaviors to occur, on average, once a week for three months. Specifiers of Purging Type and Nonpurging Type have been eliminated, as they had very little diagnostic reliability, and instead *DSM-5* has added a specifier of **Partial Remission** for individuals who once met full criteria for Bulimia Nervosa, but currently, some, but not all, of the criteria have been sustained for a period of time. The **In Full**

Remission specifier is available in those situations where a full criteria for Bulimia Nervosa were previously met, but none of the criteria have been met for a sustained period of time. Severity specifiers of **Mild, Moderate, Severe, and Extreme** are to be utilized based on the number of episodes of inappropriate compensatory behaviors per week.

Individuals whose binge-eating behavior occurs only during episodes of Anorexia Nervosa are given the diagnosis of Anorexia Nervosa, Binge-Eating/Purging Type, and should not be given the additional diagnosis of Bulimia Nervosa. For individuals with an initial diagnosis of Anorexia Nervosa who binge and purge, but no longer meet the full criteria for Anorexia Nervosa, Binge-Eating/Purging Type (e.g., when weight is normal), a diagnosis of Bulimia Nervosa should be given only when all criteria for Bulimia Nervosa have been met for at least three months.

Borderline Personality Disorder may also involve binge-eating along with other characteristic features of Borderline Personality disorder (e.g., self-mutilation, unstable relationships). In contrast, the diagnosis of Bulimia Nervosa also requires inappropriate compensatory behaviors after the binge-eating as well as over concern with body shape and weight. If criteria are met for Bulimia Nervosa and Borderline Personality Disorder, both should be diagnosed.

A major change in the eating and feeding disorders has been the inclusion of **Binge-Eating Disorder** in *DSM-5*. Binge-Eating Disorder is characterized by recurrent episodes of binge-eating without the recurrent use of compensatory behaviors. It was listed in Appendix B (Criteria Sets and Axes Provided For Further Study) of *DSM-IV-TR*, and the *DSM-5* Eating Disorders Workgroup recommended that Binge-Eating Disorder should achieve full disorder status. The distinction between Binge-Eating Disorder and Bulimia Nervosa is sometimes unclear, and the two categories may represent different stages of the same underlying disorder. *DSM-5* criteria call for recurrent episodes of binge eating as characterized by eating, in a discrete period of time, an amount of food that is definitely larger than what most people would eat, and a sense of lack of control over eating episodes. The binge eating episodes are associated with three of the following: eating more rapidly than normal, eating until uncomfortably full, eating when not physically hungry, eating alone because of embarrassment, or feeling disgusted with oneself, depressed or very guilty after binge eating. The binge eating occurs, on average, at least once a week for three months and is not associated with compensatory behaviors as in Bulimia Nervosa.

A specifier of **Partial Remission** is reserved for individuals who met full criteria for binge eating disorder, but currently binge-eating occurs at an average frequency of less than one episode per week, for a sustained period of time. The **In Full Remission** is available in those situations where a full criteria for Binge-Eating Disorder were previously met, but none of the criteria have been met for a sustained period of time. Severity specifiers of **Mild, Moderate, Severe, and Extreme** are to be utilized based on the frequency of binge eating episodes per week, and the degree of functional disability.

Both Binge-Eating Disorder and Bulimia Nervosa are characterized by recurrent binge eating, but in Bulimia Nervosa, there are recurrent, inappropriate compensatory behaviors (e.g., purging, driven periods of exercise). In terms of clinical presentation, the recurrent, inappropriate compensatory behaviors seen and Bulimia Nervosa are absent in Binge-Eating Disorder. Unlike individuals with Bulimia Nervosa, individuals with Binge-Eating Disorder typically do not show sustained dietary restriction designed to influence body weight and shape. They may, however, report frequent attempts at dieting. If criteria are met for Binge-Eating Disorder and Borderline Personality Disorder, both diagnoses should be given.

DSM-5 also contains a category of **Other Specified Feeding Or Eating Disorder.** This category applies when a feeding or eating disorder is present and interferes with functioning, but does not meet the full criteria for any of the disorders in the feeding and eating disorders category. This may include such things as atypical anorexia nervosa, bulimia nervosa (of low-frequency and/or limited duration), binge eating disorder (of low-frequency and or limited

Haarman

duration), purging disorder, and night eating syndrome. The Other Specified Feeding or Eating Disorder category is used in situations where the clinician chose to communicate the specific reason that the presentation does not meet diagnostic criteria for a specific diagnosis.

Section XI: Elimination Disorders: Chapter 11

The criteria for **Enuresis** and **Encopresis,** contained in *DSM-5*, remain virtually identical to what was identified in *DSM-IV-TR*. A diagnosis of Enuresis or Encopresis is not made if it is better explained as a medical condition or a side effect of medication.

Section XII: Sleep-Wake Disorders: Chapter 12

The *DSM-5* classification of sleep-wake disorders is intended for use by the general mental health and medical clinicians. Sleep wake disorders encompass 10 disorders in the sleep wake disorder group: **Insomnia Disorder, Hypersomnolence Disorder, Narcolepsy, Breathing-Related Sleep Disorders, Circadian Rhythm Sleep-Wake Disorders, Non-Rapid Eye Movement Sleep Arousal Disorders, Nightmare Disorder, Rapid Eye Movement Sleep Behavior Disorder, Restless Leg Syndrome, and Substance/Medication-Induced Sleep disorder.** The revisions in *DSM-5* present a clinically useful approach to diagnosis. In *DSM-IV-TR*, sleep disorders required a determination of whether or not the sleeping problem was a primary issue, or a consequence of another problem. In *DSM-5*, the use of the term primary has been dropped in favor of simply listing the disorder if the criteria are met. Coexisting mental and physical disorders are listed, but without the use of the terms such as related to, or due to, which were used in *DSM-IV-TR*.

Insomnia is the most common sleep complaint of the general population. Insomnia can be either acute or chronic. Among those who report insomnia, maintaining sleep is the most frequent problem, followed by difficulty falling asleep, and/or an early-morning awakening. Three *DSM-IV-TR* disorders – Primary Insomnia, Insomnia Related To Another Mental Disorder, and Sleep Disorder Due To A Medical Condition – have been merged into a single *DSM-5* diagnostic category of **Insomnia Disorder**. The criteria require a predominant complaint of dissatisfaction with sleep quantity or quality, in terms of either difficulty initiating sleep, difficulty maintaining sleep, or early-morning awakening. This causes significant distress or impairment in functioning and occurs at least three nights per week. Criteria also call for symptoms to have persisted for at least three months. *DSM-5* also provides for specifiers of **With Non-Sleep Disorder Mental Co-morbidity, With Other Medical Co-morbidity, and With Other Sleep Disorder.** Specifiers related to chronicity include **Episodic** (lasting one month but less than three months), **Persistent** (symptoms last three months or longer) **and Recurrent** (two or more episodes within the past year). A **coding note** also indicates that acute and short-term insomnia (i.e., Symptoms lasting less than

Haarman

three months, but otherwise meeting criteria) should be coded as an **Other Specified Insomnia Disorder.**

Insomnia Disorder is not diagnosed if the difficulties initiating and maintaining sleep are better explained by or occur exclusively with Circadian Rhythm Sleep-Wake Disorder, Restless Leg Syndrome, Breathing-Related Sleep Disorders, Narcolepsy, or, Parasomnia

Hypersomnolence Disorder is a broad diagnostic term, including symptoms of excessive quantities of sleep, deteriorated quality of wakefulness, and sleep inertia (a period of impaired performance and reduced vigilance following awakening from regular sleep). Substantial changes in this category have been made between *DSM-IV-TR* and *DSM-5*. The new criteria call for self-reported excessive sleepiness despite a maintenance sleep period (lasting at least seven hours), as evidenced by recurrent lapses into sleep during the day, a prolonged main sleep episode of more than nine hours that is non-restorative, and difficulty being fully alert and awake after awakening. The hypersomnolence occurs at least three times per week, for at least three months, and significantly interferes with other areas of functioning. A series of new specifiers addressing co-morbidity, duration, and severity have been added. These include **With Mental Disorder, With Medical Condition, With Another Sleep Disorder, Acute** (less than one month), **Subacute** (1 to 3 months), **Persistent** (more than three months). Specifiers related to severity include **Mild** (1 to 2 days per week), **Moderate** (3 to 4 days per week), and **Severe** (5 to 7 days per week).

Hypersomnolence Disorder is not diagnosed if the difficulties initiating and maintaining sleep are better explained by or occur exclusively with Insomnia Disorder, Circadian Rhythm Sleep-Wake Disorder, Restless Leg Syndrome, Breathing-Related Sleep Disorders, Narcolepsy, or, Parasomnia

Narcolepsy is a disorder that leads to instability in the sleep-wake cycle. It can cause excessive daytime sleepiness and leads to a sudden onset of REM sleep. Evidence has shown that narcolepsy is associated with a lowered amount of hypocretin in the brain. A number of specific changes have occurred in diagnostic criteria, including periods of irresistible sleep, lapsing into sleep, or napping occurring at least three times per week over a three month period. Criteria also call for cataplexy (i.e., brief episodes of sudden bilateral loss of muscle tone), hypocretin deficiency in cerebrospinal fluid, or polysomnography showing REM sleep latency of less than 15 minutes. A series of new specifiers have been added, including: **Narcolepsy without Cataplexy but with Hypocretin Deficiency, Narcolepsy with Cataplexy but without Hypocretin Deficiency, Autosomnal Dominant Cerebellar Ataxia, Deafness, and Narcolepsy, Autosomnal Dominant Narcolepsy, Obesity, and Type 2 Diabetes,** and **Narcolepsy Secondary to Another Medical Condition.** Additional specifiers address the issue of severity, including **Mild** (infrequent cataplexy, need for naps only once or twice per day, and less disturbed nocturnal sleep), **Moderate** (cataplexy daily, or every few days, disturbed nocturnal sleep, and need for multiple naps), and **Severe** (drug-resistant cataplexy with multiple daily attacks, nearly constant sleepiness, and disturbed nocturnal sleep).

Hypersomnolence and Narcolepsy are similar with respect to the degree of daytime sleepiness, age at onset, and stability over time, but can be distinguished based on clinical and laboratory features. Individuals with hypersomnolence typically have longer and less disrupted nocturnal sleep, greater difficulty awakening, and more persistent daytime sleepiness (as opposed to the more discrete "sleep attacks" seen in Narcolepsy.

The Breathing-Related Sleep Disorder category of *DSM-IV-TR* has been eliminated and three new categories, **Obstructive Sleep Apnea Hypopnea, Central Sleep Apnea, and Sleep-Related Hypoventilation** have differentiated that disorder in *DSM-5*.

Haarman

In **Obstructive Sleep Apnea Hypopnea** breathing repeatedly stops and starts during sleep. An absence of airflow is called Apnea and a decrease in airflow is called Hypopnea. Breathing disruptions impair the ability to reach the deep restful stages of sleep, often resulting in sleepiness during wakeful hours. Criteria call for either: evidence by polysomnography of at least 5 apneas or hypopneas per hour and either 1) breathing disturbances (i.e. Snoring, snorting, or breathing pauses) or 2) daytime sleepiness or fatigue, or evidence by polysomnography of at least 15 apneas or hypopneas per hour, regardless of other symptoms. A specifier of **Mild** (apnea hypopnea index is less than 15), **Moderate** (apnea or hypopnea index is 15 - 30), or **Severe** (apnea hypopnea index is more than 30).

Individuals with Obstructive Sleep Apnea Hypopnea must be differentiated from individuals with primary snoring. Individuals with Obstructive Sleep Apnea Hypopnea typically report nocturnal gasping and choking. The presence of sleepiness or other daytime symptoms may suggest a diagnosis of Obstructive Sleep Apnea Hypopnea, but this differentiation typically requires polysomnography. Obstructive Sleep Apnea Hypopnea can be differentiated from Narcolepsy by the absence of cataplexy and sleep paralysis. Daytime sleep episodes observed in Narcolepsy are characteristically shorter and associated with dreaming. A diagnosis of Obstructive Sleep Apnea Hypopnea does not exclude a diagnosis of Narcolepsy as the two conditions may co-occur.

In *DSM-IV-TR*, **Central Sleep Apnea** was included in the Breathing-Related Sleep Disorder diagnosis and did not have separate criteria. Specific diagnostic criteria for Central Sleep Apnea have been developed, as Central Sleep Apnea is viewed as a disruption in breathing because the brain fails to send proper signals to the muscles. This is in contrast to Obstructive Sleep Apnea Hypopnea where breathing is disrupted due to an obstruction of the upper airway. Criteria call for evidence by polysomnography of at least 5 central sleep apneas per hour. Specifiers include: **Idiopathic Central Sleep Apnea, Cheyne-Stokes Breathing, or Central Sleep Apnea Co-morbid with Opioid Use,** and these specifiers are coded as G codes or R codes.

Haarman

Central Sleep Apnea can be distinguished from Obstructive Sleep Apnea Hypopnea by the presence of at least five central apneas per hour of sleep. The conditions may co-occur, but Central Sleep Apnea is considered to dominate when the ratio of central to obstructive respiratory events exceeds 50%.

Sleep-Related Hypoventilation is the result of decreased respiration associated with elevated carbon dioxide levels during sleep. Sleep-Related Hypoventilation is characterized by frequent episodes of shallow breathing lasting longer than 10 seconds, and is a new disorder in *DSM-5*. Criteria require polysomnography episodes of decreased respiration associated with carbon dioxide levels and cannot be better explained by another sleep disorder. Specific specifiers include **Idiopathic Hypoventilation, Congenital Central Alveolar Hypoventilation,** or **Co-morbid Sleep-Related Hypoventilation.** These specifiers are coded as G codes, or R codes.

Sleep-Related Hypoventilation can be distinguished from Obstructive Sleep Apnea Hypopnea and Central Sleep Apnea. Sleep-Related Hypoventilation typically shows more sustained periods of oxygen desaturation rather than the periodic episodes seen in Obstructive Sleep Apnea Hypopnea and Central Sleep Apnea.

Circadian Rhythm Sleep-Wake Disorder is a persistent or recurring pattern of sleep disruption resulting either from the altered sleep-wake schedule or from an inequality between a person's natural sleep-wake cycle and the sleep related demands of lifestyle. Criteria call for a persistent or recurrent pattern of sleep disruption that is primarily due to an alteration of the circadian system. This may be a misalignment of the natural sleep cycle and the person's physical environment or social or professional schedule. The sleep disruption leads to excessive sleepiness, insomnia, or both. A major change in *DSM-5* is the specifiers and the manner in which they are coded. A **Delayed Sleep Phase Type** specifier can be further clarified as either **Familial** or **Overlapping With Non-24 Hour Sleep-Wake Type.**

Haarman

Additional specifiers include**, Advanced Sleep Phase Type, Irregular Sleep-wake Type, Non-24-Hour Sleep-Wake Type, Shift Work Type,** and **Unspecified Type.** Circadian Rhythm Sleep-Wake Disorder can also be specified along the dimension of severity by using specifiers of **Episodic** (symptoms last at least one month but less than three months), **Persistent** (symptoms last three months or longer)**,** and **Recurrent** (two or more episodes occurred within the space of a year). These specifiers are coded as G codes.

In *DSM-5*, the Sleep Terror Disorder and Sleepwalking Disorder of *DSM-IV-TR* have been combined into a new category entitled **Non-Rapid Eye Movement (NREM) Sleep Arousal Disorder.** Sleepwalking and sleep terrors represent both elements of wakefulness and non-REM sleep, a combination that results in the appearance of complex motor behavior without conscious awareness. The overlap of these conditions in people and animals is well-established. Criteria call for recurrent episodes of incomplete awakening from sleep, usually occurring during the first third of of the major sleep cycle, and accompanied by either sleepwalking or sleep terrors. Little or no dream imagery is recalled, as well as amnesia for the behavioral episodes. Coding is based on the specifiers of either **Sleepwalking Type** or **Sleep Terror Type**, and the Sleepwalking Type specifier is further delineated **With Sleep-Related Eating** or **With Sleep-Related Sexual Behavior (Sexsomnia).**

In contrast to individuals with NREM Sleep Arousal Disorders. individuals with Nightmare Disorder typically awaken easily and completely, report vivid dreams, and tend to have episodes later in the night. NREM Sleep Arousal Disorders occur during NREM sleep, whereas nightmares usually occur during REM sleep. REM Sleep Behavior Disorder may be difficult to distinguish from NREM Sleep Arousal Disorders. REM Sleep Behavior Disorder is characterized by episodes of prominent, complex movements, often involving personal injury during sleep. Individuals with REM Sleep Behavior Disorder awaken easily and report more detailed and vivid dream content than do individuals with NREM

Sleep Arousal Disorder. REM Sleep Behavior Disorder individuals often report that they "act out their dreams."

Nightmare Disorder has undergone limited changes in *DSM-5*. Nightmare disorder is characterized by recurrent dreams that feel threatening or frightening, the person becomes fully oriented when waking up, and can usually remember the dreams. In *DSM-5*, an extensive number of specifiers have been added, including, **During Sleep Onset, With Associated Non-Sleep Disorder, With Associated Other Medical Condition,** and **With Associated Other Sleep Disorder.** Additional specifiers to describe chronicity and severity have also been included, including: **Acute** (duration of nightmares for at least one month or less), **Subacute** (duration of nightmares is greater than one month but less than six months), and **Persistent** (the duration of nightmares is six months or greater). Severity is specified as either **Mild** (less than one episode per week), **Moderate** (one or more episodes per week but less than nightly), or **Severe** (episodes occur nightly).

Both Nightmare Disorder and Sleep Terror Disorder include awakenings, or partial awakenings, with fearfulness and autonomic activation, but the two disorders are differentiable. Nightmares typically occur later in the night, during REM sleep, and produce vivid, story like dreams, mild autonomic arousal, and complete awakening. Sleep terrors arise in the first third of the night during stage three or four of NREM sleep, and produce either no dream recall or images without a story. There is usually amnesia for the event in the morning.

Rapid Eye Movement Sleep Behavior Disorder has been added in *DSM-5*. REM Sleep Behavior Disorder is well-established and has the potential to cause dramatic and potentially violent or injurious behaviors during REM sleep. Its clinical features, polysomnography findings and a response to medication have been well-established. REM Sleep Behavior Disorder criteria call for repeated episodes of arousal during sleep, associated with

Haarman

vocalizations, and complex motor behaviors. These behaviors arise during REM sleep and typically occur more than 90 minutes after sleep onset, are more frequent during the later portions of the sleep period, and uncommonly occur during daytime naps. Upon awakening from these episodes, the individuals are awake, alert and not confused or disoriented. Additionally, one of the following must be present: 1) REM sleep without atonia or 2) a history of neurological conditions.

Sleepwalking and sleep terrors can easily be confused with REM Sleep Behavior Disorder. These disorders occur typically in younger individuals, and unlike REM Sleep Behavior Disorder, arise from deep NREM sleep, and therefore tend to occur in the early portion of the sleep cycle.

Another new disorder in *DSM-5* is **Restless Legs Syndrome.** *DSM-IV-TR* included a brief summary of Restless Legs Syndrome within the broader category of Dyssomnia Not Otherwise Specified, but in *DSM-5*, Restless Legs Syndrome has been elevated to disorder status. Criteria require a compulsive urge to move the legs without accompanying unpleasant sensations. It is characterized by the following: an urge to move the legs begins or worsens during periods of rest or inactivity, the urge to move the legs is partially or totally relieved by movement, and the urge to move the legs is worse in the evening or at night than during the day. Symptoms must occur three times per week, have persisted for at least three months, cause considerable impairment in functioning, and are not attributable to another disorder.

Substance/Medication-Induced Sleep Disorder criteria have remained relatively unchanged and a note has remained that indicates this diagnosis should be made only when the symptoms of a severe sleep disturbance are sufficiently severe to warrant clinical attention. Specifiers of **Insomnia Type, Daytime Sleepiness Type, Parasomnia Type,** and **Mixed Type** have been continued in *DSM-5* as well as **With Onset During Intoxication** and **With Onset During Discontinuation/Withdrawal**. Coding has become significantly more complicated based on whether or not there is a co-morbid substance use disorder present. The fourth digit is an indicator of the level of use disorder present and if there is no co-morbid substance use disorder present, the fourth position character is a "9" and only the substance induced anxiety disorder is narrated. When more than one substance is judged to play a significant role in the development of the sleep disturbance, each should be listed separately (e.g., F10.282 Severe Alcohol Use Disorder with Alcohol-induced Sleep Disorder, with Onset During Intoxication, Insomnia Type; F14.282 Severe Cocaine Use Disorder with Cocaine-Induced Sleep Disorder, with Onset During Intoxication, Insomnia Type).

Section XIII: Sexual Dysfunctions: Chapter 13

A major structural change between the *DSM-IV-TR* and *DSM-5* has occurred in how sexual disorders are handled. In *DSM-IV-TR*, Sexual Dysfunctions, Paraphilias, and Gender Identity Disorders were included in the same chapter. In *DSM-5,* Sexual Dysfunctions, Gender Dysphoria, and Paraphilic Disorders have each been given a separate chapter. The Sexual Dysfunctions chapter includes: **Delayed Ejaculation, Erectile Disorder, Female Orgasmic Disorder, Female Sexual Interest/Arousal Disorder, Genito-Pelvic Pain/Penetration Disorder, Male Hypoactive Sexual Desire Disorder, Premature (Early) Ejaculation, and Substance/Medication-induced Sexual Dysfunction.** During the *DSM-5* deliberations, there was controversy about the possibility of including Hypersexual Disorder (commonly referred to as either "sex addiction" or "compulsive sexual behavior") and Paraphillic Coercive Disorder (a sexual preference for coerced sexual activity). After considerable discussion, the decision was made not to include these disorders in *DSM-5.*

DSM-5 states that sexual dysfunctions are a heterogeneous group of disorders that are typically characterized by a disturbance in the person's ability to respond sexually or to experience sexual pleasure. An individual may have several sexual dysfunctions concurrently, and in such cases, all of the dysfunctions should be diagnosed. Clinical judgment should be used to determine if the sexual difficulties are the result of inadequate sexual stimulation, and in these cases the sexual dysfunction diagnosis would not be made. Clinical judgment about the diagnosis of sexual dysfunction should take into consideration cultural factors, partner factors, relationship factors, medical factors, and individual vulnerability. If severe relationship distress, partner violence, or other stressors better explain the sexual difficulties, then a sexual dysfunction diagnosis is not made, but an appropriate Z code may be listed.

Criteria for **Delayed Ejaculation** require that there is a marked delay in ejaculation, infrequency of ejaculation, or absence of ejaculation occurring on almost all occasions (approximately 75% to 100%) of partnered sexual activity. Criteria also call for the requirement that symptoms of delayed ejaculation have persisted for approximately 6 months, and cause clinically significant distress for the individual. Specifiers regarding the onset, circumstances, and severity are also utilized, including **Lifelong, Acquired, Generalized, Situational, Mild, Moderate,** and **Severe.**

The major differential diagnosis is between delayed ejaculation fully explained by another medical illness and delayed ejaculation with psychogenic, idiopathic, or combined psychological and medical etiology. Situational aspects of the complaint are typically suggestive of a psychological basis for the problem. A number of pharmacological agents, such as antidepressants, antipsychotics, and opioid drugs can cause ejaculatory problems.

Male Erectile Disorder of *DSM-IV-TR* has been changed to **Erectile Disorder** in *DSM-5*. In addition to the general changes in the overall category of sexual dysfunctions, the diagnosis of Erectile Disorder underwent several specific changes. Whereas, *DSM-IV-TR* stated that the disorder was an "inability to attain, or to maintain until completion of sexual activity, an adequate erection," *DSM-5* requires one of three possible symptoms: marked difficulty in obtaining an erection during sexual activity, marked difficulty in maintaining an erection until the completion of sexual activity, or marked decrease in erectile rigidity. The disorder has also been quantified to require experiencing symptoms on almost all occasions (75%-100%) of the time. Specifiers regarding the onset, circumstances, and severity are also utilized, including **Lifelong, Acquired, Generalized, Situational, Mild, Moderate,** and **Severe.**

The most difficult aspect of the differential diagnosis of Erectile Disorder is ruling out erectile problems that are fully explained by medical factors. Such cases, should not receive a diagnosis of a mental disorder. Erectile problems that are situational and inconsistent and that have an acute onset after a stressful life event are most often due to psychological issues. An age of less than 40 years, is also suggestive of a possible psychological etiology to the difficulty. Another major differential is whether the erectile problem is secondary to substance/medication use.

Haarman

Female Orgasmic Disorder involves a recurrent delay in, marked infrequency of, or absence of orgasm, or markedly reduced intensity of orgasmic sensations. *DSM-5* includes three significant changes to Female Orgasmic Disorder. "Marked infrequency" of orgasms and "reduced intensity of orgasmic sensations" have been added as symptoms, either of which can fulfill the diagnosis. The addition of "markedly reduced intensity of orgasmic sensations" reflects the fact that orgasm is not an all or nothing phenomenon, and that diminished intensity of orgasm is problematic for some women. In addition, in *DSM-5*, the phrase "following a normal sexual excitement phase" has been deleted due to the variability of the sexual excitement phase from person-to-person. This disorder has also been quantified to require the presence of symptoms being experienced on almost all (75%-100%) occasions of sexual activity. As with most of the other disorders in this section, specifiers regarding the onset, circumstances, and severity are also utilized, including **Lifelong, Acquired, Generalized, Situational, Never Experienced Orgasm, Mild, Moderate,** and **Severe.**

A Major Depressive Disorder typically involves diminished interest or pleasure in all, or most all, activities and may explain Female Orgasmic Disorder. If the orgasmic difficulties are better explained by a Major Depressive Disorder, a diagnosis of Female Orgasmic Disorder should not be made. In some instances substance/medication use may also explain the orgasmic difficulty. A diagnosis of Female Orgasmic Disorder is also not appropriate if the problems are a result of inadequate sexual stimulation.

DSM-IV–TR categories of Female Hypoactive Sexual Desire Disorder and Female Sexual Arousal episode have been combined into a new category in *DSM-5* called **Female Sexual Interest/Arousal Disorder.** This diagnosis implies a woman has either a lack of interest in sexual activity or an inability to obtain or maintain arousal. Terminology utilized in *DSM-IV-TR* such as "desire" has been changed to "interest"in *DSM-5*. *DSM-IV-TR* language of "inability to attain, or to maintain until completion of the sexual activity, an adequate lubrication-swelling response of sexual excitement" has been eliminated and replaced with "absent/reduced genital or non-genital sensations during sexual activity in almost all (75%-100%) sexual encounters." Symptoms must have persisted for a minimum of six months and must cause clinically significant distress in the individual. This diagnosis also carries with it, specifiers including, **Lifelong, Acquired, Generalized, Situational, Mild, Moderate,** and **Severe.**

A Major Depressive Disorder typically involves "markedly diminished interest or pleasure in all, or almost all, activities most of the day, nearly every day," and may explain the lack of sexual interest/arousal. If the lack of interest and arousal are better explained by a Major Depressive Disorder, a diagnosis of Female Sexual Interest/Arousal Disorder should not be made. In some instances substance/medication use may also explain the lack of sexual interest. A diagnosis of Female Sexual Interest/Arousal Disorder is also not appropriate if the problems are a result of inadequate sexual stimulation. Similarly, transient alterations in sexual functioning that are secondary to a significant life or personal event must also be considered as a part of the differential diagnosis.

In *DSM-IV-TR*, two distinct disorders –Dyspareunia and Vaginismus – were used to diagnose sexual pain disorders. These have now been subsumed within a single new category, **Genito-Pelvic Pain/Penetration Disorder.** The primary rationale for this change was that Dyspareunia and Vaginismus were unreliable diagnoses that were difficult for clinicians to distinguish between on a reliable basis. The new combined diagnosis requires difficulties in vaginal penetration, vaginal or pelvic pain during intercourse, anxiety about pain in anticipation of intercourse, or a marked tension or tightening of the pelvic floor muscles during vaginal penetration. Criteria require for symptoms to have persisted a minimum of six months and to cause clinically significant distress in the individual. Specifiers for this disorder vary slightly from other sexual disorders in that only **Lifelong, Acquired, Mild, Moderate,** and **Severe** are available.

Male Hypoactive Sexual Desire Disorder has not been substantially changed in *DSM-5,* with the exception of the requirement for a minimum duration of six months and that the disorder causes clinically significant distress

Haarman

in the individual. As with almost all other disorders in this section, specifiers regarding the onset, circumstances, and severity are also utilized, including **Lifelong, Acquired, Generalized, Situational, Mild, Moderate,** and **Severe.**

A Major Depressive Disorder typically involves "markedly diminished interest or pleasure in all, or almost all, activities most of the day, nearly every day," and may explain the lack of sexual desire. If the lack of desire is better explained by a Major Depressive Disorder, a diagnosis of Male Hypoactive Sexual Desire Disorder should not be made. In some instances substance/medication use may also explain the lack of sexual interest. A diagnosis of Male Hypoactive Sexual Desire Disorder is also not appropriate if the problems are a result of interpersonal or contextual factors. The presence of another sexual dysfunction does not rule out a diagnosis of Male Hypoactive Sexual Desire Disorder; however, if the man's a low desire is explained by self identification as asexual, then a diagnosis of Male Hypoactive Sexual Desire Disorder is not made.

The criteria for a diagnosis of **Premature (Early) Ejaculation** have been operationalized and quantified in *DSM-5*. Criteria now call for "a persistent or recurrent pattern of ejaculation, occurring during partner sexual activity, within approximately 1 minute following vaginal penetration and before the individual wishes it." As with other *DSM-5* diagnoses, the symptoms must have been present for at least six months, must be experienced in almost all (75%-100%) occasions of sexual activity, and must cause clinically significant distress in the individual. As with almost all other disorders in this section, specifiers regarding the onset, circumstances, and severity are also utilized, including **Lifelong, Acquired, Generalized, Situational, Mild, Moderate,** and **Severe.**

When problems with Premature Ejaculation are due exclusively to substance use, intoxication, substance withdrawal, or situational factors, Premature Ejaculation should not be diagnosed.

Haarman

Section XIV: Gender Dysphoria: Chapter 14

In response to criticisms that the term Gender Identity Disorder, as used in *DSM-IV-TR*, was stigmatizing, a decision was made to rename the disorder **Gender Dysphoria** in *DSM-5*. Gender Dysphoria is characterized by a marked incongruence between the persons assigned gender and their expressed gender. Although not all individuals will experience distress as a result of such incongruence, many individuals are distressed if the desired physical intervention by means of hormones and/or surgery are not available. It is hoped that the *DSM-5* terminology is more descriptive than the previous *DSM-IV-TR* term Gender Identity Disorder and focuses on the dysphoria as a clinical problem, not identity per se.

Gender Dysphoria in Children has undergone substantial changes in criteria both in terms of the conceptualization of the disorder as well as symptomatology. Gender Dysphoria in Children requires marked incongruence between one's experienced/expressed gender and assigned gender. In *DSM-IV-TR*, criteria required four of five symptoms; whereas, the *DSM-5*, criteria require six of eight symptoms, one of which must include a strong desire to be of the other gender or an insistence that one is the other gender. Criteria also require clinically significant distress or impairment in social, school, or other important areas of functioning. A specifier of **With a Disorder of Sex Development** can be used for individuals with congenital adrenal genital disorders such as congenital adrenal hyperplasia, androgen insensitivity syndrome, or other intersex conditions.

Gender Dysphoria in Adolescence and Adults is manifested by symptoms such as a stated desire to be the other gender, frequent passing as the other gender, desire to live as the other gender, and a conviction that the person has the typical feelings and reactions of the other gender. Criteria call for a marked incongruence between an individual's experienced/expressed gender and assigned gender for a period of six months duration, and at least two of six symptoms are required for the diagnosis. Consistent with Gender Dysphoria in Children, a specifier of **With a Disorder of Sex**

Development can be used for individuals with congenital adrenal genital disorders. An additional specifier of **Posttransition** is utilized where an individual has transitioned to full-time living in the desired gender and has undergone (or is preparing to undergo) at least one cross sex medical procedure.

Gender Dysphoria is distinguished from simple nonconformity to stereotypical gender role behavior by the strong desire to be another gender than the assigned one. The diagnosis is not meant to describe simple nonconformity. Given the increased openness to atypical gender expression, it is important that the clinical diagnosis be limited to those individuals whose distress and impairment meet the specific criteria. An individual with Transvestic Disorder who also has clinically significant distress and impairment and meets criteria for Gender Dysphoria can be given both diagnoses.

Section XV: Disruptive, Impulse-Control, and Conduct Disorders: Chapter 15

The Disruptive, Impulse-Control, and Conduct Disorders chapter in *DSM-5* includes conditions involving problems of self control of emotions and behaviors. While other disorders also involve problems in emotional and/or behavioral regulation, the disorders in this chapter are unique in terms of repetitiveness and etiology. These problems manifest in behaviors that violate the rights of others and/or bring the individual into significant conflict with societal norms or authority figures. The underlying causes of the problems can vary greatly across the disorders in this chapter, and among individuals within a given diagnostic category. The disorders are unified by the presence of impaired self-regulation that results in difficult, disruptive, aggressive, or antisocial behavior. This chapter includes **Oppositional Defiant Disorder, Intermittent Explosive Disorder, Conduct Disorder, Antisocial Personality Disorder, Pyromania, and Kleptomania.**

Oppositional Defiant Disorder has undergone some cosmetic changes, as well as some conceptual changes, compared to what had been presented in *DSM-IV-TR*. Oppositional Defiant Disorder is characterized by irritability, anger, defiance, and temper outbursts. *DSM-5* considers Oppositional Defiant Disorder to be a developmental antecedent for some youth to the development of a full blown Conduct Disorder. This suggests that the disorders are on a continuum, and may reflect different stages of the same spectrum of disruptive behavior. However, Oppositional Defiant Disorder does not necessarily always develop into Conduct Disorder. *DSM-5* presents Oppositional Defiant Disorder, Conduct Disorder, and Antisocial Personality Disorder in level of severity and developmentally to reflect age-dependent expressions of the same disorder. At least four symptoms of angry/irritable mood, argumentative/defiant behavior, and vindictiveness must be present for at least six months. The same eight symptoms that were utilized in *DSM-IV-TR* are retained in *DSM-5*, but have been reordered under general categories of Angry/Irritable Mood, Argumentative/Defiant Behavior, and Vindictiveness.

An interesting addition to *DSM-5* criteria is the requirement that symptoms are present during interactions with at least one individual who is not a sibling. In addition, the past exclusion for individuals who also met criteria for Conduct Disorder and Antisocial Personality Disorder has been dropped, and now individuals who meet both sets of criteria will carry both diagnoses. An additional **coding note** has been added in *DSM-5* to make the criteria more age, gender, and culture sensitive. Under *DSM-IV-TR*, many very young children were being inappropriately diagnosed as Oppositional Defiant Disorder, when in reality their oppositional behavior was more a result of situational or developmental variability. In an attempt to correct this, *DSM-5* has required age specific criteria. For children younger than five years, the behaviors should occur *on most days* for a period of at least six months; whereas, for individuals five years or older, the behavior should occur at least once per week for at least six months. Severity is specified as either **Mild** (confined to only one setting), **Moderate** (symptoms are present in at least two settings), or **Severe** (symptoms are present in three or more settings).

Conduct Disorder and Oppositional Defiant Disorder are both related to conduct problems that bring the individual in conflict with authority figures. The behaviors of Oppositional Defiant Disorder are typically less severe, and do not include aggression, destruction of property, or a pattern of theft or deceit. Furthermore, Oppositional Defiant Disorder includes problems of emotional dysregulation (i.e., angry and irritable mood) that are not included in the definition of Conduct Disorder. ADHD is often comorbid with Oppositional Defiant Disorder. Intermittent Explosive Disorder also involves high levels of anger; however, individuals with this disorder show serious aggression towards others, which is not part of the definition of Opositional Defiant Disorder.

Oppositional Defiant Disorder shares with Disruptive Mood Dysregulation Disorder the symptoms of chronic, negative mood, and temper outbursts. However, the severity, frequency, and chronicity of temper outbursts are more severe in individuals with Disruptive Mood Dysregulation Disorder. When the mood disturbance is severe enough to meet criteria for Disruptive Mood Dysregulation Disorder, a diagnosis of Oppositional Defiant Disorder is not given, even if all the criteria for Oppositional Defiant Disorder are met.

Haarman

Intermittent Explosive Disorder has been moved from the *DSM-IV-TR* chapter on Impulse-Control Disorders Not Elsewhere Classified to the Disruptive, Impulse-Control, and Conduct Disorders chapter in *DSM-5*. In attempting a greater specificity, **Intermittent Explosive Disorder** in *DSM-5* has had extensive criteria change. A significant change in this disorder is that *DSM-IV-TR* required physical aggression; whereas, in *DSM-5,* verbal aggression and nondestructive/non-injurious physical aggression also meet criteria.

Aggressive outbursts in this disorder are characterized by rapid onset and short duration, and there are little or no anticipatory indications. Episodes involve verbal assault, destructive and nondestructive property assault, or injurious or non-injurious physical assault. These recurrent behavioral outbursts represent a failure to control aggressive impulses as manifested by: 1) verbal aggression or physical aggression towards property, animals, or individuals, occurring twice weekly for a period of three months, that does not result in damage to property or physical injury or 2) outbursts resulting in damage to property and/or a physical assault involving physical injury occurring within a 12 month period. The aggressiveness expressed during these outbursts is grossly out of proportion to the provocation or precipitating stressors, is not premeditated, and the individual is, at least six years of age (or equivalent developmental level). The outbursts are not better explained by another disorder or viewed as part of an adjustment disorder. A **coding note** indicates that a diagnosis of Intermittent Explosive Disorder can be made in addition to a diagnosis of Attention-Deficit/Hyperactivity Disorder, Conduct Disorder, Oppositional Defiant Disorder, or Autism Spectrum Disorder when aggressive outbursts are in excess of those usually seen in individuals with these disorders.

A diagnosis of Intermittent Explosive Disorder should not be made when impulsive aggressive outbursts are attributable to another medical condition, or the physiological effects of substances. This diagnosis should also not be made in children and adolescents when the impulsive aggressive outbursts occur in the context of an Adjustment Disorder. Individuals with ADHD, CD, ODD, or Autism Spectrum Disorder typically exhibit impulsive aggressive behaviors. Individuals with ADHD are typically impulsive and may exhibit impulsive aggressive outbursts and while individuals with Conduct Disorder can exhibit aggressive outbursts, the form of the aggression is characterized as proactive and predatory. Aggression in Oppositional Defiant Disorder is typically characterized by temper tantrums and verbal arguments with authority figures. The level of impulsive, aggressive behaviors in individuals with a history of one or more of these disorders is typically lower than individuals whose symptoms also meet criteria for Intermittent Explosive Disorder. Accordingly, if the impulsive aggressive outbursts warrant independent clinical attention, a comorbid diagnosis of Intermittent Explosive Disorder may also be given with the other four disorders.

Intermittent Explosive Disorder, which is characterized by recurrent behavioral outbursts that are grossly out of proportion to the provocation, must be differentiated from Disruptive Mood Dysregulation Disorder (DMDD). Disruptive Mood Dysregulation Disorder is characterized by aggressive outbursts that are accompanied by a persistently negative mood state, most of the day, nearly every day, between impulsive aggressive outbursts and has an onset before age 10. Intermittent Explosive Disorder is not diagnosed if the aggressive outbursts are better explained by a diagnosis of Disruptive Mood Dysregulation Disorder.

The basic criteria for a **Conduct Disorder** are essentially unchanged from *DSM-IV-TR*. *DSM-5* has maintained the age of onset subtypes: **Childhood-Onset Type**, the individual shows at least one symptom prior to 10 years of age, **Adolescents-Onset Type**, the individual shows no symptoms of the disorder prior to age 10, and added **Unspecified Onset**. Traditional severity specifiers of **Mild** (few problems in excess of those required to make the diagnosis are present), **Moderate** (the number of problems and the effect on others are intermediate between mild and severe, and **Severe** (many problems in excess of those required to make a diagnosis present or caused considerable harm to others) are also retained. Conduct Disorder can now also be diagnosed in adults, provided they do not meet criteria for an Antisocial Personality Disorder diagnosis.

Haarman

A major addition to the criteria for Conduct Disorder has been the inclusion of a specifier **With Limited Prosocial Emotions**. Discussions in the literature have persisted for years about a subset of individuals within the Conduct Disorder diagnosis who display calloused and unemotional traits. The new specifier has been added to describe the childhood equivalent of adults with psychopathy (a distinct syndrome that falls within the antisocial spectrum and is characterized by a lack of empathy and concern for the feelings, wishes, and well-being of others). The specifier of Limited Prosocial Emotions reflects the individual's typical pattern of interpersonal and emotional functioning, and not just occasional occurrences. In order to assess the criteria for this specifier, multiple information sources are necessary, in addition to the individual's self report.

To qualify for this specifier, the individual must have displayed two of the following characteristics persistently over at least 12 months, in multiple relationships, and in multiple settings: 1) **lack of remorse or guilt** (the individual does not feel guilty when he or she does something wrong and shows a general lack of concern about the negative consequences of his or her actions), 2) **callous-lack of empathy** (the individual is unconcerned about the feelings of others, is described as cold and uncaring, and appears more concerned about the effects of his or her actions on himself), 3) **unconcerned about performance** (the individual shows no concern about poor performance at school or work, does not put forth the effort necessary to perform well, and blames others for his or her poor performance), and 4) **shallow or deficient affect** (the individual does not express feelings or show emotions to others except in ways that seem insincere and superficial, or when emotional expressions are used for gain and manipulation).

In contrast to Conduct Disorder, Oppositional Defiant Disorder involves disruptive behaviors that are typically of a less severe nature than those with Conduct Disorder. Additionally, Oppositional Defiant Disorder does not include aggression towards individuals, destruction of property, or a pattern of theft or deceit. Moreover, Oppositional Defiant Disorder includes problems of emotional dysregulation that are not part of the definition of Conduct Disorder. If criteria are met for both conditions, both can be diagnosed under *DSM-5*. The diagnosis of an Adjustment Disorder (with disturbance of conduct or with mixed disturbance of emotions and conduct) should be considered if conduct problems do not meet criteria for Conduct Disorder and are developed in clear association with the onset of a psychosocial stressor, and do not resolve within six months of the termination of the stressor. Conduct Disorder is diagnosed only when conduct problems represent a repetitive and persistent pattern that is associated with an impairment in social, academic, or occupational functioning. In those cases where an individual meets criteria for a Major Depressive Disorder or Bipolar Disorder and also meets criteria for a Conduct Disorder, both diagnoses can be given.

Antisocial Personality Disorder is detailed in the chapter on Personality Disorders, but it was also listed in this chapter because it is considered part of the externalizing conduct disorder spectrum. An Antisocial Personality Disorder can be diagnosed when the individual is 18 years or older. Conduct Disorder is not diagnosed if the individual is age 18 or older and, if criteria are not met for Antisocial Personality Disorder.

Although there was some discussion of eliminating the diagnoses of **Pyromania** and **Kleptomania**, as they rarely occur in isolation, but are almost always in the context of a Conduct Disorder, a Manic Episode, or an Antisocial Personality Disorder, the diagnoses of Pyromania and Kleptomania were retained in *DSM-5*, essentially unchanged. It is important to rule out other causes of fire setting before giving the diagnosis of Pyromania. Intentional fire setting may occur for profit, sabotage, revenge, to conceal a crime, or as an act of terrorism or protest. Kleptomania should be distinguished from ordinary acts of theft or shoplifting, which are motivated by the usefulness of the object or its monetary worth. Kleptomania is exceedingly rare, whereas shoplifting is relatively common.

Section XVI: Substance-Related and Addictive Disorders: Chapter 16

The substance-related disorders encompass ten separate classes of drugs: **alcohol, caffeine, cannabis, hallucinogens, inhalants, opioids, sedatives, hypnotics and anxiolytics, stimulants, tobacco, and other substances**. These ten classes are not fully distinct, as all drugs that are taken in excess have in common direct activation of the brain reward system, which is involved in the reinforcement of behaviors. Many substances described in this chapter can also cause substance-induced disorders that resemble independent mood or anxiety disorders, psychotic disorders, or other disorders, except that the substance-induced disorders are usually transitory and temporary. The chapter is organized such that disorders (i. e., Use Disorders, Intoxication, and Withdrawal) are placed in the *DSM-5* according to substance. Stimulants-Related Disorder diagnoses replaced the categories for amphetamine and cocaine use disorders. Cannabis Use Disorders and Cannabis Withdrawal are new to *DSM-5*. Caffeine Withdrawal is elevated to the status of an independent disorder from *DSM-IV-TR* for Further Study and nicotine use disorders are now called Tobacco-Related Disorders.

Perhaps the most important change in *DSM-5* is that a distinction is no longer made between "abuse" and "dependence" and the two diagnoses sets have been merged. In fact, the term dependence is not used anywhere in *DSM-5* to avoid overlap with the use of the term "dependence" to describe pharmacological tolerance and withdrawal. There were several reasons for combining abuse and dependence. First, clinicians traditionally had trouble distinguishing the syndromes of abuse and dependence. Whereas, studies showed that test-retest reliability of the *DSM-IV-TR* terminology of "dependence" was uniformly very good to excellent, the reliability of *DSM-IV-TR* "abuse," was lower and more variable. Many falsely assumed that abuse was often a prodromal phase of dependence, but several studies show this was not the case. Second, studies showed that the most common way alcohol abuse was diagnosed with *DSM-IV-TR* was with a single criteria (A2, hazardous use). Although this behavior is certainly unwise and risky, basing a psychiatric diagnosis on a single symptom is questionable. Third, the division between abuse and dependence led to "diagnostic orphans," whereby a person could meet the criteria for dependence, but not for abuse. Considering this evidence, the Workgroup recommended that abuse and dependence be combined into a single disorder of graded clinical severity, with two criteria required for diagnosis (Black and Grant, 2014).

Another major controversy in this chapter was the inclusion of Gambling Disorder. While Pathological Gambling was listed in *DSM-IV-TR* in the "Impulse Control Disorder Chapter", the disorder has been moved to the chapter on "Substance-Related and Addictive Disorders" as a result of evidence showing that gambling activates the same brain reward system as drugs, with effects similar to those produced by drugs of abuse (Potenza, 2006). Other behaviors (the so-called behavioral addictions), such as Internet Use, Sex Addiction, Exercise Addiction, and Compulsive Shopping appear to have a similar effect on the reward system, but the Workgroup concluded that the research on these disorders was insufficient for inclusion in this chapter. *DSM-5* has specifically chosen to avoid the terminology of *addiction* in favor of a more neutral terminology *Use Disorder*.

Another complication with the approach taken by *DSM-5* is an intricate coding and recording procedure. Clinicians are directed to use the code that applies to the class of substances, but record the name of the *specific substance*. For example, the diagnosis should be recorded F13.20 Moderate Alprazolam Use Disorder, rather than F13.20 Moderate Sedative, Hypnotic, or Anxiolytic Use Disorder. For substances that do not fit any of the classes (e.g. Steroids), the appropriate Other Substance Use Disorder should specify the *specific substance,* F19.10 Mild Anabolic Steroid Use Disorder. If criteria are met for more than one substance use disorder, all should be diagnosed (e.g. F11.20 Severe Heroin Use Disorder, F14.20 Moderate Cocaine Use Disorder, F10.10 Mild Alcohol Use Disorder). **To further complicate the situation, the appropriate ICD-10-CM coding for a Substance Use Disorder depends on whether or not there is a co-morbid substance-induced disorder.** Because ICD-10-CM codes for substance-induced disorder indicate the presence, or absence, and severity of the substance induced disorder, ICD-10-CM codes for substance use disorders can be used, only in the absence of a substance-induced disorder. **If a substance intoxication, substance withdrawal, or substance-induced mental disorder is present, do not use the specific codes** for a Use Disorder, instead, the co-morbid Use Disorder *is indicated by the 4th character* of the Substance Intoxication, Substance Withdrawal, or Substance-Induced Mental Disorder.

Alcohol-Related Disorders indicated in *DSM-5* include **Alcohol Use Disorder, Alcohol Intoxication, Alcohol Withdrawal, Other Alcohol-Induced Disorders, and Unspecified Alcohol-Related Disorders.** The *DSM-IV-TR* categories of Alcohol Abuse and Alcohol Dependence have been eliminated in favor of a diagnosis of **Alcohol Use Disorder,** which is a merger of the criteria for Alcohol Abuse and Alcohol Dependence with the elimination of the recurrent substance-related legal problems criteria and the inclusion of a new criteria of *craving, or a strong desire or urge to use alcohol.* Whereas, the diagnosis of Alcohol Abuse required one of four symptoms, and the diagnosis of Alcohol Dependence required three of seven symptoms, the diagnostic bar for Alcohol Use Disorder has been set at two of 11 symptoms. Diagnostic criteria call for a problematic pattern of alcohol use leading to significant impairment or distress by at least two symptoms occurring within a 12 month period. Severity specifiers of **Mild** (F10.10 presence of 2-3 symptoms), **Moderate** (F10.20 presence of 4-5 symptoms), or **Severe** (F10.20 presence of six or more symptoms) are stated. An additional specifier of **In a Controlled Environment** is used if the individual is in an environment where access to alcohol is restricted. Remission specifiers are also available in those situations where the person once met the criteria for Alcohol Use Disorder, but no longer meets criteria. **In Early Remission** indicates that the individual previously met full criteria for Alcohol Use Disorder, but now none of the criteria for Alcohol Use Disorder (with the exception of craving) have been met for at least 3 months, but for less than 12 months. **In Sustained Remission** is utilized for an individual who previously met full criteria for Alcohol Use Disorder, but now none of the criteria for Alcohol Use Disorder (with the exception of craving) have been met for a period of 12 months or longer.

Alcohol Intoxication is the result of recent ingestion of alcohol creating significant problematic behavior or psychological changes involving motor, speech, or cognitive issues. The coding of this disorder is dependent on

Haarman

whether or not Alcohol Intoxication is co-morbid with Alcohol Use Disorder. If there is no co-morbid Alcohol Use Disorder, it is coded as F10.929; if Mild Alcohol Use Disorder is co-morbid, use F10.129; and if Moderate or Severe Alcohol Use Disorder is co-morbid, F10.229 is used.

Alcohol Withdrawal is indicated by the presence of a characteristic syndrome after the cessation of use that has been heavy and prolonged. Two or more specific symptoms, only slightly modified from *DSM-IV-TR*, are required for a diagnosis. The **With Perceptual Disturbances** specifier has been slightly modified in *DSM-5*, but still requires hallucinations with intact reality testing, or auditory, visual, or tactile illusions in the absence of delirium. The ICD-10-CM code for **Alcohol Withdrawal without Perceptual Disturbances** is F10.239, and the ICD-10-CM code for **Alcohol Withdrawal With Perceptual Disturbances** is F10.232. *It is not permissible to code a co-morbid Alcohol Use Disorder with an Alcohol Withdrawal Disorder since Alcohol Withdrawal assumes an underlying Alcohol Use Disorder.*

Caffeine-Related Disorders indicated by *DSM-5* include **Caffeine Intoxication, Caffeine Withdrawal, Other Caffeine-Induced Disorders, and Unspecified Caffeine-Related Disorders.** Available scientific evidence supports the diagnoses of Caffeine Intoxication and Caffeine Withdrawal. Some caffeine users display symptoms consistent with problematic use, but scientific data to support a diagnostic category of Caffeine Use Disorder are not available. Caffeine Use Disorder criteria are included in the *DSM-5* "Conditions for Further Study Chapter."

Caffeine Intoxication includes the recent consumption of caffeine (in excess of 250 mg.) and five of 12 symptoms (unchanged from *DSM-IV-TR*). **Caffeine Withdrawal** is new to *DSM-5* and was included in *DSM-IV-TR's* "Criteria Sets and Axes Provided for Further Study." It was not included in *DSM-IV-TR* since it was not considered serious enough to warrant clinical attention. A body of research is now available that demonstrate that caffeine withdrawal can produce distress and impairment. Criteria call for prolonged use of caffeine, with cessation producing at least three symptoms, including: headaches, fatigue or drowsiness, dysphoric or irritable mood, difficulty concentrating, and/or flu-like symptoms.

Cannabis-Related Disorders indicated by DSM-5 include **Cannabis Use Disorder, Cannabis Intoxication, Cannabis Withdrawal, Other Cannabis-Induced Disorders, and Unspecified Cannabis-Related Disorders.** The *DSM-IV-TR* categories of Cannabis Abuse and Cannabis Dependence have been eliminated in favor of a diagnosis of **Cannabis Use Disorder,** which is a merger of the criteria for Cannabis Abuse and Cannabis Dependence with the elimination of the recurrent substance-related legal problems criteria and the inclusion of a new criteria of *craving, or a strong desire or urge to use cannabis.* Diagnostic criteria call for a problematic pattern of Cannabis use leading to significant impairment or distress by at least two symptoms occurring within a 12 month period. Severity specifiers of **Mild** (F12.10 presence of 2-3 symptoms), **Moderate** (F12.20 presence of 4-5 symptoms), or **Severe** (F12.20 presence of six or more symptoms) are utilized. An additional specifier of **In a Controlled Environment** is used if the individual is in an environment where access to Cannabis is restricted. Remission specifiers are also available in those situations where the person once met the criteria for Cannabis Use Disorder, but no longer meets the criteria. **In Early Remission** indicates that the individual previously met full criteria for Cannabis Use Disorder, but now none of the criteria for Cannabis Use Disorder (with the exception of craving) have been met for at least 3 months, but for less than 12 months. **In Sustained Remission** is utilized for an individual who previously met full criteria for Cannabis Use Disorder, but now none of the criteria for Cannabis Use Disorder (with the exception of craving) have been met for a period of 12 months or longer.

Cannabis Intoxication develops during or shortly after cannabis use, creating significant problematic behavior or psychological changes involving motor coordination, euphoria, anxiety, time distortion, impaired judgment, or social changes. Symptoms of increased appetite, dry mouth, and/or tachycardia are also observed. The **With Perceptual Disturbances**

specifier has been slightly modified *in DSM-5*, but still requires hallucinations with intact reality testing, or auditory, visual, or tactile illusions in the absence of delirium. The coding of this disorder is dependent on whether or not Cannabis Intoxication is accompanied by perceptual disturbances or co-morbid with Cannabis Use Disorder. In situations **where there are perceptual disturbances**, if there is no co-morbid Cannabis Use Disorder, it is coded as F12.922; if Mild Cannabis Use Disorder is co-morbid, use F12.122; and if Moderate or Severe Cannabis Use Disorder is co-morbid, F12.222 is used. If **perceptual disturbances are not present** and there is no co-morbid Cannabis Use Disorder, it is coded as F12.929; if Mild Cannabis Use Disorder is co-morbid, use F12.129; and if Moderate or Severe Cannabis Use Disorder is co-morbid, F12.229 is used.

Cannabis Withdrawal is new to *DSM-5* and was not included in *DSM-IV-TR*. Studies have shown that the syndrome can be reliably identified in both humans and animals (Black and Grant, 2014). Criteria call for cessation of cannabis use that has been heavy and prolonged (almost daily over several months) and is evidenced by three of the following: irritability, anxiety, sleep disturbances, decreased appetite, restlessness, depressed mood, and shakiness/sweats/fever/chills/headaches. The ICD-10-CM code for Cannabis Withdrawal is F12.288. *It is not permissible to code a co-morbid Cannabis Use Disorder with a Cannabis Withdrawal Disorder since Cannabis Withdrawal assumes an underlying moderate to severe Cannabis Use Disorder.*

Hallucinogen-Related Disorders indicated by *DSM-5* include **Phencyclidine Use Disorder, Other Hallucinogen Disorder, Phencyclidine Intoxication, Other Hallucinogen Intoxication, Hallucinogen Persisting Perception Disorder, Other Phencyclidine-Induced Disorders, Other Hallucinogen-Induced Disorders, Unspecified Phencyclidine-Related Disorders, and Unspecified Hallucinogen-Related Disorders.** The *DSM-IV-TR* categories of Phencyclidine Abuse and Phencyclidine Dependence have been eliminated in favor of a diagnosis of **Phencyclidine Use Disorder**, which is a merger of the criteria for Phencyclidine Abuse and Phencyclidine Dependence with the elimination of the recurrent substance-related legal problems criteria and the inclusion of a new criteria of *craving, or a strong desire or urge to use phencyclidine.* Withdrawal symptoms have not been established for phencyclidines, so this criteria does not apply. Diagnostic criteria call for a problematic pattern of phencyclidine use leading to significant impairment or distress by at least two symptoms occurring within a 12 month period. Severity specifiers of **Mild** (F16.10 presence of 2-3 symptoms), **Moderate** (F16.20 presence of 4-5 symptoms), or **Severe** (F16.20 presence of six or more symptoms) are to be considered. An additional specifier **In a Controlled Environment** is used if the individual is in an environment where access to phencyclidine is restricted. Remission specifiers are also available in those situations where the person once met the criteria for Phencyclidine Use Disorder, but no longer meets the criteria. **In Early Remission** indicates that the individual previously met full criteria for Phencyclidine Use Disorder, but now none of the criteria for Phencyclidine Use Disorder (with the exception of craving) have been met for at least 3 months, but for less than 12 months. **In Sustained Remission** is utilized for an individual who previously met full criteria for Phencyclidine Use Disorder, but now none of the criteria for Phencyclidine Use Disorder (with the exception of craving) have been met for a period of 12 months or longer.

Other Hallucinogen Use Disorder, which is a merger of *DSM-IV-TR* criteria for Hallucinogen Abuse and Hallucinogen Dependence with the elimination of the recurrent substance-related legal problems criteria and the inclusion of a new criteria of *craving, or a strong desire or urge to use hallucinogens*. Withdrawal symptoms have not been established for hallucinogens, so this criteria, present in other substance use disorder diagnoses, does not apply. Diagnostic criteria call for a problematic pattern of hallucinogen use leading to significant impairment or distress by at least two symptoms occurring within a 12 month period. ICD-10-CM coding is the same for Phencyclidine Use Disorder and Other Hallucinogen Use Disorder. Severity specifiers of **Mild** (F16.10 presence of 2-3 symptoms), **Moderate** (F16.20 presence of 4-5 symptoms), or **Severe** (F16.20 presence of six or more symptoms) are provided by DSM-5. An additional specifier of **In a Controlled Environment** is used if the individual is in an environment where access to other hallucinogens is restricted. Remission specifiers are also available in those situations where the person once met the criteria for Other Hallucinogen Use Disorder, but no longer meets criteria. **In Early Remission** indicates that the individual previously met full criteria for Other Hallucinogen Use

Disorder, but now none of the criteria for Other Hallucinogen Use Disorder (with the exception of craving) have been met for at least 3 months, but for less than 12 months. **In Sustained Remission** is utilized for an individual who previously met full criteria for Other Hallucinogen Use Disorder, but now none of the criteria for Other Hallucinogen Use Disorder (with the exception of craving) have been met for a period of 12 months or longer. The clinician is to specify the particular hallucinogen as part of the diagnosis despite using only one ICD-10-CM code.

Phencyclidine Intoxication is the result of recent use of phencyclidine creating significant problematic behavior or psychological changes, typically within an hour, involving: motor, speech, or cognitive issues. The coding of this disorder is dependent on whether or not Phencyclidine Intoxication is co-morbid with Phencyclidine Use Disorder. If there is no co-morbid Phencyclidine Use Disorder, it is coded as F16.929; if Mild Phencyclidine Use Disorder is co-morbid, use F16.129; and if Moderate or Severe Phencyclidine Use Disorder is co-morbid, F16.229 is used.

Other Hallucinogen Intoxication is the result of recent ingestion of a hallucinogen creating significant problematic behavior or psychological changes involving: motor, speech, or cognitive issues and perceptual changes occurring in a state of full wakefulness. The coding of this disorder is dependent on whether or not Hallucinogen Intoxication is co-morbid with Hallucinogen Use Disorder. If there is no co-morbid Hallucinogen Use Disorder, it is coded as F16.929; if Mild Hallucinogen Use Disorder is co-morbid, use F6.129; and if Moderate or Severe Hallucinogen Use Disorder is co-morbid, F16.229 is used. Note that the ICD-10-CM numbering is the same for both disorders. Specify the particular hallucinogen.

Hallucinogen Persisting Perception Disorder involves the re-experiencing one or more of the perceptual symptoms that were experienced while intoxicated with a hallucinogen. Criteria require that, following the cessation of use of a hallucinogen, one or more of the perceptual symptoms are re-experienced. Examples might include: geometric hallucinations, false

Haarman

perceptions of movement, flashes of color, positive afterimages, halos, and macropsia or micropsia.

Paint thinner, airplane glue, and gasoline are just a few of the inhalants that are commonly abused. People who regularly use hydrocarbon-based inhalants may develop most of the diagnostic features of a substance use disorder, with the exception of withdrawal. **Inhalant Use Disorder, Inhalant Intoxication, Other Inhalant-Induced Disorder, and Unspecified Inhalant-Related Disorder** are included in the *DSM-5*.

Inhalant Use Disorder, which is a merger of the *DSM-IV-TR* criteria for Inhalant Abuse and Inhalant Dependence, with the elimination of the recurrent substance-related legal problems criteria, and the inclusion of a new criteria of *craving, or a strong desire or urge to use an inhalant.* Whereas, the diagnosis of Inhalant Abuse required one of four symptoms, and the diagnosis of Inhalant Dependence required three of seven symptoms, the diagnostic bar for Inhalant Use Disorder has been set at two of 11 symptoms. Diagnostic criteria call for a problematic pattern of inhalant use leading to significant impairment or distress as evidenced by at least two symptoms occurring within a 12 month period. Severity specifiers of **Mild** (F18.10 presence of 2-3 symptoms), **Moderate** (F18.20 presence of 4-5 symptoms), or **Severe** (F18.20 presence of six or more symptoms) are to be utilized. An additional specifier, **In a Controlled Environment** is used if the individual is in an environment where access to inhalants is restricted. Remission specifiers are also available in those situations where the person once met the criteria for Inhalant Use Disorder, but no longer meets criteria. **In Early Remission** indicates that the individual previously met full criteria for Inhalant Use Disorder, but now none of the criteria for Inhalant Use Disorder (with the exception of craving) have been met for a period of at least 3 months, but for less than 12 months. **In Sustained Remission** is utilized for an individual who previously met full criteria for Inhalant Use Disorder, but now none of the criteria for Inhalant Use Disorder (with the exception of craving) have been met for a period of 12 months or longer. Specify the particular inhalant involved (e.g. Solvent Use Disorder).

Haarman

Inhalant Intoxication is the result of recent, intended or unintended, short-term, high dosage exposure to inhalants, particularly hydrocarbons, creating significant problematic behavior or psychological changes involving motor, speech, or cognitive issues. Coding of this disorder is dependent on whether or not Inhalant Intoxication is co-morbid with Inhalant Use Disorder. If there is no co-morbid Inhalant Use Disorder, it is coded as F18.929; if Mild Inhalant Use Disorder is co-morbid, use F18.129; and if Moderate or Severe Inhalant Use Disorder is co-morbid, F18.229 is used.

The *DSM-5* Opioid-Related Disorders includes **Opioid Use Disorder, Opioid Intoxication, Opioid Withdrawal, Other Opioid-Induced Disorders, and Unspecified Opioid-Related Disorders.** The *DSM-IV-TR* categories of Opioid Abuse and Opioid Dependence have been eliminated in favor of a diagnosis of **Opioid Use Disorder**, which is a merger of the criteria Opioid Abuse and Opioid Dependence with the elimination of the recurrent substance-related legal problems criteria and the inclusion of a new criteria of *craving, or a strong desire or urge to use an opioid.* Whereas, the diagnosis of Opioid Abuse required one of four symptoms, and the diagnosis of Opioid Dependence required three of seven symptoms, the diagnostic bar for Opioid Use Disorder has been set at two of 11 symptoms. Diagnostic criteria call for a problematic pattern of opioid use leading to significant impairment or distress by at least two symptoms occurring within a 12 month period. Severity specifiers of **Mild** (F11.10 presence of 2-3 symptoms), **Moderate** (F11.20 presence of 4-5 symptoms), or **Severe** (F11.20 presence of six or more symptoms), and an additional specifier **In a Controlled Environment** is used if the individual is in an environment where access to opioids is restricted. Remission specifiers are also available in those situations where the person once met the criteria for Opioid Use Disorder, but no longer meets criteria. **In Early Remission** indicates that the individual previously met full criteria for Opioid Use Disorder, but now none of the criteria for Opioid Use Disorder (with the exception of craving) have been met for at least 3 months, but for less than 12 months. **In Sustained Remission** is utilized for an individual who previously met full criteria for Opioid Use Disorder, but now none of the criteria for Opioid Use Disorder (with the exception of craving) have been met for a period of 12 months or longer. The clinician must also specify if the individual is **On Maintenance Therapy** *including prescribed agonist medication.*

Opioid Intoxication is the result of recent use of opioids creating significant problematic behavior or psychological changes involving motor, speech, or cognitive issues. Coding of this disorder is dependent on whether or not Opioid Intoxication is co-morbid with Opioid Use Disorder and whether or not there are perceptual disturbances. The **With Perceptual Disturbances** specifier has been slightly modified in *DSM-5*, but still requires hallucinations with intact reality testing, or auditory, visual, or tactile illusions in the absence of delirium. The ICD-10-CM codes for Opioid Intoxication, **without perceptual disturbances** is F11.929 if there is no co-morbid Opioid Use Disorder; if Mild Opioid Use Disorder is co-morbid, use F11.129; and if Moderate or Severe Opioid Use Disorder is co-morbid, F11.229 is used. The ICD-10-CM codes for Opioid Intoxication, **with perceptual disturbances** is F11.922 if there is no co-morbid Opioid Use Disorder; if Mild Opioid Use Disorder is co-morbid, use F11.122; and if Moderate or Severe Opioid Use Disorder is co-morbid, F11.222 is used.

Opioid Withdrawal is indicated by the presence of a characteristic withdrawal syndrome after the cessation of use that has been heavy and prolonged. Three or more specific symptoms, essentially the same as in *DSM-IV-TR,* are required for a diagnosis. The ICD-10-CM code for Opioid Withdrawal is F11.23. *It is not permissible to code a co-morbid Opioid Use Disorder with an Opioid Withdrawal Disorder since Opioid Withdrawal assumes an underlying Opioid Use Disorder.*

Sedative, hypnotic, or anxiolytic-Related Disorders indicated by *DSM-5* include **Sedative, Hypnotic, or Anxiolytic Use Disorder, Sedative, Hypnotic, or Anxiolytic Intoxication, Sedative, Hypnotic, or Anxiolytic Withdrawal, Other Sedative, Hypnotic, or Anxiolytic-Induced Disorders, and Unspecified Sedative, Hypnotic, or Anxiolytic-Related Disorders.** The *DSM-IV-TR* categories of Sedative, Hypnotic, or Anxiolytic Abuse and Sedative, Hypnotic, or

Anxiolytic Dependence have been eliminated in favor of a diagnosis of **Sedative, Hypnotic, or Anxiolytic Use Disorder**, which is a merger of the *DSM-IV-TR* criteria for Sedative, Hypnotic, or Anxiolytic Abuse and Sedative, Hypnotic, or Anxiolytic Dependence with the elimination of the recurrent substance-related legal problems criteria and the inclusion of a new criteria of *craving, or a strong desire or urge to use sedative, hypnotic, or anxiolytics.* Whereas, the diagnosis of Sedative, Hypnotic, or Anxiolytic Abuse required one of four symptoms, and the diagnosis of Sedative, Hypnotic, or Anxiolytic Dependence required three of seven symptoms, the diagnostic bar for Sedative, Hypnotic, or Anxiolytic Use Disorder has been set at two of 11 symptoms. Diagnostic criteria call for a problematic pattern of sedative, hypnotic, or anxiolytic use leading to significant impairment or distress as evidenced by at least two symptoms, occurring within a 12 month period. Criteria are not considered being met for individuals taking sedatives, hypnotics, or anxiolytics under medical supervision. Severity specifiers of **Mild** (F13.10 presence of 2-3 symptoms), **Moderate** (F13.20 presence of 4-5 symptoms), or **Severe** (F13.20 presence of six or more symptoms) are based on the number of symptoms. An additional specifier, **In a Controlled Environment** is used if the individual is in an environment where access to sedative, hypnotic, or anxiolytics drugs is restricted. Remission specifiers are also available in those situations where the person once met the criteria for Sedative, Hypnotic, or Anxiolytic Use Disorder, but no longer meets the criteria. **In Early Remission** indicates that the individual previously met full criteria for Sedative, Hypnotic, or Anxiolytic Use Disorder, but now none of the criteria for Sedative, Hypnotic, or Anxiolytic Use Disorder (with the exception of craving) have been met for at least 3 months, but for less than 12 months. **In Sustained Remission** is utilized for an individual who previously met full criteria for Sedative, Hypnotic, or Anxiolytic Use Disorder, but now none of the criteria for Sedative, Hypnotic, or Anxiolytic Use Disorder (with the exception of craving) have been met for a period of 12 months or longer.

Sedative, Hypnotic, or Anxiolytic Intoxication is the result of recent use of sedative, hypnotic, or anxiolytics creating significant problematic behavior or psychological changes involving motor, speech, or cognitive issues. Coding of this disorder is dependent on whether or not Sedative, Hypnotic, or

Anxiolytic Intoxication is co-morbid with Sedative, Hypnotic, or Anxiolytic Use Disorder. If there is no co-morbid Sedative, Hypnotic, or Anxiolytic Use Disorder, it is coded as F13.929; if Mild Sedative, Hypnotic, or Anxiolytic Use Disorder is co-morbid, use F13.129; and if Moderate or Severe Sedative, Hypnotic, or Anxiolytic Use Disorder is co-morbid, F13.229 is used.

Sedative, Hypnotic, or Anxiolytic Withdrawal is indicated by the presence of a characteristic syndrome after the cessation of use. Two or more specific symptoms, only slightly modified from DSM-IV-TR, are required for a diagnosis. The **With Perceptual Disturbances** specifier has been slightly modified in *DSM-5*, but still requires hallucinations with intact reality testing, or auditory, visual, or tactile illusions in the absence of delirium. The ICD-10-CM code for Sedative, Hypnotic, or Anxiolytic Withdrawal Without Perceptual Disturbances is F13.239, and the ICD-10-CM code for Sedative, hypnotic, or Anxiolytic Withdrawal With Perceptual Disturbances is F13.232. *It is not permissible to code a co-morbid Sedative, Hypnotic, or Anxiolytic Use Disorder with a Sedative, Hypnotic, or Anxiolytic Withdrawal Disorder since Sedative, Hypnotic, or Anxiolytic Withdrawal assumes an underlying Sedative, Hypnotic, or Anxiolytic Use Disorder.*

The *DSM-IV-TR* categories of Amphetamine Abuse, Amphetamine Dependence, Cocaine Abuse, and Cocaine Dependence have been combined and eliminated in favor of a single diagnosis of **Stimulant Use Disorder**. This is a merger of the abuse and dependence categories with the elimination of the recurrent substance-related legal problems criteria and the inclusion of a new criteria of *craving, or a strong desire or urge to use stimulant.* Whereas, the diagnoses of Amphetamine Abuse and Cocaine Abuse required one of four symptoms, and the diagnoses of Amphetamine Dependence and Cocaine Dependence required three of seven symptoms, the diagnostic bar for Stimulant Use Disorder has been set at two of 11 symptoms. Diagnostic criteria call for a problematic pattern of stimulant use leading to significant impairment or distress as evidenced by at least two symptoms occurring within a 12 month period. Criteria exclude those individuals taking stimulants under appropriate medical supervision, such as medications for Attention-Deficit/Hyperactivity Disorder or Narcolepsy. Severity specifiers for this category must also spell out the substance involved for proper ICD-10-CM coding. **Mild** (presence of 2-3 symptoms) F15.10 Amphetamine-type Substance Use Disorder, Mild, F14.10 Cocaine Use Disorder, Mild, or F15.10 Other or Unspecified Stimulant Use Disorder, Mild; **Moderate** (presence of 4-5 symptoms) F15.20 Amphetamine-type Substance Use Disorder, Moderate, F14.20 Cocaine Use Disorder, Moderate, or F15.20 Other or Unspecified Stimulant Use Disorder, Moderate; or **Severe** (presence of six or more symptoms) F15.20 Amphetamine-type Substance Use Disorder, Severe, F14.20 Cocaine Use Disorder, Severe, or F15.20 Other or Unspecified Stimulant Use Disorder, Severe. An additional specifier of **In a Controlled Environment** is used if the individual is in an environment where access to stimulants is restricted. Remission specifiers are also available in those situations where the person once met the criteria for Stimulant Use Disorder, but no longer meets criteria. **In Early Remission** indicates that the individual previously met full criteria for Stimulant Use Disorder, but now none of the criteria for Stimulant Use Disorder (with the exception of craving) have been met for at least 3 months, but for less than 12 months. **In Sustained Remission** is utilized for an individual who previously met full criteria for Stimulant Use Disorder, but now none of the criteria for Stimulant Use Disorder (with the exception of craving) have been met for a period of 12 months or longer.

Stimulant Intoxication is the result of recent use of an amphetamine-type substance, cocaine, or other stimulants creating significant problematic behavior or psychological changes involving motor, speech, or cognitive issues. Clinicians must specify the intoxicant. Coding of this disorder is dependent on whether or not Stimulant Intoxication is co-morbid with Stimulant Use Disorder and whether or not there are perceptual disturbances. The **With Perceptual Disturbances** specifier has been slightly modified in DSM-5, but still requires hallucinations with intact reality testing, or auditory, visual, or tactile illusions in the absence of delirium. The ICD-10-CM codes for Stimulant Intoxication, **without perceptual disturbances** is F15.929, if there is no co-morbid Amphetamine or Stimulant Use Disorder; if Mild Amphetamine or Stimulant Use Disorder is co-morbid, use F15.129; and if Moderate or Severe Amphetamine Stimulant Use Disorder is co-morbid, F15.229 is used. Similarly, Stimulant Intoxication, **without perceptual disturbances** is F14.929 if there is no co-morbid Cocaine Use Disorder; if Mild Cocaine Use Disorder is co-morbid, use F14.129; and if Moderate or Severe Cocaine Use Disorder is co-morbid, F14.229 is used. The ICD-10-CM codes for Stimulant Intoxication, **with perceptual disturbances** is F15.922 if there is no co-morbid Amphetamine or Stimulant Use Disorder; if Mild Amphetamine or Stimulant Use Disorder is co-morbid, use F15.122; and if Moderate or Severe Amphetamine or Stimulant Use Disorder is co-morbid, F15.222 is used. Likewise, utilize F14.929 if there is no co-morbid Cocaine Use Disorder; if Mild Cocaine Use Disorder is co-morbid, use F14.122; and if Moderate or Severe Cocaine Use Disorder is co-morbid, F14.222 is used.

Stimulant Withdrawal is indicated, after cessation of use, by dysphoric mood and the presence of at least two of the following: fatigue, unpleasant dreams, insomnia or hypersomnia, increased appetite, and motor changes. The clinician must specify the substance that causes the withdrawal syndrome. The ICD-10-CM code for Amphetamine or Another Stimulant Withdrawal is F15.23. The code for Cocaine Withdrawal is 14.23. *It is not permissible to code a co-morbid Amphetamine, Cocaine, or Other Stimulant Use Disorder with an Amphetamine, Cocaine, or Other Stimulant Withdrawal Disorder, since Amphetamine, Cocaine, or Other Stimulant Withdrawal assumes an underlying Amphetamine, Cocaine, or Other Stimulant Use Disorder.*

DSM-5 has renamed Nicotine-Related Disorders as Tobacco-Related Disorders. Tobacco-Related Disorders include: **Tobacco Use Disorder, Tobacco Withdrawal, Other Tobacco-Induced Disorders, and Unspecified Tobacco-Related Disorders.** The DSM-IV-TR category of Tobacco Dependence has been eliminated in favor of a diagnosis of **Tobacco Use Disorder**, which is parallel with other substance use disorder criteria, including the inclusion of a new criteria of *craving, or a strong desire or urge to use tobacco.* Diagnostic criteria call for a problematic pattern of tobacco use leading to significant impairment or distress by at least two symptoms occurring within a 12 month period. Severity specifiers of **Mild** (F11.10 presence of 2-3 symptoms), **Moderate** (F11.20 presence of 4-5 symptoms), or **Severe** (F11.20 presence of six or more symptoms) have been included. An additional specifier of **In a Controlled Environment** is used if the individual is in an environment where access to tobacco is restricted. Remission specifiers are also available in those situations where the person once met the criteria for Tobacco Use Disorder, but no longer meets criteria. **In Early Remission** indicates that the individual previously met full criteria for Tobacco Use Disorder, but now none of the criteria for Tobacco Use Disorder (with the exception of craving) have been met for at least 3 months, but for less than 12 months. **In Sustained Remission** is utilized for an individual who previously met full criteria for Tobacco Use Disorder, but now none of the criteria for Tobacco Use Disorder (with the exception of craving) have been met for a period of 12 months or longer. The clinician must also specify if the individual is **On Maintenance Therapy** and is taking long-term maintenance medication, such as nicotine replacement medication.

Tobacco Withdrawal is indicated, after cessation of daily use of tobacco for several weeks, by the presence of four of the following: irritability, anxiety, difficulty concentrating, insomnia or hypersomnia, increased appetite, restlessness, or depressed mood. The ICD-10-CM code for Tobacco Withdrawal is F15.23. *It is not permissible to code a co-morbid Tobacco Use Disorder with Tobacco Withdrawal Disorder since Tobacco Withdrawal assumes an underlying Tobacco Use Disorder.*

Disordered gambling behavior was first officially recognized in *DSM-III*, as Pathological Gambling. In *DSM-IV-TR*, Pathological Gambling was categorized as one of the Impulsue-Control Disorders along with Pyromania, Kleptomania, and Trichotillomania. In *DSM-5*, the disorder is now included in the chapter on substance use disorders because of consistently high rates of co-morbidity, similar presentation of some symptoms, and physiological and genetic overlap. The criteria have had only minor changes from *DSM-IV-TR*. Importantly the name has changed from **Pathological Gambling** to **Gambling Disorder** and the number of symptoms required for the diagnosis has been reduced.

Gambling Disorder is persistent and recurrent gambling behavior leading to impairment or distress as indicated by at least four of the following: increasing amounts gambled, restlessness when attempting to stop, unsuccessful efforts to control or stop, a preoccupation with gambling, gambling when distressed, chasing one's losses, concealing gambling, jeopardized or lost relationships or job, and relies on others to provide money for desperate financial situations. Severity specifiers of **Mild** (presence of 4-5 symptoms), **Moderate** (presence of 6-7 symptoms), or **Severe** (presence of 8-9 symptoms) are to be utilized. Remission specifiers are also available in those situations where the person once met the criteria for Gambling Disorder, but no longer meets criteria. **In Early Remission** indicates that the individual previously met full criteria for Gambling Disorder, but now none of the criteria for Gambling Disorder have been met for at least 3 months, but for less than 12 months. **In Sustained Remission** is utilized for an individual who previously met full criteria for Gambling Disorder, but now none of the criteria for Gambling Disorder have been met for a period of 12 months or longer. Chronicity specifiers are also available including, **Episodic** - meeting criteria at more than one point in time, with symptoms subsiding between periods of Gambling Disorder for at least several months, and **Persistent** - experiencing continuous symptoms meeting diagnostic criteria for multiple years.

Gambling Disorder must be distinguished from professional and social gambling. In professional gambling, the risks are limited and discipline is a central factor to the successful professional gambler. Social gambling typically occurs with friends or colleagues, last for a limited period of time, and has an acceptable level of losses. Some individuals can experience problems associated with gambling that do not meet the full criteria for Gambling Disorder and should not be diagnosed. Loss of judgment in excessive gambling may occur during a Manic Episode, and an additional diagnosis of Gambling Disorder should be given only if the behavior is not better explained by the Manic Episode. Problems with gambling may occur in individuals with Antisocial Personality Disorder and other personality disorders. If criteria are met for both disorders, both can be diagnosed.

Section XVII: Neurocognitive Disorders: Chapter 17

The DSM-5 Chapter on Neurocognitive Disorders encompasses a number of disorders that have cognitive impairment as their presenting problem. These include: **Delirium, Mild or Major Neurocognitive Disorder Due to Alzheimer's Disease, Mild or Major Frontotemporal Neurocognitive Disorder, Mild or Major Neurocognitive Disorder with Lewy Bodies, Mild or Major Vascular Neurocognitive Disorder, Mild or Major Neurocognitive Disorder Due to Traumatic Brain Injury, Substance/Medication-Induced Mild or Major Neurocognitive Disorder, Mild or Major Neurocognitive Disorder Due to HIV Infection, Mild or Major Neurocognitive Disorder Due to Prion Disease, Mild or Major Neurocognitive Disorder Due to Parkinson's Disease, Mild or Major Neurocognitive Disorder Due to Huntington's Disease, Mild or Major Neurocognitive Disorder Due to Another Medical Condition, and Mild or Major Neurocognitive Disorder Due to Multiple Etiologies.** In *DSM-IV-TR*, the chapter was called "Delirium, Dementia, Amnestic and Other Cognitive Disorders." *DSM-5* refers to those disorders that are acquired (i.e.Those attributable to medical conditions or the effects of drug abuse or medications) or are degenerative (i.e. Those that reflect a decline from a previous level) rather than disorders that are congenital or apparent in childhood. The title was selected to avoid the stigma associated with the word dementia. The neurocognitive disorders are divided into three syndromes: delirium, major neurocognitive disorder, and mild neurocognitive disorder. The major change to this diagnostic group is the concept of "major" and "mild" neurocognitive disorders, which can still be a focus of care.

Delirium is a disturbance in the level of awareness or attention, marked by the acute onset of cognitive changes attributable to a general medical condition. Delirium tends to have an acute onset, relatively brief duration, and fluctuating course. It is distinguished from Major or Mild Neurocognitive Disorders on the basis of its core characteristics: 1) a disturbance in the level of awareness, and 2) the reduced ability to direct, focus, sustain, and shift attention. Although some level of disturbance in awareness and attention is observed in all neurocognitive disorders, these disturbances are not prominent in Major or Mild Neurocognitive Disorder. The diagnostic criteria in *DSM-5*

Haarman

Delirium are not substantially changed from what was included in *DSM-IV-TR*. One exception is an additional criteria requiring that disturbances in attention and cognition are not better explained by another pre-existing or evolving neurocognitive disorder, and do not occur in the context of a severely reduced level of arousal such as a coma.

Schizophrenia Spectrum and Other Psychotic Disorders, Bipolar Disorders, and Depressive Disorders may involve delusions, hallucinations, or agitation, but they are not due to the direct physiological effects of a general medical condition, or substance use. They are not accompanied by a disturbance in attention and awareness, and the additional disturbances in cognition, language, or visual spatial ability that are characteristic of Delirium.

There are multiple subtypes for the diagnosis of Delirium that address the neurological issues. Two subtypes indicate whether the delirium is due to substance intoxication or substance withdrawal, or another possible subtype of medication-induced delirium, or multiple etiologies. Specifiers related to chronicity and activity level are also included. **Substance Intoxication Delirium** is diagnosed Instead of substance intoxication, when the symptoms of changing attention and cognition dominate the clinical picture. Coding has become significantly more complicated based on whether or not there is a co-morbid substance use disorder present. The fourth digit is an indicator of the level of use disorder present and if there is no co-morbid substance use disorder present, the fourth position character is a "9" and only the substance induced anxiety disorder is narrated. If a Mild Substance Use Disorder is co-morbid with the Substance Intoxication Delirium, the fourth position character is "1," and the diagnosis should be recorded as "Mild Substance Use Disorder with Substance Intoxication Delirium." If a Moderate, or Severe Substance Use Disorder is co-morbid with the Substance Intoxication Delirium, the fourth position character is "2," and should be recorded as "Moderate Substance Use Disorder with Substance Intoxication Disorder.

Substance Withdrawal Delirium is diagnosed instead of Substance Withdrawal when the symptoms of changing attention and cognition are sufficiently severe to warrant clinical attention. Coding is dependent upon the specific substance involved.

Medication-Induced Delirium is diagnosed when the symptoms of attention and cognition arise as a side effect of the medication taken as prescribed. Coding for this disorder also is dependent upon the specific medication involved. **Delirium Due to Multiple Etiologies** is utilized when there is evidence from history, physical examination, or laboratory findings that the delirium has more than one etiology. Coding requires the use of multiple separate codes reflecting the specific delirium etiologies and the medical condition involved. Specifiers are also available to address the chronicity, **Acute** (lasting a few hours or days) or **Persistent** (lasting weeks or months). Specifiers are also available to indicate the overall activity level of the individual: **Hyperactive** (increased psychomotor activity accompanied by mood, agitation, and/or refusal to cooperate), **Hypoactive** (a reduced level of psychomotor activity accompanied by sluggishness and lethargy that may approach a stupor), and **Mixed Level of Activity** (a normal level of psychomotor activity, but attention and awareness are disturbed or individuals whose activity level rapidly fluctuates).

Major or Mild Neurocognitive Disorder, what was formally known in *DSM-IV-TR* as dementia**,** is an acquired disorder with significant cognitive decline in one or more of the following domains: complex attention, executive functioning, learning and memory, language, perceptual-motor ability, or social cognition. Unlike *DSM-IV-TR* criteria for Dementia, the *DSM-5* Major Neurocognitive Disorder criteria do not require memory to be one of the impaired domains and allow cognitive deficit to be limited to one domain. The distinction between Major Neurocognitive Disorder and Mild Neurocognitive Disorder is one of severity. In Major Neurocognitive Disorder, the individual experiences a significant cognitive decline and a significant disruption in independence and everyday activity. In Mild Neurocognitive Disorder, the individual experiences a modest cognitive decline and deficits do not interfere with the capacity for independence and everyday life activities. Specifiers for both Major Neurocognitive Disorder and Mild Neurocognitive Disorder are based on the assumed etiology, and include: Alzheimer's Disease, Frontotemporal Lobar Degeneration, Lewy Body Disease, Vascular Disease, Traumatic Brain Injury, Substance/Medication Use, HIV Infection, Prion Disease, Parkinson's Disease, Huntington's Disease, Another Medical Condition, Multiple Etiologies, and Unspecified.

Intellectual Disability is characterized by intellectual and adaptive functioning deficits that have their onset during the early developmental period. Major or Mild Neurocognitive Disorders represent a significant decline in cognitive functioning over time. Schizophrenia may also involve cognitive impairment and deterioration in intellectual functioning, but typically involves an earlier age of onset, less severe cognitive impairment, and a symptom pattern that is not due to the direct effects of a medical condition, or substance/medication use. Major Depressive Disorder involves memory deficits, difficulty concentrating, and other cognitive impairments, but these deficits improve when the depression remits, are associated with other characteristic depressive symptoms, and are not due to the direct effects of a general medical condition, or substance/medication use. Major or Mild Neurocognitive Disorder should be distinguished from normal age related cognitive decline which is characterized by cognitive impairment that is in keeping with what would be expected given the individual's age.

Major or Mild Neurocognitive Disorder Due to Alzheimer's Disease is a neurodegenerative disorder. It typically occurs late in life, but can occur earlier. It is marked by an insidious onset, gradual decline and typically in early prominent memory loss. The diagnosis of Alzheimer's specifier must be made on clinical grounds, in the absence of brain biopsy. Alzheimer's disease has a characteristic pattern of onset and progressive cognitive decline. Criteria require an insidious onset and gradual progression in impairment of one or more cognitive domains. For Mild Neurocognitive Disorder Due to Alzheimer's Disease, impairment in only one domain is required. Impairment in at least two domains is required for a diagnosis of Major Neurocognitive Disorder Due to Alzheimer's Disease.

A specifier of **Probable Alzheimer's Disease** is available for Major Neurocognitive Disorder Due to Alzheimer's disease and should be utilized when appropriate. The Probable Alzheimer's Disease specifier is utilized for Major Neurocognitive Disorder Due to Alzheimer's disease if either 1) there is evidence of a causative Alzheimer's disease genetic mutation from family history or genetic testing or 2) there is clear evidence of a decline in memory and at least one other cognitive domain, there has been a steadily progressive, gradual decline in cognition, without extended plateaus, and there is no evidence of a mixed etiology. Otherwise, Major Neurocognitive Disorder due to Alzheimer's Disease has a specifier of **Possible Alzheimer's Disease.**

A specifier of **Probable Alzheimer's Disease** is available for Mild Neurocognitive Disorder Due to Alzheimer's Disease and should be utilized when appropriate. The Probable Alzheimer's Disease specifier is utilized for Mild Neurocognitive Disorder Due to Alzheimer's Disease if there is no evidence of a causative Alzheimer's disease genetic mutation from family history or genetic testing. A specifier of **Possible Alzheimer's Disease** is utilized for Mild Neurocognitive Disorder Due to Alzheimer's disease if there is no clear evidence of a causative Alzheimer's disease genetic mutation from family history or genetic testing and all three of the following: a decline in memory, a steadily progressive, gradual decline in cognition, without extended plateaus, and there is no evidence of a mixed etiology.

Coding Note: for **Probable Major Neurocognitive Disorder due to Alzheimer's Disease, With Behavioral Disturbance**, code first: **G 30.9** Alzheimer's Disease, followed by **F02.81 Major Neurocognitive Disorder Due to Alzheimer's Disease.** For **Probable Neurocognitive Disorder Due to Alzheimer's Disease, Without Behavioral Disturbance**, code first: **G 30.9** Alzheimer's Disease, followed by **F02.80 Major Neurocognitive Disorder Due to Alzheimer's Disease, Without Behavioral Disturbance.** For **Possible Major Neurocognitive Disorder Due to Alzheimer's Disease,** code **G31.9 Possible Alzheimer's Disease. Note** do not use additional code for Alzheimer's Disease.

Haarman

Major or Mild Frontotemporal Neurocognitive Disorder is a neurodegenerative disorder thought to be caused by frontotemporal lobar degeneration. It is characterized by behavioral and personality changes and language impairment. *DSM-5* recognizes both behavioral and language variants. It can be very difficult to distinguish from other Major or Mild Neurocognitive Disorders or Psychiatric disorders, such as schizophrenia and bipolar disorder. Neuroimaging and genetics can be particularly useful in documenting anomalies in the frontal and temporal regions. For Mild Frontotemporal Neurocognitive Disorder, impairment in only one domain is required and cognitive deficits do not interfere with the capacity for independence in everyday activities. Impairment in at least two domains, such as language and cognitive deficits that interfere with independence and everyday activities are required for a diagnosis of Major Frontotemporal Neurocognitive Disorder.

A specifier of **Probable Frontotemporal Neurocognitive Disorder** is available. Probable Frontotemporal Neurocognitive Disorder is utilized if either 1) there is evidence of a causative Frontotemporal Neurocognitive Disorder of genetic mutation from family history or genetic testing or 2) there is clear evidence of a disproportionate frontal and/or temporal lobe involvement from neuroimaging. Otherwise, **Possible Frontotemporal Neurocognitive Disorder** is utilized if there is no evidence of a genetic mutation, and neural imaging has not been performed.

Coding Note: for **Probable Major Neurocognitive Disorder due to Frontotemporal Degeneration, With Behavioral Disturbance,** code first: **G 31.09 Frontotemporal Disease,** followed by **F02.81 Probable Major Neurocognitive Disorder Due to Frontotemporal Lobar Degeneration, With Behavioral Disturbance.** For **Probable Major Neurocognitive Disorder Due to Frontotemporal Lobar Degeneration, Without Behavioral Disturbance**, code first: **G31.09 Frontotemporal Disease,** followed by **F02.80 Probable Major Neurocognitive Disorder Due to Frontotemporal Lobar Degeneration, Without Behavioral Disturbance.**

Haarman

For **Possible Major Neurocognitive Disorder Due to Frontotemporal Lobar Degeneration**, code **G31.9** Possible Major Neurocognitive Disorder Due to Frontotemporal Lobar Degeneration. Note do not use additional code for **Frontotemporal Disease**. *Behavioral disturbance cannot be coded, but should still be indicated in writing in the diagnosis.*

For **Mild Neurocognitive Disorder Due to Frontotemporal Lobar Degeneration**, code: **G31.84.** Do not use the additional code for Frontotemporal Disease. Behavioral disturbance cannot be coded, but should still be indicated in writing in the diagnosis.

Major or Mild Neurocognitive Disorder with Lewy Bodies is now recognized as the second most common degenerative dementia in older adults. The *DSM-5* diagnostic criteria call for prominent visual hallucinations and Parkinsonian features occurring early in the illness. The course is often slightly more rapid than in Alzheimer's Disease. Individuals with this form of neurocognitive disorder are very sensitive to the side effects of conventional antipsychotics.

Probable Major or Mild Neurocognitive Disorder with Lewy Bodies requires that the individual has two core features or one suggested feature and one core feature. Core features include: 1) fluctuating cognition with variations in attention or alertness, 2) recurrent visual hallucinations, and 3) spontaneous features of Parkinsonism. Suggestive features include, 1) rapid eye movement sleep behavior disorder and 2) severe neuroleptic sensitivity. **Possible Major or Mild Neurocognitive Disorder with Lewy Bodies** requires that the individual who has only one core feature, or one or more suggested features.

Coding Note: for **Probable Major Neurocognitive Disorder with Lewy Bodies, With Behavioral Disturbance**, code first: **G 31.83 Lewy Body Disease**, followed by **F02.81 Probable Major Neurocognitive Disorder** with Lewy Bodies, With Behavioral Disturbance. For **Probable Major Neurocognitive Disorder with Lewy Bodies, Without Behavioral Disturbance,** code first: **G31.83 Lewy Body Disease,** followed by **F02.80** Probable Major Neurocognitive Disorder with Lewy Bodies, Without Behavioral Disturbance.

For **Possible Major Neurocognitive Disorder with Lewy Bodies**, code **G31.9 Possible Major Neurocognitive Disorder with Lewy Bodies. Note** do not use additional code for **Lewy Body Disease**. *Behavioral disturbance cannot be coded, but should still be indicated in writing in the diagnosis.*

For **Mild Neurocognitive Disorder with Lewy Bodies,** code: **G31.84.** Do not use the additional code for Lewy Body Disease. Behavioral disturbance cannot be coded, but should still be indicated in writing in the diagnosis.

Major or Mild Vascular Neurocognitive Disorder has changed the concept of vascular dementia as introduced in *DSM-IV-TR*. The concept of multi-infarct dementia has been replaced by a much broader concept of dementia attributed to both small and large blood vessel disease. Assessment of cerebral vascular disease relies on history, physical examination, and neural imaging. The new criteria are consistent with those of the other neurocognitive disorders, as well as, with the prevailing view regarding cognitive disorders caused by vascular disease, which lie on a continuum.

Probable Vascular Neurocognitive Disorder requires that the individual has one or more of the following: 1) Criteria are supported by neural imaging evidence, 2) the neurocognitive syndrome is temporarily related to one or more documented cerebrovascular events, or 3) both clinical and genetic evidence of cerebrovascular disease is present.

Possible Vascular Neurocognitive Disorder is diagnosed if the individual meets the overall criteria, but neuroimaging is not available and the temporal relationship of the neurocognitive syndrome with one or more cerebrovascular events is not established. oding Note: for **Probable Major Vascular Neurocognitive Disorder, With Behavioral Disturbance**, code first: **F01.51**. For **Probable Major Vascular Neurocognitive Disorder, Without Behavioral Disturbance,** code **F01.50**. For **Possible Major Vascular Neurocognitive Disorder, with or without Behavioral Disturbance**, code **G31.9**. An additional medical code for the cerebrovascular disease is not needed.

For **Mild Vascular Neurocognitive Disorder,** code: **G31.84**. Do not use the additional code for the vascular Disease. *Behavioral disturbance cannot be coded, but should still be indicated in writing in the diagnosis.*

Major or Mild Neurocognitive Disorder Due to Traumatic Brain Injury is caused by an impact to the head or with rapid movement or brain displacement within the skull. The clinical characteristics of the disorder depend on the location, severity, and duration of the trauma. This diagnosis may be difficult in individuals with Substance Use Disorders because such individuals are at risk both for repeated head injuries and for Substance-Induced Neurocognitive Disorders. Posttraumatic stress may co-occur with this disorder. There must be evidence of a traumatic brain injury as indicated by at least one or more of the following: 1) loss of consciousness, 2) posttraumatic amnesia, 3) disorientation and confusion, and 4) neurological signs.

Coding Note: for **Major Neurocognitive Disorder, due to Traumatic Brain Injury, With Behavioral Disturbance**, code first: **S06.2X9S, Diffuse Traumatic Brain Injury,** followed by **F02.81 Major Neurocognitive Disorder Due to Traumatic Brain Injury, With Behavioral Disturbance.** For **Major Neurocognitive Disorder, Due to Traumatic Brain Injury, Without Behavioral Disturbance,** code first: **S06.2X9S, Diffuse Traumatic Brain Injury,** followed by **F02.80 Major Neurocognitive Disorder, Due to Traumatic Brain Injury, Without Behavioral Disturbance.**

Haarman

For **Mild Neurocognitive Disorder Due to Traumatic Brain Injury,** code: **G31.84.** Do not use the additional code for Traumatic Brain Injury. *Behavioral disturbance cannot be coded, but should still be indicated in writing in the diagnosis.*

Major or Mild Neurocognitive Disorder Due to HIV Infection can be due to any number of associated diseases. This diagnosis should be given only when cognitive impairment is judged to be due to the direct central nervous system effects of HIV.

Coding Note: for **Major Neurocognitive Disorder, due to HIV Infection, With Behavioral Disturbance,** code first: **B20,** HIV Infection, followed by **F02.81** Major Neurocognitive Disorder Due to HIV Infection, With Behavioral Disturbance. For **Major Neurocognitive Disorder, Due to HIV Infection, Without Behavioral Disturbance,** code first: **B20,** HIV Infection, followed by **F02.80** Major Neurocognitive Disorder, Due to HIV Infection, Without Behavioral Disturbance.

For **Mild Neurocognitive Disorder Due to HIV Infection,** code: **G31.84.** Do not use the additional code for HIV Infection. Behavioral disturbance cannot be coded, but should still be indicated in writing in the diagnosis.

Major or Mild Neurocognitive Disorder Due to Prion Disease. This disorder due to prion disease is rare, and the most common type is Creutzfeldt-Jakob disease. The disease is accompanied by ataxia, myoclonus, chorea, and dystonia. The course is rapidly progressive, over as little as six months, and the diagnosis can be confirmed with brain biopsy.

Coding Note: for **Major Neurocognitive Disorder, due to Prion Disease, With Behavioral Disturbance,** code first: **A81.9, Prion Disease,** followed by **F02.81** Major Neurocognitive Disorder Due to Prion Disease, With Behavioral Disturbance. For **Major Neurocognitive Disorder, Due to Prion Disease, Without Behavioral Disturbance**, code first: **A81.9**, Prion Disease, followed by **F02.80** Major Neurocognitive Disorder, Due to Prion Disease, Without Behavioral Disturbance.

For **Mild Neurocognitive Disorder Due to Prion Disease**, code: **G31.84**. Do not use the additional code Prion Disease. *Behavioral disturbance cannot be coded, but should still be indicated in writing in the diagnosis.*

Major or Mild Neurocognitive Disorder Due to Parkinson's Disease. The essential feature of this disorder is cognitive decline after the onset of Parkinson's Disease. As many as 75% of individuals with Parkinson's Disease will develop a major neurocognitive disorder, and 25% will have a mild neurocognitive disorder. Individuals who are older at disease onset, and those with increasing duration of the disease, appear more likely to develop a neurocognitive disorder.

A specifier of **Major or Mild Neurocognitive Disorder Probably due to Parkinson's Disease** is utilized if both 1) there is no evidence of a mixed etiology and 2) the Parkinson's disease and clearly precedes the onset of the neurocognitive disorder. Otherwise, **Major or Mild Neurocognitive Disorder Possibly due to Parkinson's Disease** is utilized if either one or two is met.

Coding Note: for **Major Neurocognitive Disorder Probably due to Parkinson's Disease, With Behavioral Disturbance,** code first: **G20**, Parkinson's Disease, followed by **F02.81** Major Neurocognitive Disorder Probably Due to Parkinson's Disease, With Behavioral Disturbance. For **Major Neurocognitive Disorder Probably Due to Parkinson's Disease, Without Behavioral Disturbance**, code first: **G20** Parkinson's

Disease, followed by **F02.80 Major Neurocognitive Disorder Probably Due to Parkinson's, Without Behavioral Disturbance.** For **Major Neurocognitive Disorder Possibly Due to Parkinson's**, code **G31.9 Major Neurocognitive Disorder Possibly Due to Parkinson's Disease. Note** do not use additional code for **Parkinson's Disease.** *Behavioral disturbance cannot be coded, but should still be indicated in writing in the diagnosis.*

For **Mild Neurocognitive Disorder Due to Parkinson's Disease,** code: **G31.84.** Do not use the additional code for Parkinson's Disease. *Behavioral disturbance cannot be coded, but should still be indicated in writing in the diagnosis.*

Major or Mild Neurocognitive Disorder Due to Huntington's Disease. Cognitive and neural changes often precede motor abnormalities of bradykinesia and chorea. Diagnoses of Huntington's disease are based on the extrapyramidial motor abnormalities in a person with a family history of Huntington's, or by genetic testing. Coding Note: for **Major Neurocognitive Disorder, due to Huntington's Disease, With Behavioral Disturbance**, code first: **G10, Huntington's Disease,** followed by **F02.81 Major Neurocognitive Disorder Due to Huntington's Disease, With Behavioral Disturbance.** For **Major Neurocognitive Disorder, Due to Huntington's Disease, Without Behavioral Disturbance**, code first: **G10, Huntington's Disease,** followed by **F02.80 Major Neurocognitive Disorder, Due to Huntington's Disease, Without Behavioral Disturbance.**

For **Mild Neurocognitive Disorder Due to Huntington's Disease,** code: **G31.84.** Do not use the additional code for Huntington's Disease. *Behavioral disturbance cannot be coded, but should still be indicated in writing in the diagnosis.*

Section XVIII: Personality Disorders: Chapter 18

Maladaptive character traits have been recognized for an extensive period of time. Formal attempts to list the variety of personality dysfunctions actually began in *DSM-I*, where eight different types of personality disorders were listed. The list was expanded to ten personality disorders in DSM-II, where they were briefly described, but no criteria were listed. *DSM-III* personality disorders were given prominence by being coded on a separate axis (Axis II) on the multiaxial system. Criteria for 11 different personality disorders were included and the concept of personality disorder "clusters," where disorder types were grouped by their predominant symptom pattern, was introduced. The number of disorders was pared down to ten in *DSM-IV-TR* with the elimination of the Passive Aggressive Personality Disorder.

During the development of *DSM-5*, the Personality and Personality Disorders Work Group conceived a model of personality disorders that attempted to combine categorical diagnosis with optional dimensional ratings. The Workgroup recommended reducing the number of personality disorders to six, by eliminating the Dependent, Histrionic, Paranoid, and Schizoid types. The proposal received much criticism, in part because of its complexity, and the perception that it would be overly time-consuming for clinicians. As a resolution to the controversy, the American Psychiatric Association Board of Trustees voted to move the new schema to Chapter III (Emerging Measures and Models) and to essentially continue the 10 specific *DSM-IV-TR* personality disorders, with minor edits. Discussion also clarified situations where the person's presentation meets the general diagnostic criteria for a personality disorder, but does not meet criteria for a specific disorder. In those situations, the diagnosis of either Other Specified Personality Disorder or Unspecified Personality Disorder should be used.

The personality disorders continue to be grouped into three clusters on the basis of their descriptive similarity. Cluster A includes Paranoid, Schizoid, and Schizotypal Personality Disorders and the dominant symptom similarity for these individuals is that they often appear odd or eccentric. Cluster B included Antisocial, Borderline, Histrionic, and Narcissistic Personality Disorders, as many of these individuals appear dramatic, emotional, or erratic. Cluster C includes Avoidant, Dependent, and Obsessive-Compulsive Personality Disorders and is dominated by symptoms of anxiety or fearfulness.

Paranoid Personality Disorder remains essentially unchanged and describes individuals who are chronically suspicious and distrustful of others. In response to their paranoid beliefs, they can be irritable, hostile, and avoidant. They can develop hypervigilance towards their environment, finding conspiracies against them wherever they turn. Research suggests that the paranoid personality disorder lies within the schizophrenia spectrum and results from a common genetic predisposition (Black and Grant, 2014). Coding Note: If criteria are met prior to the onset of schizophrenia, add "**(premorbid).**"

Other personality disorders may be confused with Paranoid Personality Disorder because they have certain features in common. Paranoid Personality Disorder and Schizotypal Personality Disorder share the traits of suspiciousness, interpersonal aloofness, and paranoid ideation, but Schizotypal Personality Disorder also includes symptoms such as magical thinking, unusual perceptual experiences, and odd thinking and speech. Individuals with Schizoid Personality Disorder are often perceived as strange, eccentric, cold, and aloof, but typically they do not have prominent paranoid ideation. The tendency of individuals with Paranoid Personality Disorder to react to minor stimuli with anger is also seen in the Borderline and Histrionic Personality Disorders, but underlying motivation for the reaction is different. The Paranoid Personality Disorder can be distinguished from Delusional Disorder, Schizophrenia, and Bipolar or Major Depressive Disorder with Psychotic Features, because these disorders are all characterized by persistent psychotic symptoms, not normally seen in the Paranoid Personality Disorder.

Schizoid Personality Disorder describes people who have difficulty achieving intimacy or developing emotionally meaningful relationships. People with Schizoid Personality Disorder typically choose solitary activities and tend to have no close relationships, including family members. These individuals rarely experience strong emotions, express little desire for sexual intimacy, tend to be indifferent to praise or criticism, and display a constricted affect. They may come across to other individuals as dull, emotionally constricted, and aloof. *The disorder is not normally diagnosed in persons with schizophrenia or other psychotic disorders because these conditions are not typically accompanied by a seclusive lifestyle.*

The distinction between Schizoid Personality and Avoidant Personality Disorder can sometimes be difficult to identify, but it rests solely on the motivation underlying the person's tendency to avoid interpersonal relationships. Avoidant Personality disordered individuals avoid relationships out of fear of rejection or hurt; whereas, Schizoid Personality disordered individuals avoid relationships out of indifference or a lack of finding meaningful rewards in relationships. Coding Note: If criteria are met prior to the onset of schizophrenia, add "**(premorbid).**"

Schizotypal Personality Disorder is characterized by a pattern of peculiar behavior, odd speech and thinking, and unusual perceptual experiences. Individuals with these symptoms may appear odd and unusual, but they are not psychotic. Because a high proportion of people diagnosed with Schizotypal Personality Disorder develop Schizophrenia, their schizotypal traits may be early (or prodromal) manifestations of Schizophrenia. The placement of Schizotypal Personality Disordered alongside the psychotic disorders was debated during *DSM-IV-TR* and these arguments were revisited during *DSM-5* deliberations. The result was, that it is listed both in the chapter on Schizophrenia Spectrum and other Psychotic Disorders and in the section on Personality Disorders. Schizotypal Personality Disorder is common with onset in childhood and the offspring of people with Schizophrenia. Some individuals who meet this description in adolescence go on to develop Schizophrenia. After the age risk for Schizophrenia, 18 to 25, these individuals rarely develop Schizophrenia and the symptoms may diminish with advancing age. Coding Note: If criteria are met prior to the onset of schizophrenia, add "**(premorbid).**"

The Schizotypal Personality disorder is typically characterized by more severe social problems and stereotyped behaviors than individuals with Autism Spectrum Disorder. The Paranoid Personality Disorder and Schizoid Personality Disorder are typified by a lack of cognitive or perceptual distortions and a lack of marked eccentricity or "weirdness" that is seen in the Schizotypal Personality Disorder. Avoidant Personality Disorder is characterized by a desire for relationships that is constrained by a fear of embarrassment or rejection, in contrast to the indifference toward social interaction that is typically associated with Schizotypal Personality Disorder.

Antisocial Personality Disorder is characterized by a pervasive pattern of poor social conformity, deceitfulness, impulsivity, criminality, and a lack of remorse. It is more common in men than women and is often found in psychiatric and correctional settings. In *DSM-I*, it was described as "sociopathic personality disturbance," and criteria slowly evolved until *DSM-IV-TR*. *DSM-5* criteria are relatively unchanged. As in *DSM-IV-TR*, *DSM-5* criteria call for evidence of a Conduct Disorder, with onset before age 15 years.

Individuals with Antisocial Personality Disorder and Narcissistic Personality Disorder share tendencies to be tough-minded, glib, superficial, exploitative, and lacking in empathy. However, the Narcissistic Personality Disorder does not include characteristics of impulsivity, aggression, and deceit, which are the hallmarks of the Antisocial Personality Disorder. In addition, individuals with Antisocial Personality Disorder typically are not as needy and have a history of Conduct Disorder in childhood, or criminal behavior as adults. Individuals with Antisocial Personality Disorder and Histrionic Personality Disorder share tendencies to be impulsive, superficial, excitement seeking, reckless, seductive, and manipulative, but persons with Histrionic Personality Disorder tend to be more exaggerated in their emotions and do not characteristically engage in antisocial behaviors. Individuals with Histrionic, and Borderline Personality Disorder are manipulative to gain nurturance; whereas, those with Antisocial Personality Disorder are manipulative to gain profit, power, control or material advantages. Individuals with Antisocial Personality Disorder tend to be less emotionally unstable and more directly aggressive and goal-driven than those with Borderline Personality Disorder.

Haarman

Borderline Personality Disorder shows evidence of a profound identity disturbance, unstable moods, and difficult interpersonal relationships. Core symptoms include a pervasive pattern of anger dyscontrol, affective instability, impulsive behavior, and unstable and overly intense interpersonal relationships. Individuals with Borderline Personality Disorder often hurt themselves - for example, by cutting or burning - and frequently attempt suicide. An estimated 8 to 10% of persons with Borderline Personality Disorder eventually successfully commit suicide.

Borderline Personality Disorder often co-occurs with Bipolar Disorders, and when criteria for both are met, both diagnoses can be given. Because the situational presentation of Borderline Personality Disorder can mimic a Depressive or Bipolar Disorder, care should be given to avoid an additional diagnosis of Bipolar Personality Disorder without a documented pattern of behavior that had both an early onset and a long-standing course.

Although Histrionic Personality Disorder can also be characterized by attention seeking, manipulative behavior, and rapidly shifting emotions, the Borderline Personality Disorder is distinguished by self-destructiveness, angry disruptions in close relationships, and chronic feelings of emptiness and loneliness. Although Antisocial Personality Disorder and Borderline Personality Disorder are both characterized by manipulative behavior, individuals with Antisocial Personality Disorder are manipulative to gain profit, power, or gratification; whereas, the Borderline Personality Disorder is directed towards gaining the concern, sympathy and response of caretakers.

Both the Dependent Personality Disorder and Borderline Personality Disorder are characterized by fear of abandonment; however, the individual with Borderline Personality Disorder reacts to abandonment with feelings of emotional emptiness, rage, and unrealistic demands. This is in stark contrast to the individual with Dependent Personality Disorder who reacts with increasing appeasement and submissiveness, or who is driven to immediately seek a "replacement relationship" that can provide the required caregiving and support.

Haarman

Histrionic Personality Disorder is characterized by a pattern of excessive emotionality and attention seeking behavior, and includes such symptoms as excessive concern with appearance and wanting to be the center of attention. Histrionic persons can be gregarious and charming, but they can also be manipulative, vain, and demanding. The disorder has a prevalence rate of 2% in the general population, and is more frequently diagnosed in women. Diagnostic criteria remained unchanged from *DSM-IV-TR*.

Although Borderline Personality Disorder can also be characterized by attention seeking, manipulative behavior, and rapidly shifting emotions, it is distinguished from Histrionic Personality Disorder by self destructiveness, angry disruptions in close relationships, and chronic feelings of emptiness. Individuals with Antisocial Personality Disorder are motivated by a desire for profit, reward, or material gain rather than a desire for attention and approval, which dominates the Histrionic Personality Disorder.

Individuals with Narcissistic Personality Disorder crave attention from others, but what they usually want is praise for their "superiority," whereas, individuals with Histrionic Personality Disorder are willing to be seen as fragile or dependent if this will gain them the attention they seek. In the Dependent Personality Disorder, the individual is excessively dependent on others for praise and guidance, but is without the flamboyant, exaggerated, emotional features of individuals with Histrionic Personality Disorder.

Narcissistic Personality Disorder derives its name from Narcissus, the Greek mythological God, who fell in love with his own reflection. Freud used the term to describe persons who were self-absorbed and who needed to bolster his or her self-esteem through grandiose fantasy, exaggerated ambition, exhibitionism, and feelings of entitlement. The prevalence of this disorder may be as high as 6.2% in the general population, and most persons receiving the diagnosis are male.

The need for attention, which is a dominant aspect of the Narcissistic Personality Disorder is also observed in individuals with Histrionic Personality

Disorder but is more related to the need for approval as opposed to a need for admiration seen in the Narcissistic Personality Disorder. This need for attention is also observed in individuals with Borderline Personality Disorder, but is more characterized by instability in self-image, self destructiveness, impulsivity, and abandonment concerns. The perfectionism, which is seen in Obsessive-Compulsive Personality Disorder, is reflected as a striving to attain perfection; whereas, in the Narcissistic Personality Disorder, many of these individuals believe that perfection has already been achieved and their efforts are to have their "perfection" recognized by others.

Avoidant Personality Disorder was created to distinguish individuals who avoid social interaction due to fear of rejection from other individuals. Avoidant Personality Disorder is characterized by low self-esteem, reluctance to engage in activities, and avoidance of social activities and interpersonal interactions. The disorder is also characterized by anxious preoccupation with social evaluation and a general lack of positive engagement. Many of these traits are present from early childhood and persist into adulthood. There is considerable overlap with several of the anxiety disorders, such as Social Anxiety Disorder, and the disorder is equally prevalent in men and women, with an overall prevalence rate of approximately 2.4% of the general population. The criteria for Avoidant Personality Disorder are unchanged in *DSM-5*.

Both Avoidant Personality Disorder and Dependent Personality Disorder are characterized by feelings of inadequacy, hypersensitivity criticism, and a need for reassurance. Although the primary focus of concern in Avoidant Personality Disorder is the avoidance of humiliation and rejection, in Dependent Personality Disorder, the focus is on being taken care of by someone. The Schizoid Personality Disorder and Schizotypal Personality Disorder are characterized by social isolation. However, individuals with Avoidant Personality Disorder may be socially isolated, they want to have relationships with others and feel their loneliness and isolation deeply, whereas those with Schizoid or Schizotypal Personality Disorders may be content with and even prefer social isolation.

Dependent Personality Disorder reveals a pattern of relying excessively on others for emotional support and in making everyday decisions. Psychoanalytic oriented clinicians have linked dependency to a fixation at the oral stage of development; whereas, other experts have tied the dependent personality to the disruption of attachments early in life, or to overprotective and parental authoritarianism experienced in childhood. Dependent Personality Disorder has a prevalence of around 0.5% in the general population and is diagnosed more frequently in women. Some experts believe the disorder is not sufficiently distinctive to stand alone and point to the fact that over dependency on others, commonly occurs in people with other personality disorder types as well.

Although many personality disorders are characterized by dependent features, the Dependent Personality Disorder is distinguished by its predominately submissive, reactive, and clinging features. Both Dependent Personality Disorder and Borderline Personality Disorder are characterized by a fear of abandonment; however, the individual with Borderline Personality Disorder reacts to abandonment with feelings of emotional emptiness, rage, and unrealistic demands, whereas, the individual with Dependant Personality Disorder reacts with increasing appeasement, submissiveness, and urgently seeks a replacement relationship to provide caregiving and support. Individuals with Histrionic Personality Disorder, and those with Dependent Personality Disorder have strong needs for reassurance, approval, and may appear childlike and clinging. However, unlike the Dependent Personality Disorder, which is characterized by self-effacing and docile behavior, the Histrionic Personality Disorder is characterized by a gregarious flamboyance with active demands for attention.

Obsessive-Compulsive Personality Disorder is to be distinguished from Obsessive-Compulsive Disorder. Obsessive-Compulsive Personality Disorder is conceptualized as a chronic maladaptive pattern of excessive perfectionism, preoccupation with orderliness and detail, and the need for control of one's emotions and environment. It contributes to significant distress or impairment, particularly in interpersonal functioning. The disorder is relatively common having a prevalence in the general population as high as 7.9%. It occurs more commonly in men than women.

Haarman

In contrast to Obsessive-Compulsive Personality Disorder, Hoarding Disorder is characterized by a persistent difficulty discarding or parting with possessions, regardless of their value. In Hoarding Disorder, as opposed to Obsessive-Compulsive Personality Disorder, the inability to discard items dominates the clinical picture and results in excessive accumulation of possessions that clutter active living areas. If criteria are met for both conditions, both disorders can be diagnosed

Other Specified Personality Disorder replaces the category of **Personality Disorder Not Otherwise Specified** in an attempt to provide greater diagnostic specificity. This category applies to presentations in which symptoms and characteristics of a personality disorder, cause significant distress or impairment in important areas of functioning, but do not meet the full criteria for any of the Personality Disorders. The Other Specified Personality Disorder category is used in situations where the clinician chooses to communicate the specific reasons that the presentation does not meet the criteria for any specific personality disorder. This is done by recording "other specified personality disorder, followed by the specific reasons (e.g., Mixed personality features). This residual diagnosis can be used when an individual, who otherwise meets the general personality disorder criteria, does not meet criteria for one of the ten specific disorders, or when there is insufficient information to make a more specific diagnosis.

Section XIX: Paraphilic Disorders: Chapter 19

The Paraphilic Disorders included in *DSM-5* are **Voyeuristic Disorder, Exhibltionistic Disorder, Frotteuristic Disorder, Sexual Masochism Disorder, Sexual Sadism Disorder, Pedophilic Disorder, Fetishlstic Disorder, and Transvestic Disorder.** These disorders have traditionally been selected for listing in the *DSM* for two main reasons: they are relatively common, and some of them involve actions that are noxious or potentially harmful to others. The eight listed disorders do not exhaust the list of possible paraphilic disorders. Dozens of distinct paraphilias have been identified, and almost any of them, by virtue of the negative consequences for the individual or for others, could rise to the level of a Paraphilic Disorder. The diagnosis of Other Specified Paraphilia Disorder is therefore indispensable and will be required in many cases. A Paraphilic Disorder is a paraphilia that is currently causing distress or impairment in the individual or a paraphilia, the satisfaction of which, entails personal harm or risk of harm to others. A paraphilia is a necessary, but not sufficient condition for having a Paraphilia Disorder. A paraphilia by itself does not necessarily justify or require clinical intervention.

Voyeuristic Disorder is characterized by recurrent, intense sexual arousal from watching an unsuspecting person who is naked or in the process of undressing. Voyeuristic Disorder requires the person to have acted upon these sexual urges with a nonconsenting person, and the perpetrator must be at least 18 years of age. Specifiers of **In a Controlled Environment** (is applicable to individuals living in an institutional, or other settings, where opportunities are restricted) and **In Full Remission** (where the individual has not acted on the urges for at least five years in an uncontrolled environment) are to be used as appropriate. Voyeuristic Disorder is differentiated from Conduct Disorder, or Antisocial Personality Disorder by the addition of many other norm-breaking and antisocial behaviors in addition to the specific sexual interest in secretly watching an unsuspecting individual.

Exhibitionistic Disorder requires that for a period of at least six months, recurrent, intense sexual arousal from the exposure of one's genitals to an unsuspecting person has been manifested in fantasies, urges, or behaviors. The individual must have acted on the urges with a non-consenting person. New *DSM-5* specifiers of: **Sexually Aroused by Exposing Genitals to Prepubertal Children, Sexually Aroused by Exposing Genitals to Physically Mature Individuals, or Sexually Aroused by Exposing Genitals to Prepubertal Children and to Physically Mature Individuals** are to be used as appropriate. Specifiers of **In a Controlled Environment** (is applicable to individuals living in an institutional, or other settings, where opportunities are restricted) and **In Full Remission** (where the individual has not acted on the urges for at least five years in an uncontrolled environment) are to be used as appropriate. Exhibitionistic Disorder is differentiated from Conduct Disorder, or Antisocial Personality Disorder by the addition of many other norm-breaking and antisocial behaviors in addition to the specific sexual interest of exposing one's genitals.

Frotteuristic Disorder requires that over a six-month period, the individual has recurrent, intense sexual arousal from touching or rubbing against a nonconsenting person as manifested by fantasies, urges, or behaviors. During this time, the individual has acted on these urges with a nonconsenting person, or the urges cause clinically significant distress and/or impairment. Specifiers of In a Controlled Environment (is applicable to individuals living in an institutional, or other settings, where opportunities are restricted) and In Full Remission (where the individual has not acted on the urges for at least five years in an uncontrolled environment) have been added in DSM-5, and are to be used as appropriate. Frotteuristic Disorder is differentiated from Conduct Disorder, or Antisocial Personality Disorder. In both of these, the addition of many other norm-breaking and antisocial behaviors are seen in addition to the specific sexual interest of touching or rubbing against a non-consenting individual.

Sexual Masochism Disorder involves recurrent, intense sexual arousal from the act of being humiliated, beaten, bound, or otherwise made to suffer for a period of six months. This is manifested by fantasies, urges, or behaviors, and these behaviors cause clinically significant distress or impairment. New specifiers have been added in *DSM-5*, including: **With Asphyxiophilia** (the practice of achieving sexual arousal realted to restriction of breathing), **In a Controlled Environment** (is applicable to individuals living in an institutional, or other settings, where opportunities to engage in masochistic behaviors are restricted) and **In Full Remission** (where the individual has not acted on the urges for at least five years in an uncontrolled environment) have been added in *DSM-5*, and are to be used as appropriate.

Sexual Sadism Disorder involves recurrent, intense sexual arousal from the physical or psychological suffering of another person, as manifested by fantasies, urges, or behavior. The urges have persisted for a period of at least six months and that the individual has acted on these urges with a non-consenting person or in a way that causes significant distress or impairment. Specifiers of **In a Controlled Environment** (is applicable to individuals living in an institutional, or other settings, where opportunities are restricted) and **In Full Remission** (where the individual has not acted on the urges for at least five years in an uncontrolled environment) have been added in DSM-5, and are to be used as appropriate.

Pedophilia Disorder requires, for a period of at least six months, recurrent, intense sexually arousing fantasies, urges, or behaviors involving sexual activity with a prepubescent child or children (generally age 13 years or younger). The individual has acted on these urges, or experiences marked distress or interpersonal difficulty as a result of these urges. The perpetrator is at least 16 years of age, and at least five years older than the child (note, do not include an individual in late adolescence involved in an ongoing sexual relationship with a 12 or 13-year-old). *DSM-5* has provided multiple specifiers for this disorder, including: **Exclusive Type, Nonexclusive Type, Sexually Attracted to Males, Sexually Attracted to Females, Sexually Attracted to Both,** and **Limited to Incest.** Many of the conditions that could be differential diagnoses for Pedophilia Disorder also, sometimes occur as comorbid diagnoses. It is therefore generally necessary to evaluate the evidence for Pedophilic Disorder and other possible conditions as separate questions.

Haarman

Fetishistic Disorder involves recurrent, intense sexual arousal from either the use of nonliving objects or a highly specific focus on non-genital body parts, as evidenced in fantasies, urges or behaviors, for a period of at least six months. The fantasies, sexual urges, or behaviors cause significant distress or impairment. The fetish objects are not limited to articles of clothing used in cross-dressing or devices specifically designed for the purpose of tactile genital stimulation. *DSM-5* has provided multiple specifiers for this disorder, including: **Body Parts, Nonliving Objects,** and **Other.** Specifiers of **In a Controlled Environment** (is applicable to individuals living in an institutional, or other settings, where opportunities are restricted) and **In Full Remission** (where the individual has not acted on the urges for at least five years in an uncontrolled environment) have been added in *DSM-5,* and are to be used as appropriate.

The nearest diagnostic neighbor of Fetishistic Disorder is Transvestic Disorder. As noted in the diagnostic criteria, Fetishistic Disorder is not diagnosed when fetish objects are limited to articles of clothing exclusively worn during cross-dressing, or when the object is genitally stimulating because it has been designed for that purpose (e.g.,vibrators or dildos). Fetishes can co-occur with other paraphilic disorders.

Transvestic Disorder involves recurrent, intense sexual arousal from cross-dressing, as manifested by fantasies, urges, or behaviors that have continued for a period of six months and cause clinically significant distress or impairment. *DSM-5* provides additional specifiers **With Fetishism** (if sexually aroused by fabrics, materials, or garments) and **With Autogynephilia** (if sexually aroused by thoughts or images of self as female). Specifiers of **In a Controlled Environment** (is applicable to individuals living in an institutional, or other settings, where opportunities are restricted) and **In Full Remission** (where the individual has not acted on the urges for at least five years in an uncontrolled environment) have been added in *DSM-5,* and are to be used as appropriate. Distinguishing Transvestic Disorder from other paraphilias depends on the individual's specific thoughts during the activity and the presence of other fetishes. Individuals with Transvestic Disorder do not

Haarman

report an incongruence between their experienced gender or assigned gender, nor a desire to be the other gender which is seen in Gender Dysphoria. Individuals with a presentation that meets full diagnostic criteria for Transvestic Disorder as well as Gender Dysphoria should be given both diagnoses.

Other Specified Paraphilic's Disorder applies to presentations in which symptoms of a paraphilic disorder cause clinically significant distress or impairment, but do not meet the full criteria for any of the named disorders. The Other Specified Paraphilia Disorder category is used in situations where the clinician chooses to communicate the specific reason that the presentation does not meet criteria. This is done by recording "Other Specified Paraphilia Disorder" followed by the specific reason (e.g., zoophilia, scatologia, necrophilia, coprophilia, klismaphilia, urophilia, etc.).

Other Conditions That May Be a Focus of Clinical Attention: Chapter 20

DSM-5 recognizes other conditions and problems that may be a focus of clinical attention. These may otherwise affect the diagnosis, course, prognosis, or treatment of a patient's mental disorder. It is recognized that certain problems may motivate people to seek psychiatric care, but that these conditions are not mental illnesses. What once had been identified in the multiaxial system as axis IV or V codes in *DSM-5* are now to be coded as Z codes. A condition or problem may be coded as the reason for the current visit to help to explain the need for a test, procedure, or treatment. Conditions and problems in this chapter may also be included in the medical record as useful information or circumstances that may affect the patient's care, regardless of their relevance to the current visit. The conditions and problems listed in this chapter are not mental disorders. Their inclusion in *DSM-5* is meant to draw attention to the scope of additional issues that may be encountered in routine practice and to provide a systematic listing which may be useful to clinicians in documenting these issues. *DSM-5* groups these conditions by specific problems and provides specific "Z" Codes, including:

Problems Related to Family Upbringing
Other Problems Related to Primary Support Group
Child Maltreatment and Neglect problems
Child Sexual Abuse
Child Neglect
Child Psychological Abuse
Spouse for Partner Violence, Physical
Spouse or Partner Violence, Sexual
Spouse or Partner Neglect
Spouse or Partner Abuse, Psychological
Adult Abuse by Nonspouse or Nonpartner
Educational Problems
Occupational Problems
Housing Problems

Economic Problems

Other Problems Related to the Social Environment

Problems Related to Crime or Interaction With the Legal System

Other Health Service Encounters for Counseling and Medical Device

Problems Related to Other Psychosocial, Personal, and Environmental Circumstances

Chapter Seven: Case Studies and Diagnostic Drills

The final Chapter of this book contains 20 case examples that have been prepared to highlight some of the differences between *DSM-IV-TR* diagnoses and *DSM-5* diagnoses. Since the *DSM-III*, the system of classification has been symptom based and symptom specific. In order to arrive at an accurate diagnosis, clinicians have had to identify symptoms, the length of time the symptoms have been present, the number of symptoms consistent with a specific disorder criteria, the onset of symptoms, whether the symptoms resulted in a significant dysfunction or impairment, and whether symptoms once existed, but have fallen into remission or below diagnostic criteria.

In the following section, a case is present and the reader's task is to identify the symptoms and dysfunctions, propose diagnostic categories that might fit that symptom presentation, and then make a differential diagnosis to arrive at an appropriate diagnosis. This system of symptom identification and differential diagnosis can lead to more accurate diagnoses, which will hopefully lead to more evidence based treatment approaches tailored to a specific diagnosis. A great resource in arriving at a differential diagnosis is: *DSM-5 Handbook of Differential Diagnosis* by Dr. Michael First. In his book, he provides Differential Diagnosis Decision Trees for arriving at an appropriate decision based on symptom presentation. His book also contains Differential Diagnostic Tables that contrast and point out the key differences between specific disorders. His book is highly recommended for those who would like to improve their diagnostic sophistication and accuracy.

After each case study, a protocol for working through the diagnostic decision is provided, as well as space for readers to record their analysis of the case. A listing of answers and diagnoses for each case study is provided at the end of the chapter.

Haarman

CASE STUDY #1
Stephen Sandstone

Stephen was referred to a local Family Services agency by his pediatrician as a result of a history of over activity, behavior problems in school, and poor social relationships. His mother indicated that Steven was particularly active as an infant and a toddler. Stephen's teachers found him difficult to control and they see him as being extremely impulsive and distractable, moving from one activity to the next. His teachers report that he does not seem to listen even when spoken to directly and has difficulty organizing tasks and losing things necessary to complete tasks. He often talks excessively and is reported to be constantly on "the go." His teacher reports that he is immature and restless, responds best in a structured one-on-one situation, and is considered the class "pest" as he is constantly annoying other children. He frequently blurts out answers before the questions are asked and interrupts the work of other students

At age 8, he currently knows his alphabet and has a sight vocabulary of approximately 20 words. He cannot read a full sentence and his math skills are also minimal. Because of these learning difficulties Stephen is in a small, self-contained class for learning disabled children and has failed to progress. He often fails to give close attention to details and makes careless mistakes in schoolwork.

Since the start of the school year, he has soiled his pants, two to three times per week. He does not have any friends and has been reported by the bus driver for fighting with other children. His mother reports that Stephen responds well to discipline, but lately he has started talking back and swearing at her. He frequently throws temper tantrums, especially if she asks him to do something or denies a request. His constant whining is irritating for her, especially since her husband has been in the hospital for the past six months. Because of his illness, his father has been minimally involved with Stephen's discipline for the last two years.

Haarman

Primary Symptoms /Dysfunctions

_____

_____

_____

_____

_____

Differential Diagnoses to be Considered

_____

_____

_____

_____

_____

Diagnosis:

_____

_____

_____

_____

_____

CASE STUDY # 2
James Red

James is a five-year-old who shows significant delays in social and self-help skills. He makes a variety of sounds, but has yet to form them into intelligible words. At times he uses peculiar finger movements and flaps his hands when he is either very happy or very angry. His parents report that sometimes he is very affectionate, but does not play appropriately with other children very well. A variety of inappropriate behaviors make him a difficult child to manage and he often has temper tantrums and screams without cause. He does not react to spankings and does not cry.

His family tolerates his minor daily rituals, but interruptions cause them considerable distress. His father feels that he is "babied and catered to," but his mother feels that she must do everything possible, and that sometimes, "she can't ignore him." His mother does not feel supported by her husband and feels that she is "in this by herself." At this point, James does not yet dress himself and wears diapers day and night. He is very attached to a stuffed bear, but is easily separated from his mother. Often he will engross himself for long periods of time twisting tissues or blades of grass in front of his face. His parents are concerned that he is oblivious to danger and may cause harm to himself unless he is constantly supervised. They report that he rarely complies with commands or expected tasks.

When James was 18 months old his parents began to suspect that he was different. He seemed "too good" and, at the same time, not responsive enough. Intellectual functioning cannot be assessed, but the examiner felt that there are some impairments. A hearing evaluation was normal.

On a recent clinic visit James continued to display poor social relations. He easily took the interviewer's hand, but did not discriminate between his mother and other strangers in the waiting room. An occasional grimace momentarily altered his somewhat otherwise bland expression. He appears to tune out and be disinterested in most things about him. The background noise in the clinic agitated him, and he frequently put his fingers in his ears. When he became upset, he butted his head against his mother and resisted her attempts to comfort him.

Haarman

Primary Symptoms/Dysfunctions

_____

_____

_____

_____

_____

Differential Diagnoses to be Considered

_____

_____

_____

_____

_____

Diagnosis:

_____

_____

_____

_____

_____

CASE STUDY # 3

Dante Purple

Dante, an eleven-year-old child, was brought to the clinic by his mother (at the request of his school) because of continued fighting and bullying. His mother claims that Dante has always been a "handful," but now feels that he gets out of line too often and that she can no longer control him. She recently found numerous items in his room that she believes to be stolen, and she has received several reports from the neighbors about property damage. He lies constantly, even when caught and confronted. When confronted, he shows no remorse or guilt. He was recently suspended from school along with two friends for having set up a blockade to get younger kids on their way home from school. They then made demands for money, but Dante claimed that they intended no harm. There was, however, an incident in which a younger girl was pushed off her bike "but Dante saw it as no big deal".

Dante has repeated both first and second grades. His teachers report that he is easily frustrated, and is failing most subjects. He is constantly out of his seat, creating a disruption. He usually looks unhappy and upset, but is unconcerned about his poor performance. His behavior is viewed as attention seeking. He works much better in a small, resource class to which he is assigned two hours a day for help in reading. Most of the rest of the day is spent in the principal's office. Dante is described as showing no empathy, no remorse, and no emotion.

Dante is the second oldest of four children in a single parent home. His natural father left over two years ago and his mother works two part-time jobs to make ends meet. This means that the children are left unsupervised, a good part of the day, with Dante's older sister taking most of the responsibility. Dante does not get along with his sister and will hit and bite her if she tries to manage him. During the interview Dante said little and looked "absent." When asked, he denied feeling "blue" but complained that his sister is "mean" to him. He stated that his sister once hit him with a bat, but she got a "whooping" for it. Prior testing showed that Verbal IQ equals 57, Performance IQ equals 78, and Full Scale IQ equals 66.

Haarman

Primary Symptoms/Dysfunctions

_____

_____

_____

_____

_____

Differential Diagnoses to be Considered

_____

_____

_____

_____

_____

Diagnosis:

_____

_____

_____

_____

_____

CASE STUDY # 4

Susan Yellow

Six-year-old Susan was brought to the clinic by her parents who stated that their child was ruining their marriage. The father feels that the mother spoils the child with inconsistent discipline. The mother feels that she tries her best without success and that the father is extremely harsh and critical. Ms. Yellow reports that their marriage was "rocky" from the very beginning and has just gotten worse with Susan's disruptive behavior. Mother acknowledges that she has been diagnosed with major depression and wonders if she passed this on to Susan.

For the past three years, Susan has been "extremely difficult." She is willful and the "terrible twos" were never outgrown. Her mother states in the past year she is angry and resistive "all the time, and no one wants to have anything to do with her." Susan often spoils family events by her misbehavior. At the private school she attends the teachers often have her play quietly by herself because she irritates and annoys the other children. In turn, the other children who attempt to respond to her are met with aggression such as throwing things or slapping them. She lisps, has difficulty sounding out "d's," and stutters when excited, but this has improved somewhat in the past year. Developmental milestones have been reached within normal limits. She is considered quite bright in school, but her behavior makes learning difficult.

During the clinic interview, Susan seemed to enjoy the individual attention shown her, but was demanding and destructive of the toys in the room. At the end of the interview, she tried to keep the toys, even though she was told she couldn't. She refused to help clean up at the end of the session stating she " just don't feel like it." Both parents appear to be substantially invested in their child, but are finding her violent temper tantrums more and more difficult to handle.

Primary Symptoms/Dysfunctions

_____

_____

_____

_____

_____

Differential Diagnoses to be Considered

_____

_____

_____

_____

_____

Diagnosis:

_____

_____

_____

_____

_____

CASE STUDY # 5

Betty Blue

Betty is a 15-year-old girl who lives with her parents and is seeking therapy because her parents found her hanging from her closet door with a belt around her neck. Her parents came to her rescue only because they heard her violently kicking the door. Betty states that she changed her mind about wanting to die "and the belt hurt my neck." Betty has a history of "eating when she is upset" but no sustained history of purging or other compensatory efforts. Her weight has ranged from 160 pounds at age 14 to the current low of 125. She has a tendency to be slightly heavy but is five feet six inches tall. She's an excellent athlete, jogs 6 miles a day, and plays competitive basketball on her high school team.

There are periods when she feels depressed, because of the way she looks and the friction at home between her parents. "I can't take it any more." She is more likely to binge during these times, eating in secret, rapidly devouring huge quantities of food, usually junk food, even though she is not hungry She has been known to eat an entire chicken at one setting, only to later purge through self-induced vomiting. She then becomes depressed about how fat she looks and refuses dates because of her embarrassment. She has been binging several times a week for months. She reports having a "stash" of junk hidden in her closet that her father does not know anything about. She is afraid that if he discovers the "stash," he'll constantly pull room checks and increase his anger at her daily "weigh ins." She feels a great deal of pressure from her father to win an athletic scholarship.

She is a good student and is curious about the psychological basis for binging. She says she now understands how an alcoholic must feel because she knows that binging is bad for her, but she simply can't stop when she starts to eat. "Something must be terribly wrong with me. Sometimes I am amazed that any human can eat that much" She has kept her binging a secret from her parents and only one of her friends knows about her habits.

Haarman

Primary Symptoms/Dysfunctions

_____

_____

_____

_____

_____

Differential Diagnoses to be Considered

_____

_____

_____

_____

_____

Diagnosis:

_____

_____

_____

_____

_____

Case Study #6
Helen Black
Helen, a five-year-old, was referred by her caseworker after several disrupted placements in foster care. She was in the 15th percentile for weight, although her height was normal. The caseworker was struck by Helen's sad expression and lack of interest in toys. She moved around the room in almost a frenzy with a constant stream of verbalizing and attempts to get all the adults to focus on her. When the social worker attempted to talk to the foster mother, Helen began going through the social worker's purse.

Helen's existence had been chaotic since birth. Having been born to a chronic paranoid schizophrenic mother, who has now been institutionalized, Helen had minimal care from her mother. Her father is unknown. A landlady who took an interest in Helen provided some level of care as her mother's illness deteriorated. Her mother had been hallucinating and delusional since Helen's birth, and it was doubtful whether she would ever be able to provide adequate care. Helen was literally passed from person to person in the neighborhood and the mother would allow her to be on the streets at all hours of the night. She shows no real connection to her biological mother even though she was in the room for the interview.

During the interview Helen was constantly interrupted the examiner. She moved from lap to lap of any adult who came in the room. She attempted to remove a broach that the caseworker was wearing while she sat in her lap. The mother of a little boy in the waiting room accused Helen of acting inappropriately by trying to kiss her son on the mouth. At one point she wandered out of the office and was found in another worker's office playing with a stuffed animal. She was encouraged to play with the other children in the waiting room, but refused and sat in the corner playing with her fingers in a repetitive fashion. Motor development appears to be normal.

Primary Symptoms/Dysfunctions

_____

_____

_____

_____

_____

Differential Diagnoses to be Considered

_____

_____

_____

_____

_____

Diagnosis:

_____

_____

_____

_____

_____

CASE STUDY # 7
Laura Lemon

Laura, age 9, was brought to the clinic for excessive shyness, difficulty going to sleep, and an inability to be alone in the house. In addition, she had begun to brood that the family dog might get sick and die. She looked very sad and her affect was generally very flat. Her mother had just returned home following three months of psychiatric hospitalization for severe depression. The mother's illness had followed her husband's separation from the family in order to live with a younger woman whom he intends to marry.

Laura had been reluctant to attend school when in kindergarten and first grade, but the school had handled this by setting limits about school attendance. At home, she often attempted to sleep in her parents' bed. In the past two years, the problems have worsened considerably. Frequently, Laura would fake illness on school days, and she had begun to do poorly academically. Recent testing had revealed reading difficulties that were thought to be long-standing, and tutoring had been initiated. This academic year she was repeating third grade. Laura has taken this poorly and has no friends in her current class.

During the interview, Laura spoke with reluctance and appeared sad. She seemed preoccupied with her dog, named Mandy, and feared that the dog might fall ill. When asked directly, she said she did not sleep well, unless she was in the same bed as her mother. Although she admitted that she could not stay in her house alone for even 10 minutes, she claimed this was almost never a problem as long as her older sister, a neighbor, or a baby sitter was with her, which was almost all the time. She admitted she wanted to have more friends, but was reluctant to spend much time in their houses, except for a girl who lived next door, from whose house she could see her own house.

Haarman

Primary Symptoms/Dysfunctions

_____

_____

_____

_____

_____

Differential Diagnoses to be Considered

_____

_____

_____

_____

_____

Diagnosis:

_____

_____

_____

_____

_____

CASE STUDY # 8

Paula Pear

Paula is a four-year-old female who currently lives in a foster home. She had been in foster care on several prior occasions as a result of physical and emotional abuse. Recently she had been reunited with her biological mother and her father, who had been diagnosed as a paranoid schizophrenic. Four months ago, she witnessed her father shoot her mother and then threaten to kill Paula before finally turning the gun on himself and making her watch as he pulled the trigger.

Since that time she has had repeated nightmares where she re-experiences the evening again. She repeatedly talks about the experience and seems unable to talk about other subjects. Her father's brother has made inquiries about adopting her, however, whenever he visits she cries continually. When her uncle visits, she claims that her name is "Angel" and that God is watching over her. Her uncle is threatening to make her live with them and has hired an attorney to fight the State for custody. She refuses to go back to her hometown even for a short visit with her former classmates and neighbors.

Paula has become increasingly irritable, has difficulty falling asleep, and has difficulty concentrating in school. She has become excessively afraid of blood and has been known to pass out at school if one of her classmates is injured in a minor fashion. At school, she does not participate in class and tends to isolate herself on the playground. She refuses to be left alone in a room, and follows her foster mother from room to room.

Haarman

Primary Symptoms/Dysfunctions

_____

_____

_____

_____

_____

Differential Diagnoses to be Considered

_____

_____

_____

_____

_____

Diagnosis:

_____

_____

_____

_____

_____

CASE STUDY # 9

Adam Apple

Adam is a well-groomed 16-year-old male whose hands are badly chapped and the color of dusty bricks. He states that, "whenever I go to the bathroom, I get this feeling that there could be some semen on my hands and it might get some girl pregnant, even if I only shook hands with her. I get this urge to wash my hands, but then after I have washed them, I'm afraid to turn off the water because I touched the handle with my "dirty" hands. At times I am afraid to come out of the bathroom because I may have touched the door, on my way in and "it may have semen on it."

Adam was extremely bright and a good student, however, recently his grades had been slipping. Adam attributed this to his hand washing rituals. Whenever he thought he might have accidentally contaminated his hands with semen, he felt compelled to scrub them thoroughly. A year earlier, this had only meant three or four minutes with a bar of soap and water as hot as he could stand it. Now he carries surgical soap with him and may wash for 15 minutes at a time. "I know it seems crazy, but if I don't wash, the pressure just won't let up and builds until I *have* to wash them. Washing is the only thing that relieves the pressure."

Adam denied being depressed, although he was visibly saddened and upset about his behavior. He acknowledges that he has been "drinking to relax," but he finds himself drinking to the point of passing out. He recently just escaped being stopped by the police after drinking to relax with friends. He reported that when he thinks about girls and sex he starts tapping his fingers and makes a "clucking" sound in the back of his throat. His friends have been ridiculing him for it. The one girl who was interested in him now wants nothing to do with him. He can't explain why he has to "cluck" and I "just can't help myself." His sleep and appetite had been normal; he denies hallucinations or delusions; and he did not feel guilty or suicidal. He did acknowledge that his father was a minister, and it would "absolutely kill him" if he got a girl pregnant, even by accident.

Primary Symptoms/Dysfunctions

_____

_____

_____

_____

_____

Differential Diagnoses to be Considered

_____

_____

_____

_____

_____

Diagnosis:

_____

_____

_____

_____

_____

CASE STUDY # 10

Rick Red

For the past three months, nine-year-old Rick has expressed fears about attending an after school program. In spite of being an excellent student, he becomes upset at the prospect of spending time in after school care. He reports a mixture of worries about failure and complains of stomachaches and headaches. Primarily, he feels sad, and for the past few weeks he has been unable to enjoy his usual school activities. Going to sleep is problematic also, because he is worried about doing poorly in school and he is frequently awakened several times during the night. At the same time, his school performance has begun to decline, because of missing school and difficulty in concentrating. He has become very blue and on several occasions he has burst into tears for no apparent reason.

His mother has had three Major Depressive Episodes. During their 20 years of marriage, his parents have had continuing marital problems. Rick and his two brothers have often been at the center of their disputes. Although shy, he is a likeable child and has always been a good student. In the past, he has attended summer camp, and, though he was somewhat home sick, he seemed to enjoy the activities. He has stayed overnight several times with friends who live nearby, but does appear to be somewhat tied to his mother.

During the interview, Rick suddenly began to sob and said that he felt terrible all the time. He said that at times he felt he would be better off if he were dead. Although he denied any specific suicide plan, he indicated that he just didn't want to wake-up in the morning. He feels guilty that he is a problem to his parents and feels responsible for many of their marital difficulties.

Haarman

Primary Symptoms/Dysfunctions

_____

_____

_____

_____

_____

Differential Diagnoses to be Considered

_____

_____

_____

_____

Diagnosis:

_____

_____

_____

_____

Case Study #11
Charles Cabbage

Charles, a 14-year-old whose parents had been divorced since he was 8, was evaluated because in the past two months he had been breaking a variety of school rules. He had consistently been getting into fights with other children, which was quite unlike his previous behavior. He was recently arrested for shoplifting. His mother says that he "has gone totally crazy." This appeared to start after his return from summer vacation.

Charles has a long history of being "difficult." His chronic anger was identified almost immediately by his parents who joking referred to him as "Charles Manson." His temper outbursts are almost legendary, and by age five he had been expelled from eight daycare centers. In elementary school his temper would put him in the principal's office on an almost daily basis. Even when he is not "pitching a fit he is a difficult child to be around, and it has only gotten worse as he has gotten older." He was described by his mother as a two year old in a 14 year old body. "It feels like I'm dealing with a two year old and every time I tell him no, there's a major meltdown that can go on for hours.

This year he was introduced to his father's live-in girlfriend, who the father plans to marry. Charles felt that she monopolized his father's time. She arranged Charles' schedule in California to be a series of day camps, so that she had more time with his father alone. Charles was asked to leave all but one of the camps due to his behavior.

When interviewed, Charles was friendly towards the examiner, but brash in criticizing the school and pointing out what "dopes" his friends were. His boast of being "a bad ass" is out of proportion to any of his offenses. Since being back home, he is openly defiant with his mother, has left the house without permission, and brought drug paraphernalia into the house that he was "keeping for a friend." He was caught at school smoking a joint in the bathroom and the rumors at school is that he is selling on school grounds. His mother says that she can't deal with him anymore and wants him put in a hospital, a juvenile camp, or a boarding school. Psychological testing indicates normal intelligence, but reading is approximately three years below grade level. Charles had always had difficulty with reading and is in a special reading program for high school.

Haarman

Primary Symptoms/Dysfunctions

_____

_____

_____

_____

Differential Diagnoses to be Considered

_____

_____

_____

_____

Diagnosis:

_____

_____

_____

_____

Case Study #12

Ms. D

Ms. D, a 55-year-old real estate executive, reports a history of past periods of hopelessness, sadness, despair, and melancholy, which ultimately went away without hospitalization or the use of psychotropic medications. She states that she can hardly remember a period in her life, beginning in adolescence, where she felt good about things. She began to feel poorly after the recent housing crisis. Her hopelessness became more and more pronounced until she has not been able to report to work for four weeks. She feels very guilty that she has let her partners and co-workers down, by "not being with it." She spends her days and nights lying in bed awake and staring at the ceiling. "It's as if I don't have enough energy to move."

Ms. D reports that, if she ever is able to fall asleep, she wakes up at two or three in the morning and then becomes angry and irritated that she can't fall back asleep. The worst time for her is right before dawn and that she may have thoughts of killing herself at that time, just to be "out of my misery." She has stopped eating, "because it is too much trouble to cook and I don't feel like going out." She reports dropping from 140 pounds to 115 pounds, "with no end in sight."

Her face shows no emotion as she talks about this and "there is nothing in life that is enjoyable or worth living for." Ms. D reports that there are times that she is overwhelmed with guilt, but cannot identify anything specific that she should be guilty about. She feels that she has let everyone down and that it will be her fault if the business collapses. Her business partner has started to make rumblings of wanting to dissolve the partnership. Ms. D. reports that for the last three years she can hardly remember any days where she felt normal, let alone happy. She denies any hallucinations or delusions, but "I do feel like I am dead inside and have felt that way for about three years." She states that she has felt a similar emptiness right after her mother died several years ago," but it was never anything like this." She says that it is difficult to describe her feelings and that she has an emotional ache that is "horrid beyond words."

Haarman

Symptoms:

_____

_____

_____

_____

_____

Differential Diagnoses:

_____

_____

_____

_____

_____

Diagnosis:

_____

_____

_____

_____

_____

Case Study #13

Melissa

Melissa is a 23-year-old, recently married woman who was referred for evaluation after a suicide attempt by an overdose of pills. On the night of the attempt, she had a fight with her husband of three months about his ongoing contact with a female friend. Her husband stormed out of the house, and she later wrote a note saying that she couldn't deal with his attitude and that her jewelry should be given to her sister. When her husband returned home he found her comatose and called 911.

During the last couple of months, Melissa has been crying frequently, and has lost interest in her friends, school, and work. Her grades have taken a real nose dive and she is considering dropping all her classes as "I'm so far behind it is hopeless." She has been eating constantly and has gained 20 pounds since the wedding. Her husband constantly criticizes her weight. He complains that all she ever wants to do is sleep, and they never go anywhere or hang out with friends like they did before they were married. Melissa states that she is too tired to go out and that there is nothing that is of interest to her. She is struggling with marriage and says: "I had no idea being married would be so hard."

Since early adolescence Melissa has had a pattern of getting too quickly involved in relationships and "absolutely freaking out if the guy showed any loss of interest in me, which of course ultimately led to him being annoyed and abandoning me." All of her relationships were "filled with heat initially, but then they get bored and leave me." Usually after a breakup, she reported going on spending sprees and buying a new wardrobe and then playing the bar scene to get attention. Melissa reports that she always had a "hot red-headed temper" and can go off on people. This is not her first suicide attempt, but in the past, she "told people ahead of time that she was going to do something and they stopped me."

She views herself as dumb, boring, and uninteresting, and that no one wants to spend time with her. She feels ignored and rejected by her husband and spends most of her time, alternating between crying and being angry. Melissa states that she constantly feels tense, can't concentrate because "I'm worried that my marriage is already on the rocks, and I'm afraid that I might lose total

Haarman

control of myself." She notes that these mood swings seem to tie in to her menstrual cycle, but present almost all the time, even after she has completed her period. "I don't want to be this way, but I just can't help it. It's just not worth continuing to live."

Symptoms:

_____

_____

_____

_____

Differential Diagnoses:

_____

_____

_____

_____

Diagnosis:

_____

_____

_____

_____

Case Study #14

Zeke

Zeke is a 45-year-old married accountant who was recently admitted to a psychiatric hospital for evaluation for depression. He has had four prior psychiatric consultations for depression and suicidal ideation during the preceding year. At the time of admission, as in earlier admissions, he denies having any psychiatric difficulties, but according to him, is "dying" from a mysterious illness that no one has been able to diagnose. "I'm going blind, my bowels don't work, my skin is coming off, and I'm losing my hair." During the two weeks before his admission, Zeke spent most of his time lying in bed and not being able to work. His wife reports that his mood has been persistently gloomy and pessimistic and that he is frequently irritable with her.

According to his wife, throughout their marriage Zeke has always fluctuated between periods of alternating depression and sudden bursts of excessive energy, that usually only last for a few days. During his energetic periods, he stays late at work, keeping several secretaries busy with his production. He also suddenly becomes involved in volunteer activities and begins extensive exercise programs, which he quickly abandons. During his most recent energetic period, he announced that he had made arrangements for a trip to Australia in place of the family beach vacation and they were leaving in four days. While his wife accompanies him on these impromptu trips, they are usually not a pleasant experience due to the whirlwind pace and his over scheduling everything. She reports that this pattern of behavior was well established when she met him in college. He did fairly well in school, but would fluctuate between "glum" periods when he would sleep all day and miss classes, and then go on to a three-day all-nighter study binge.

Zeke's wife says that his brief outbursts of energy tend to vanish as suddenly as they come. Then he fails to follow through on activities, becoming irritable, sad, moody, and pessimistic. His wife reports that his depressive episodes have tended to "go on forever" in the fall and winter; whereas, his really energetic periods have been especially common in summer. When questioned about his energetic periods, Zeke says that he realizes that he sometimes goes too far and lose his control, but that he much prefers these to the "down times, "as he feels intensely alive, fun-loving, energetic, and can accomplish so much. He says that he can remember having these brief outbursts of productivity since

Haarman

he was in his early teens and that he's always been a "flighty" person whose moods fluctuate quickly. "I'm just like my father in that way.

Symptoms:

_____

_____

_____

_____

_____

Differential Diagnoses:

_____

_____

_____

_____

_____

Diagnosis:_____

_____

_____

_____

_

Case Study #15

Kelli

Kelli is a 30-year-old single woman who lives at home with her parents. She was brought to the hospital by her parents, with each one holding an arm and dragging her into the admissions area. She is loudly singing the "Battle Hymn of the Republic" at full volume when the psychologist enters the room. She consoles the psychologist about his misfortune of having blue eyes, but reassures him that he can change their color by trying to look through the top of his head. She rapidly switches from topic to topic in an incoherent ramble.

She reports that she recently broke up with her "dog of a boyfriend" who was secretly a Bishop in the Catholic Church who tried to sexually abuse her. Since that time, she hasn't slept in four days, has lost 8 pounds, and ordered thousands of dollars of merchandise from the Home Shopping Network, "since I was awake anyway." She reported that she has booked a flight to Paris that is scheduled to leave in three hours, "so make this fast." She reports being troubled by both male and female voices in her head that call her a "dumb whore." She reports that she hears these voices in her "down" phase.

Her parents report that Kelli was an only child who was "spoiled and pampered." She was a difficult child who could have tantrums that could last for hours. She was able to get her degree and teaches in a local kindergarten. Kelli's parents report that their daughter "drinks too much," has wrecked two cars while drinking, has been fired for drinking on the job, and always says that she is going to quit, but never does. She has an outstanding warrant and is due in court Friday for arraignment on a DUI. Relationships with men in the past have been intensely emotional at first, but eventually deteriorate into mutual hatred. "All men are heartless SOB's" who take advantage of her sexually. On several occasions, when relationships have ended, she made suicidal gestures, but always called her parents. She has had long bouts of depression when these relationships have ended and has acted out sexually by having unprotected sex with strangers who she meets in the bars. During these periods after a breakup, she tends to be unhappy, lethargic, tearful, and suicidal. These feelings tend to lift immediately after she meets a new man.

Symptoms:

_____

_____

_____

_____

_____

Differential Diagnoses:

_____

_____

_____

_____

_____

Diagnosis:

_____

_____

_____

_____

_____

Case Study #16
Annabelle
Annabelle is a 44-year-old woman whose twenty year marriage recently fell apart after the discovery that her husband and her sister had been having an ongoing sexual relationship for about 15 years. Her husband is actually the father of her niece. Annabelle was told by her sister that the father of her child was a "one night stand." Her niece's health issues triggered the search for a compatible donor and paternity was established. Upon learning the truth Annabelle "threw the rat out." She also has nothing to do with her sister who she was formerly close with, and "shared everything."

Annabelle almost immediately began having feelings of overwhelming fear and moments where she was emotionally and physically paralyzed. She became jittery and would sit at a stoplight unable to move because she was shaking so badly. " I'm always waiting for the other shoe to drop" and she wonders what else has gone on in her marriage that she will ultimately find out about. Her soon to be ex-husband travels for work and she is afraid that he might have another family somewhere. Annabelle reports that she is "crushed" and so overwhelmingly sad that she can hardly function. She has lost weight and has no appetite. She denies hallucinations, delusions, or suicidal ideation. She sees the situation as hopeless and that she can never trust another human being.

Partly as a result of the discovery and partly as a result of "I just don't give a damn any more," Annabelle began to purchase pain medications on the street, but finds that she can't afford enough to kill the pain. As a result, she has increased her drinking and has gotten a DUI. She also has gone through a series of male "drinking buddies" and occasionally brings them home to smoke weed and to use for sex "when the mood suits me." "The weed has become a real problem since I have asthma, but I do it anyway." On a recent morning, she awoke to find one of these men going through her purse and he had removed her credit cards from her wallet. She states that this isn't really her, but "I just don't give a crap about my life anymore."

Symptoms:

_____

_____

_____

_____

_____

Differential Diagnoses:

_____

_____

_____

_____

_____

Diagnosis:

_____

_____

_____

_____

_____

Case Study #17

Terri

Terri is a 28-year-old insurance executive who presents herself at the local weight loss clinic for "eating problems." She grew up in a family where both mother and father were high priced corporate attorneys. Her mother placed a great deal of emphasis on "looking good" and was on all of her daughters to avoid getting fat. At 14, Terri went to a boarding school in Boston to greater insure that she would have a chance at being accepted into an "Ivy League" school. At boarding school, she excelled both academically and athletically. She was particularly impacted by a coach's remark that if she wanted to get into an "Ivy League" school, she could guarantee her admission as a field hockey player if she would just lose some weight. At the time she was 5'7" and weighed 128 pounds.

Terri began a vigorous program of exercise and diet including 10 aerobic classes per week and eliminating all red meat and sweets. Her social relationships suffered because "she was always exercising, practicing, or studying." She dropped from 128 pounds to 90 pounds, and her menstrual cycle, which had been regular since age 13, ceased. Her body mass index was measured by her coach at 16.5 kg/m^2 who praised her dedication. At home during the summer she found her appetite uncontrollable and would set her alarm for 3:00 am to raid the refrigerator where she consumed an entire half gallon of ice cream three or four times per week and then make herself throw up. Her weight gradually returned and she was at 125 pounds by her sophomore year.

Upon graduation, she was accepted into an Ivy League school, but was not recruited for field hockey. During college, her weight increased to 150 pounds and her mother was very critical of her weight when she came home for Christmas Break. During that vacation she began to induce vomiting after her eating bouts. This pattern of eating and purging has continued fairly consistently for approximately 10 years. Terri now shares an apartment with her best friend from college, but has never told her about her eating and purging rituals. On nights when she knows her roommate will not be home, about twice a week, she usually stops at the market and buys: cookies, candy and ice cream and then eats everything quickly before her roommate gets home, and then purges. Terri spoke with great shame about this "disgusting habit" and has tried to stop, but has never gone for more than 2 weeks without purging or other compensatory behaviors.

Haarman

Symptoms:

_____

_____

_____

_____

_____

Differential Diagnoses:

_____

_____

_____

_____

Diagnosis:

_____

_____

_____

_____

_____

Case Study #18

Wanda

Wanda is a 28-year-old mortgage banker who is married and the mother of a six-year-old child. Her mother, who is an AA member convinced her to get into counseling for drinking too much and having "an enlarged liver." Wanda is the oldest of four girls and her youngest sister was diagnosed with Fetal Alcohol Syndrome. She reports that both of her parents, one of her grandfathers, and several aunts and uncles are alcoholics. "I've been around drinking my whole life, and I can handle my booze."

Wanda began drinking at age 13 and by the time she was in college "I spent every weekend drunk, but would then sober up on Sunday and study like hell to get a 3.8 GPA." She knows that she drinks too much, "but compared to my mother and my fiancee, I don't have a problem." As a young couple "we continued to drink and party every weekend, until I found out I was pregnant and then I stopped for about 10 months." She had great difficulty not drinking during her pregnancy, but got through it by reminding herself of her younger sister and not wanting to harm the baby. Wanda reports that she started drinking again after the baby was born to deal with the pressure of a new baby and a demanding job during the height of the mortgage crisis. Her drinking escalated to 5 to 10 drinks a day during the work week and 10 to 15 drinks on weekend days. She frequently called in sick on Mondays, was frequently hung over, and was arrested for a DUI. "If I get another DUI, I'll have to serve time and lose my job." Her physician diagnosed her with gastritis and has insisted that she quit drinking, but she has continued to drink. She feels terribly guilty about her child who has seen her drunk on many occasions and who begs her "Mommy don't drink."

During the interview Wanda reports that she has not had a drink in 12 hours, but is really craving a drink. She reports insomnia and drinks to fall asleep. At one point she began to cry and said that it was hopeless and "I just can't quit." Wanda reports that she has tried marijuana, but "it just doesn't do it for me." She has reported smoking two packs of cigarettes per day for 10 years, "but I can't quit those either." She denies any depressive symptoms, panic attacks, or hallucinations or delusions. She reports that she has many friends at work and in the neighborhood who think she is a lot of fun to be around.

Haarman

Symptoms:

_____

_____

_____

_____

_____

Differential Diagnoses:

_____

_____

_____

_____

_____

Diagnosis:

_____

_____

_____

_____

_____

Case Study #19

Jeremy

Jeremy is a 30-year-old married real estate broker who introduces himself as "I'm Jeremy, and I'm having a nervous breakdown." "I've always been a big worrier, but this is totally out of control." Jeremy insists that his wife is in on the interview because he is falling apart and can't think straight. His wife reports that Jeremy is always keyed up and acts as if driven by a motor. He complains that he has chronic diarrhea, a chronically upset stomach, and can't concentrate at work. At work, he misses important details, his mind is elsewhere, starts projects and doesn't finish, misses appointments, and fails to return calls. He is constantly losing things and becomes very angry at others when this happens.

Jeremy grew up "a caboose child," as the son of older parents in an affluent, privileged, and steeped in southern tradition, family. His father and grandfather attended Harvard, and Jeremy felt compelled to continue the tradition, but was an average student with average ability. He became a "legacy admission" who felt tremendous pressure to achieve and he began obsessing about grades, and the right social activities At times would become overwhelmed and literally paralyzed, to the point of inaction. "Somehow I got through, but college took a toll on me."

Once he married "the right girl" and moved back home to be employed in his parents' real estate firm, the pressure and worry lifted. Things were fine until two years ago when his father was caught in a long-term affair and was divorced by Jeremy's mother. The business, which Jeremy was running by this time almost went bankrupt in the divorce. While the company is back on its feet, Jeremy has been unable to suppress his nervousness and worry. He lies awake at night worrying about how he would support himself if the company goes "belly-up." He is obsessed about the fact that his daughter, who has significant medical issues, might not be able to get health insurance if the company goes broke and he has to take another job. He acknowledges that he comes home at night and "has a couple of beers to take the edge off," but does not feel he has a problem with alcohol. His wife agrees with this assessment, but is concerned that he could develop a drinking problem in the future if he doesn't get control of his worry. She complains that their sex life is "the pits," because he's too drunk to perform, or comes in seconds, leaving her unsatisfied, "but it's been that way our whole marriage."

Haarman

Symptoms:

_____
_____
_____
_____
_____

Differential Diagnoses:

_____
_____
_____
_____
_____

Diagnosis:

_____
_____
_____
_____
_____

Case Study #20

Fred

Fred is a 37-year-old fireman who was hospitalized for second and third degree burns over a third of his body. During the month he spent on the burn unit, he was the model, stoic patient, always cracking jokes and making the nursing staff smile. At his first follow-up appointment with the clinic he started shaking, stuttering, and became generally unresponsive. The head of the clinic called in the staff psychiatrist to consult. Upon being introduced, Fred mumbled "I sort of expected that they'd call in the shrink."

At first he continued to joke around and then suddenly burst into tears. After calming down, he explained that he cannot stop thinking about how, for the first time in his career, he entered a building alone, totally against all procedures, and nearly killed himself. "You see before you, the wreck of what used to be, a pretty good man." He states that while he was in the hospital, he was troubled by frequent nightmares about the fire, but kept it to himself since it was his fault. He assumed they would stop once he got back home, but since being home, he has been "jumpy" and nervous and the "only thing that seems to help is if I drink until I pass out. Now it takes a lot more alcohol to get there." He feels humiliated that he made a mistake at the fire, and cannot help replaying it over in his mind. He is having difficulty going to sleep for fear that the recurrent nightmares, where he is burned over and over, will start.

His co-workers invited him back to the firehouse where he was given a hero's welcome, "but I know what they were thinking, and I'm sure they were saying it was my own fault." While at the firehouse, the buzzer sounded to call out the engine in response to an alarm, and "I jumped out of my skin and started shaking all over. I left quickly saying I was sick at my stomach, but I was really just scared. I'm sure my brothers could see right through me." He voices doubt that he will ever be able to go back to work again. "I don't know if I can ever trust my judgment again, and I don't want to be responsible for one of my brothers getting hurt."

At home, he paces the floor, won't leave the house by himself, and feels detached from reality. When I try to concentrate it feels like I'm walking around in a fog, my whole life after the fire feels like a horrible dream that I'm going to wake up from, but I never do." He expresses a sense of total helplessness and is appalled by the way he looks. "I can't find any reason to go on living."

Symptoms:

_____

_____

_____

_____

Differential Diagnoses:

_____

_____

_____

_____

Diagnosis:

_____

_____

_____

_____

_____

Case Studies Sample Answers

Case Study #1 Steven:

Primary Symptoms/ Dysfunctions: Over activity, Social Problems, Impulsivity, Distractibility, Disorganization, Excessive Talking, Encopretic, Reading Problems, Limited Vocabulary, Mathematics Problems, Aggressiveness, Family Problems

Differential Diagnoses:Attention Deficit Hyperactivity Disorder, Oppositional Defiant Disorder, Specific Learning Disorder, Encopresis, Intellectual Disability, Adjustment Disorder

Diagnosis: (F90.2) Attention Deficit Hyperactivity Disorder, Combined Presentation, Moderate, (F98.1) Encopresis without constipation and overflow incontinence. Rule Out: (F81.0) Specific Learning Disability, with impairment in reading. Rule Out: (F81.2) Specific Learning Disability, with impairment in mathematics

Case Study #2 James Red Diagnosis:

Primary Symptoms/Dysfunctions:Repetitive Behaviors, Lack of autonomy, Language Development, Parental Conflict, Poor Social Relationships, Poor Communication (Pre-verbal), Motor Tics, Repetitive Behaviors, Limited Intellectual Functioning

Differential Diagnoses:Social Pragmatic Communication Disorder, Autism Spectrum Disorder, Stereotypic Movement Disorder, Intellectual Disability, Language Disorder

Diagnosis: (F84.0) Autism Spectrum Disorder, Requiring Very Substantial Support with Social Communication, Requiring Support for Restricted, Repetitive Behavior, with accompanying intellectual impairment, and with accompanying language impairment. (F79) Unspecified Intellectual Disability, lacking test data. (F88) Global Developmental Delay. (Z62.898) Child Affected by Parental Relationship Distress

Case Study #3 Dante Purple:

Primary Symptoms/Dysfunctions:Fighting/Bullying, Stealing and Lying, Aggression, Lack of empathy emotion, or remorse, Limited intellectual ability, Poor Academic Performance, Hyperactivity, Unconcerned about Performance

Differential Diagnoses:Oppositional Defiant Disorder, Intermittent Explosive Disorder, Disruptive Mood Dysregulation Disorder, Conduct Disorder, Intellectual Disability

Diagnosis: (F91.9) Conduct Disorder, Unspecified Onset, With Limited Prosocial Emotions, (F70) Intellectual Disability, Mild, Rule Out: (F81.0) Specific Learning Disability, with impairment in reading.

Case Study #4 Susan Yellow:

Primary Symptoms/Dysfunctions:Marital discord, Resistive behaviors, Aggressive behaviors, Speech sound issues, Stuttering, Temper Tantrums, Oppositional Behaviors, Sound Production Limitations, Stuttering

Differential Diagnoses:Adjustment Disorder, Conduct Disorder, Disruptive Mood Dysregulation Disorder, Oppositional Defiant Disorder, Childhood Onset Fluency Disorder, Language Disorder, Speech Sound Disorder

Diagnosis: (F91.3) Oppositional Defiant Disorder, Moderate. (F80.81) Childhood-Onset Fluency Disorder. (F80.0) Speech Sound Disorder. (Z62.898) Child Affected by Parental Relationship Distress

Case Study #5 Betty Blue:

Primary Symptoms/Dysfunctions:Suicide Attempt, Depressed Mood, Binge Eating, Anger, Parent/Child Conflict, Shame/Guilt

Differential Diagnoses:Anorexia, Bulimia Nervosa, Binge-Eating Disorder, Major Depressive Episode

Diagnosis: (F50.8) Binge-Eating Disorder, Mild, (Z62.820) Parent-Child Relational Problem

Case Study #6 Helen Black:

Primary Symptoms/Dysfunction:Disrupted Placements, Low Weight, Disruptive Behaviors, Child Neglect, Socially inappropriate Behaviors, Repetitive Behaviors

Differential Diagnoses:Attention Deficit/Hyperactivity Disorder, Post Traumatic Stress Disorder, Oppositional Defiant Disorder, Disinhibited Social Engagement Disorder, Avoidant/Restrictive Food Intake Disorder

Diagnosis: (F94.2) Disinhibited Social Engagement Disorder, Persistent. (Z69.010) Encounter for Mental Health Services for Victim of Child Neglect

Case Study #7 Laura Lemon:

Primary Symptoms/Dysfunctions:Shyness, Flattened affect, Parents' separation, Parent's hospitalization, Inability to be alone, Reading difficulties, Sleep Issues, Social Relationships, School Refusal, Separation Anxiety

Differential Diagnoses:Separation Anxiety, Generalized Anxiety, Major Depressive Disorder, Adjustment Disorder, Social Anxiety Disorder,

Specific Learning Disorder, Insomnia Disorder

Diagnosis: (F93.0) Separation Anxiety Disorder. (F43.23) Adjustment Disorder with anxiety and depressed mood, (Z63.5) Disruption of Family by Separation or Divorce

Case Study #8 Paula Pear:

Primary Symptoms/Dysfunctions:Emotional Abuse and Neglect, Experienced a trauma, Reenactment of trauma, Depersonalization, Family Conflict, Fear of blood, Social isolation, Refusal to be alone, Insomnia,

Differential Diagnoses:Post Traumatic Stress Disorder <6 years of age, Depersonalization Disorder, Separation Anxiety Disorder, Adjustment Disorder

Diagnosis: (F43.10) Posttraumatic Stress Disorder for Children 6 Years and Younger, with Dissociative Symptoms. (Z69.010) Encounter for mental health services for victim of child psychological abuse by a parent

Case Study #9 Adam Apple:

Primary Symptoms/Dysfunction:Obsessions, Compulsions, Anxiety, Saddness, Vocal Tic

Differential Diagnoses:
Obsessive Compulsive Disorder, Generalized Anxiety Disorder, Delusional Disorder

Diagnosis: (F42) Obsessive Compulsive Disorder with Good or Fair Insight, (Z62.820) Parent-Child Relational Problem

Case Study #10 Rick Red

Primary Symptoms/Dysfunction:Fearfulness, Somatic Symptoms, Sleep difficulties, Poor School Performance, Emotionality, Parental Conflict, Excessive Guilt, Passive Suicidal ideation, Weight loss

Differential Diagnoses:Major Depressive Episode, Persistent Depressive Disorder, Generalized Anxiety Disorder, Separation Anxiety Disorder

Diagnosis: (F32.0) Major Depressive Disorder, Mild, Single Episode, with Anxious Distress, Moderate, (Z62.898) Child Affected by Parental Relationship Distress

Case Study #11 Charles Cabbage:

Primary Symptoms/Dysfunction:Defiance, Aggression, Stealing, Anger, Temper Outbursts, Parental Conflict, Defiance, Academic Issues, Marijuana Use and/or Sale, Below Grade Level Academically, Reading Issues

Differential Diagnoses:Oppositional Defiant Disorder, Conduct Disorder, Disruptive Mood Dysregulation Disorder, Adjustment Disorder

Diagnosis: (F43.25) Adjustment Disorder with Mixed Disturbance of Emotions and Conduct,. Rule Out: (F34.8) Disruptive Mood Dysregulation Disorder, Rule Out (F81.0) Specific Learning Disability with impairment in Reading, (Z62.820) Parent-Child Relational Problem, Rule Out: (F12.929) Mild Cannabis Use Disorder

Case Study #12 Ms. D:

Primary Symptoms/Dysfunction:Hopelessness, despair, melancholia, symptoms existed from adolescence, unable to work, lethargy, guilt, sleep issues, suicidal ideation, weight loss, loss of appetite, current symptoms for three years, no hallucinations/delusions.

Differential Diagnoses: Major Depression, Adjustment Disorder, Persistent Depressive Disorder, Pervasive Depressive Disorder differential four symptoms: anhedonia, weight loss, worthless/guilt, suicide Major Depression: Depressed mood, anhedonia,weight loss, insomnia, fatigue, worthlessness, guilt, suicide

Diagnosis: (F33.2) Major Depressive Disorder, recurrent, severe w/o psychotic features, with melancholia, (F34.1) Persistent Depressive Disorder, with melancholic features, early onset, severe. (Z56.9) Other Problem Related to Employment, (Z63.4) Uncomplicated Bereavement

Case Study #13 Melissa:

Primary Symptoms/Dysfucntions:Suicide attempt, marital conflict, eating constantly, fatigue, adjustment issues, history of disrupted interpersonal relationships, spending sprees, mood cycling, aggression, menstrual based mood swings, hopelessness

Differential Diagnoses: Major Depressive Disorder, Bipolar Disorder, Premenstrual Dysphoric Disorder, Borderline Personality Disorder, Dependent Personality Disorder, Adjustment Disorder.

Diagnosis: (F32.1) Major Depressive Disorder, Moderate, with anxious distress, moderate, (F60.3) Borderline Personality Disorder, (Z63.0) Relationship Distress with Spouse or Intimate Partner, (Z60.0) Phase of Life Problem, Rule Out (N94.3) Premenstrual Dysphoric Disorder

Case Study #14 Zeke:

Primary Symptoms/Dysfunctions:Suicidal ideation, unexplained illness, delusions, pessimism, irritability, alternating moods, bursts of energy, impulsivity, depressive episodes, family history of mood swings and impulsivity.

Differential diagnoses: Bipolar I, Bipolar II, Cyclothymia, Illness Anxiety Disorder, ADHD, Major Depression, Histrionic Personality Disorder.

Diagnosis: (F31.81) Bipolar II Disorder, current episode depressed, moderate severity, seasonal pattern, rapid cycling, Rule Out 300.82 (F45.1) Somatic Symptom Disorder, persistent, moderate, (Z63.0) Relationship Distress with Spouse or Intimate Partner

Case Study #15 Kelli:

Primary Symptoms/Dysfunctions: Hallucinations, delusions, disorganization, tangential speech and thinking, sleep issues, impulsivity, alcohol abuse, DUI, suicidal gestures, sexual acting out

Differential Diagnoses: Bipolar I, Bipolar II, Alcohol Use Disorder, Borderline Personality Disorder, Schizophrenia, Schizoaffective Disorder

Diagnosis: (F31.2) Bipolar I, most recent episode manic, with psychotic features. (F10.20) Alcohol Use Disorder, moderate, Rule out: (F60.3) Borderline Personality Disorder, (Z63.0) Relationship Distress with Spouse or Intimate Partner, (Z65.3) Problems related to Legal Circumstances

Case Study #16: Annabelle

Primary Symptoms/Dysfunctions: Recent divorce, affair, estranged from sister, fear, somatic, weight/appetite loss, opioid use, marijuana use, impulsivity, sexual risk taking, hopelessness.

Differential Diagnoses: Adjustment Disorder, Major Depression, Bipolar Disorder, Alcohol Use, Cannabis Use, Opioid Use.

Diagnosis: (F43.25) Adjustment disorder with mixed disturbance of emotions and conduct, (F10.10) Alcohol Use Disorder, mild. (F12.10) Cannabis Use Disorder,mild, Rule Out (F11.10) Opioid Use Disorder, Mild (Z69.11) Encounter for mental health services for victim of spouse psychological abuse

Case Study #17: Terri

Primary Symptoms/Dysfunction: Eating concerns, Anorexia by history, compensatory efforts by history, low BMI by history, binge eating, purging.

Differential Diagnoses: Anorexia, Bulimia, Binge-Eating Disorder.

Diagnosis: (F50.2) Bulimia-Nervosa, purging type, mild, (F50.02) Anorexia, Binge Eating/Purging Type, moderate, in remission (by history)

Case Study #18: Wanda

Primary Symptoms/Dysfunctions:Enlarged Liver, Alcohol Use by history, Alcohol use current, gastritis, occupational issues, drinking despite potential consequences, smoking, insomnia.

Differential Diagnoses: Alcohol Use, Tobacco Use, Alcohol Withdrawal, Antisocial Personality Disorder

Diagnosis: (F10.20) Alcohol Use Disorder, severe, Enlarged Liver Problems (client report, Gastritis, (F72.0) Tobacco Use Disorder, mild, (Z65.3) Problems Related to Legal Issues

Case Study #19 Jeremy:

Primary Symptoms/Dysfunctions: Career issues, anxiety, somatic issues, inability to complete tasks, shy, socially awkward, avoidant, parents' divorce, premature ejaculation.

Differential Diagnoses: Generalized Anxiety Disorder, Social Anxiety Disorder, ADHD, Alcohol Use Disorder, Premature Ejaculation.

Diagnosis:, (F41.1) Gene/ralized Anxiety Disorder, (F40.10) Social Anxiety Disorder, (F52.4) Premature Ejaculation, Lifelong, Generalized, Severe

Case Study #20 Fred:

Primary Symptoms/Dysfunctions: Severe Burns, stuttering, crying,emotional, withdrawn, hopelessness, nightmares, Alcohol Use, dizziness, numbness, helplessness, suicidal, concentration issues.

Differential Diagnoses:Adjustment Disorder, PTSD, Acute Stress Disorder, Alcohol Use, Major Depression.

Diagnosis: (F43.10) Posttraumatic Stress Disorder, with dissociative symptoms of derealization, (F10.10) Alcohol Use Disorder, mild. Recovering from 2nd &3rd Degree Burns (Z56.9) Problem Related to Employment

Index

Haarman

About the Author

GEORGE B. HAARMAN, PSY.D., LMFT, is a Licensed Clinical Psychologist and a Licensed Marriage and Family Therapist with more than 30 years of experience. A member of the American Psychological Association and Kentucky Psychological Association, Dr. Haarman is currently in private practice in Louisville, Kentucky, and serves as a consultant to several school systems regarding the assessment of children. For 24 years, Dr. Haarman worked in the Department of Human Services in Louisville, serving as the Deputy Director for the last 12 years of his tenure there. His prior experience with DHS included working with youth detention centers, juvenile group homes, child protective services, and juvenile probation. Dr. Haarman received his doctorate in clinical psychology from Spalding University and has been an instructor at Jefferson Community College, Bellarmine University, and Spalding University. Because of his years of experience in mental health, he has presented seminars regionally and nationally on psychopathology, depression, and emotional disorders in children and adolescents. He is also the author of *School Refusal: Children Who Can't or Won't Go to School* and *Clinical Supervision: Legal, Ethical, and Risk Management Issues.*

References

Agrawal, A., Heath, A.C., & Lynskey, M. T. (2011) DSM-IV to DSM-5: The impact on the proposed revisions on diagnosis of alcohol use disorders. *Addiction. 106:1935-1943.*

Axelson, D, Birmaher,B, & Strober, M. (2006). Phenomenology of children and adolescents with bipolar spectrum disorders. *Arch Gen Psychiatry 63:1139-1148.*

Bishop, D.V. (2000). *Pragmatic language impairment: a distinct subgroup or part of the autistic continuum? Speech and Language Impairments in Children.* East Sussex, UK, Psychology Press.

Bishop, D.V. & Norbury, C.F. (2002). Exploring the borderlands of autistic disorder and language impairment. *Journal of Child Psychology and Psychiatry 43:917-929.*

Black, D.W. & Grant, J.E. (2014).*DSM-5 guidebook.* Washington, D.C.American Psychiatric Printing.

Brottman, M.A., Schmajuk, M., Rich, B.A. et al. (2006) Prevalance clinical correlates, and longitudinal course of severe mood dysregulation in children. *Biological Psychiatry 60: 991-997.*

Cumyn, L, French, L, Hechtman, L. (2009). Co-morbidity in adults with Attention Deficit Hyperactivity Disorder. *Canadian Journal of Psychiatry,* 54:673-683.

First, M.B. (2014). *DSM-5: Handbook of differential diagnosis.* Washington, DC: American Psychiatric Publishing.

Frances, A. (2010). Opening pandora's box: The 19 worst suggestions for DSM-5. *Psychiatric Times, Feb 11.*

Frances, A. (2013a). *Saving Normal.* Harper Collins New York, NY

Frances, A. (2013b).*Essentials of Psychiatric Diagnosis: Responding to the Challenge of DSM-5*. The Guilford Press, New York, NY.

Frazier, T.W., Youngstrom, E.A., Speer, L., Embacher, R, & Law, P. (2012). Validationof proposed DSM-5 criteria for autism spectrum disorder. *Journal of the American Association of Child and Adolescent Psychiatry, 51, 28-40.*

Frost, R.O., Steketee, G., & Tolin, D.F. (2012). Diagnosis and assessment of hoarding disorder. *Annual Review of Clinical Psychology, 8:219-242.*

Friedman, M.J., Resick, P. A., Bryant, R. A., (2011). Considering Post Traumatic Stress Disorder for DSM-5. *Depression and Anxiety 28:750-769.*

Hasin, D.S. & Beseler, C.L. (2009). Dimensionality of lifetime alcohol abuse, dependence and binge drinking. *Drug and Alcohol Dependence 101:53-61.*

Helzer, J.E., van den Brink, W., and Guth, S.E. (2006). Should there be both categorical and dimensional criteria for the substance use disorders in DSM-V? *Addiction* 101:17-22.

Hyman, S. (2011). Diagnosis of mental disorders in the light of modern genetics. *The Conceptual Evolution of DSM-5*. Washington, DC. American Psychiatric Publishing.

Kanner, L. (1948). *Child Psychiatry, Second Edition*. Springfield, IL., Charles Thomas, 1948

Kupfer, D.J. & Reiger, D.A. (2011). Neuroscience, clinical evidence, and the future of psychiatric classification in DSM-5. *American Journal of Psychiatry 168:172-174.*

McGee, RA, Clark, SE, Symons, DK. (2000). Does the Conner's Continuous Performance Test aid in ADGD diagnosis? *Journal of Abnormal Child Psychology 28* 415-424.

Mewton, L., Slade, T. Mcbride, O., & Teeson, M (2011). An evaluation of the proposed DSM-5 alcohol use disorder criteria using Australian national data. *Addiction 72, 811-822.*

Moffit, TE. (1993). Life course persistent and adolescence limited antisocial behavior: a developmental taxonomy. *Psychological Review* 100:674-701.
Moncrief, J. (1997). Psychiatric Imperialism - The Medicalization of Modern Living. *Surroundings,* issue 6.

Moran, M. (2013). DSM-5 provides new take on neurodevelopmental disorders. *Psychiatric News, 48,2,6-23.*

Moran, M. (2013). DSM-5 fine-tunes diagnostic criteria for psychosis, bipolar disorders. *Psychiatric News, 48 (3), 10-11.*

Moran, M. (2013). DSM-5 updates depressive, anxiety, and ocd criteria. *Psychiatric News, 48 (4), 22-43.*

Moran, M. (2013). Eating, sleep disorder criteria revised in DSM-5. *Psychiatric News, 48 (6),14-15.*

O'Brien, C.P. (2012) Rationale for changes in the DSM-5. *Journal of Studies on Alcohol and Drugs, 73(4), 705.*

Olfson, M., Blanco, C., Liu, L. et al. (2006). National trends in the outpatient treatment of children and adolescents with antipsychotic drugs. *Archives of General Psychiatry 63:679-685.*

Paris, J. (2013) . *The Intelligent Clinician's Guide to the DSM-5.* Oxford University Press, New York, NY.

Potenza, M.N. (2006). Should addictive disorders include non-substance related conditions? *Addiction 101:142-151.*

Pratt, LA, Brody, DJ, Gu, Q. (2011). Antidepressant use in persons age 12 and over: United States, 2005-2008. *NCHS data brief,* no.76. Hyattsville, MD: National Center for Health Statistics.

Volkow, N (2014). National Longitudinal Study of the Neurodevelopmental Consequences of Substance Use. *National Institute of Drug Abuse.*

Widiger, TA (2011). The DSM-5 dimensional model of personality disorder: rationale and empirical support. *Journal of Personality Disorders* 25:222-234.

Zoccolillo, M., Pickles, A., Quinton, D., & Rutter, M. (1992). The outcome of childhood conduct disorder: Implications for defining adult personality disorder and conduct disorder. *Psychological Medicine 22:971-986.*

61443872R00137

Made in the USA
Middletown, DE
19 August 2019